American Inside Out Evolution

Teacher's Book

Pre-Intermediate

SUE KAY
VAUGHAN JONES
PHILIP KERR

macmillan education

Macmillan Education

Companies and representatives throughout the world
American Inside Out Evolution. Teacher's Edition Pre-Intermediate

Written by Helena Gomm
Adapted by Simon Campbell, George Wells and Catherine Gray / Part of the writing team from The Content Station

Published under licence from Macmillan Publishers Ltd.
Macmillan is a registered trademark.
First edition published 2017

ISBN: 978-607-473-617-5

Based on New American Inside Out Teacher's Edition Pre-Intermediate
D.R. © Macmillan Publishers, S.A. de C.V. 2009
Published under license from Macmillan Publishers Ltd.

Editorial Manager: Patricia Muradas
Editorial Operations Coordinator: Veronica Teodorov Ferreira
Editor: Cintia Zaitune
Concept design: Martha Tadaieski
Page make-up: The Content Station
Graphic Production: Kelly Gobbo
Photographic research: The Content Station
Cover concept and design: Jean Aranha
Cover photo: Svetlana195| Dreamstime

We are grateful for permission to reprint the following copyright material: Page vi: Quotation from Language and Problems of Knowledge by Noam Chomsky copyright © Noam Chomsky 1988 Massachusetts Institute of Technology, reprinted by permission of The MIT Press, Cambridge, Massachusetts. Page vi: Quotation - Reproduced by permission of Oxford University Press. From Oxford Applied Linguistics: Understanding Second Language Acquisition by Rod Ellis © Rod Ellis 1985. New Edition OAL: A Study of Second Language Acquisition published 2008.

CANIEM No. 2275

Macmillan Publishers S.A. de C.V.
Insurgentes Sur 1886
Col. Florida, CP 01030
Álvaro Obregón
Ciudad de México
Tel: +52 (55) 5482 2200
elt@grupomacmillan.com

www.grupomacmillan.com
www.macmillan.com.mx
www.macmillanenglish.com

Printed in Brazil, Forma Certa, 7 2024.

Contents

Student's Book Content Map	ii
Introduction	vi
Components of the Course	vi
Practical Methodology	xiii
Teaching Pre-Intermediate Students	xiii
The Top 10 Activities for Pre-Intermediate Students	xiv
Key Concepts	xxi
Life Skills	xxxvii
The Common European Framework of Reference for Language Learning	xxxviii
CEFR Student Checklists	xxxix

Teacher's notes

1 Name	1
2 The World	13
3 Love	23
Review A	34
4 Shopping	38
5 In Shape	49
6 Job	61
Review B	72
7 Eco	75
8 Education	86
9 Smile	95
Review C	105
10 Lifestyle	109
11 Animals	118
12 Incredible	127
Review D	136

Student's Book Content Map

	Units & Topics	Speaking & Writing	Reading & Listening	Grammar, Vocabulary, & Pronunciation
page 8	1 Name **Names** **Describing people** **Memory** **Language learning**	S Names and family S Describing people S Language learning **Anecdote:** Someone who is important to you WB W Filling in a form with personal information	L Two people talking about names R What's in a name? L Remembering names R Top Five Fun: 5 Ways to Remember A Name R Today's Q&A: Dr. Sally Haines L Brad talking about somebody who is important to him **Language for Life:** Showing interest **Life Skills:** Cultural Awareness: What's in a Name?	G Tense review. *looks / looks like.* Question forms V Family. Description. Names **Focus on** names P Vowel sounds /u/, /i/, /ɑ/, /ɜr/, /ɔ/
page 16	2 The World **Home towns** **Countries** **Hotel reviews**	S Places in your country S The best things from different countries **Anecdote:** The best place you have ever visited WB W Hotel review	L Three people talking about their home towns R Hotel reviews R Everything's wrong here! L Emma talking about the best place she has ever visited **Language for Life:** Saying where you are from **Life Skills:** Prioritizing: What to do ...?	G Countable and uncountable nouns. *so/ such. very/too.* Quantity expressions V Places in a city. Adjectives. Countries, nationalities. Location. **Focus on** *like* P Word stress: countries, nationalities
page 24	3 Love **Relationships** **Stories**	S Relationships S First meetings S Telling stories WB W Linking sentences with *after/ before + ing.* Writing a story	L Walt and Betty talking about their relationship L *Get Personal* game show R How we met: A Love of Horror! R Lessons in Love: A Pink House **Language for Life:** Things in common **Life Skills:** Decision-making: A Perfect Date	G Simple past and past progressive. Adverbs of manner. V Relationship expressions. Narrative linkers. *ed/ing* adjectives. **Focus on** *get* P Irregular verbs: /æ/, /e/, /ɔ/
page 32	Review A	Pages 32, 33 **Grammar / Vocabulary / Pronunciation review** Pages 34, 35 **Reading & Listening. Writing (How I met my best friend) & Speaking**		

	Units & Topics	Speaking & Writing	Reading & Listening	Grammar, Vocabulary, & Pronunciation
page 36	**4 Shopping** **Gifts** **Clothes** **Shopping**	(S) Buying and giving gifts **Anecdote:** The last time you bought somebody a gift (S) Attitudes to shopping	(R) The Worst Gifts ... Ever! (L) Eddie talking about the last time he bought somebody a gift (L) Two men talking about shopping (R) Get the look! Runway clothes (R) Close to Edun **Language for Life:** In a clothing store **Life Skills:** Planning: A Shopping Trip	(G) Adverbs of frequency. Verb patterns. Simple present and present progressive (V) Collocations: *a bunch of ..., a box of ...*, etc. Clothes and accessories. **Focus on:** verbs used with clothes (P) Plural nouns: /s/, /z/, or /ɪz/
page 44	**5 In shape** **Fitness** **Sports** **Laughing**	(S) Extreme sports **Anecdote:** Your experiences of doing sports at school (S) Sports stars (S) What makes you laugh? (WB) (W) Organizing a text. Linking sentences with *although*. Describing a sports event	(R) Q&A with a triathlete (L) Tina talking about her experiences of doing sports at school (L) Advertisers discussing sports stars (R) How people relax (L) Laughter clubs **Language for Life:** Giving instructions **Life Skills:** Time Management: An Exercise Routine	(G) Comparative and superlatives. Phrasal verbs (V) *How* + adjective/adverb. Sports. Numbers **Focus on** verbs used with sports (P) Schwa /ə/ in expressions
page 52	**6 Job** **Work** **Experiences**	(S) Jobs (S) Best and worst experiences **Anecdote:** A person you know with a good job (W) A job application	(L) I wanted to be ... (R) Best Job in the World? (R) First jobs (L) Interview with a store owner (L) Kim talking about her friend's job **Language for Life:** Presenting yourself **Life Skills:** Sharing Tasks: Who's Doing It?	(G) Permission and obligation (*can / have to*). Present perfect and simple past (V) Jobs. Collocations (work). *should*. Office equipment **Focus on** *work* and *job* (P) Past participles (irregular verbs): vowel sounds
page 60	**Review B**	Pages 60, 61 **Grammar / Vocabulary / Pronunciation review** Pages 62, 63 **Reading & Listening. Writing (description) & Speaking**		

	Units & Topics	Speaking & Writing	Reading & Listening	Grammar, Vocabulary, & Pronunciation
page 64	7 Eco **Protests** **Environmental issues** **Volunteering**	S Climate change S Environmental issues W Writing a report S Volunteer work WB W Linking sentences with *because, as, since*. Making written suggestions	R Climate March L Four people talking about why they are protesting R Welcome to Africa Volunteers L Two conversations about volunteering **Language for Life:** On the telephone **Life Skills:** Social responsibility: How green are you?	G Subject questions. Dynamic and stative meanings. Future forms V Climate change. Opinions. *have* and *have got* **Focus on** *have* and *have got* P Word stress: words ending in *tion*
page 72	8 Education **Schools** **Families** **Social change**	S School subjects **Anecdote:** Your favorite school subject S Changes in society S What makes a perfect partner	R Run away ... and join the circus! L Andy talking about his favorite school subject R College days: The generation gap L Two generations talking about changes in society R Meet the parents L A man meets his girlfriend's parents R Top Five: Ways To Be the Perfect Partner **Language for Life:** Giving your opinion **Life Skills:** Giving advice: Education Options	G Permission and obligation (*could / had to*). *should* and *must* for advice V Education and training **Focus on** words used with education P Word stress: school subjects
page 80	9 Smile **Character** **Thailand**	S Smiling S Describing character S Vacations S Things and places you know WB W Listing points. Using adverbs of attitude. Writing a travel blog	R Your Special Smiles R Different smiles R How happy are you? R Thailand: The land of smiles L On vacation in Thailand L Living in Thailand **Language for Life:** Using body idioms **Life Skills:** Collecting information: Have you ever ...?	G Verb patterns. *for* and *since*. Present perfect: simple and progressive V The face. Character adjectives. Parts of the body **Focus on** verbs + *ing*-form or *to*-infinitive (with a change in meaning) P Sentence stress
page 88	Review C	Pages 88, 89 **Grammar / Vocabulary / Pronunciation review** Pages 90, 91 **Reading & Listening. Writing (paragraphing) & Speaking**		

	Units & Topics	Speaking & Writing	Reading & Listening	Grammar, Vocabulary, & Pronunciation
page 92	10 Lifestyle **Longevity** **Health** **Food** **Cars**	S Lifestyles S Health spas S Food and cooking **Anecdote:** The healthiest person you know S Cars **Anecdote:** Your dream car	R Secrets to a long life L A telephone inquiry R Eggplant dishes L Josh talking about the healthiest person he knows R Your First Car L Patti's dream car **Language for Life:** Idioms with food **Life Skills:** Self-knowledge: Do you have a healthy lifestyle?	G *will*. Future time clauses after *when, if, as soon as. used to* V Collocations. Food and cooking. Cars and driving **Focus on** words used with driving P Vowel sounds and spelling
page 100	11 Animals **Animals** **Pets** **People**	S Animals S Characteristics S Moral dilemmas **Anecdote:** Your pet / A pet you know WB W Linking: giving examples. Giving opinions	R Your attitude to animals L Three people talking about animals they like/dislike R Three stories about animals L People talking about their pets L Mandy talking about her friend's pet **Language for Life:** Polite requests **Life Skills:** Giving opinions: Animals: Use or abuse?	G Defining relative clauses. Unreal conditionals V Animals. Adjective + preposition. *that* **Focus on** that P Homophones (*bare/ bear*)
page 108	12 Incredible **Coincidences** **Buildings** **The weather** **Predictions**	S Strange coincidences S Best or worst hotels **Anecdote:** The most incredible building you've ever seen S The future	R Incredible but true R The World's Most Unusual Hotels L Curro talking about the most incredible building he's ever seen L North Pole weather forecast R Predicting your life? **Language for Life:** Exclaiming **Life Skills:** Achieving goals: In Five Years	G Past perfect. Passives. *will* and *might* for future possibility V Collocations with *do, get, go, have, make,* and *take*. The weather **Focus on** collocations with *do, get, go, have, make, take*
Page 116	Review D	Pages 116, 117 **Grammar / Vocabulary / Pronunciation review** Pages 118, 119 **Reading & Listening. Writing (narrative linkers) & Speaking**		

Pairwork Student A page 120 • Pairwork Student B page 125 • Grammar Extra page 130 • Audioscript page 154 • Phonetic symbols page 166 • Irregular verbs page 167

Introduction

In *American Inside Out Evolution*, meaning is central to everything we ask the students to do. Instead of basing lessons on invented people in imaginary situations, we present target language in real contexts and authentic texts. We believe that the richest "source of meaning" in any lesson is what each student brings into the classroom-their thoughts, ideas, opinions, experiences, and feelings. Our materials are therefore designed to help the teacher exploit this resource and make important and memorable connections between the target language and the students' own lives.

In addition to this fundamental core principle, here are three more important beliefs that have guided us in our teaching and writing over the years:

Sue Kay and *Vaughan Jones*

- Vocabulary should share center stage with grammar. Words are the basic building blocks of any language.
- Language skills are best acquired through lots of practice. You learn to read by reading; you learn to speak by speaking, etc. Attempts to identify and then practice discrete sub-skills are not convincing.
- There can never be enough practice activities!

Engaging Content

The American linguist and philosopher Noam Chomsky once said:
"The truth of the matter is that about 99% of teaching is making the students feel interested in the material. Then the other 1% has to do with your methods."

While we might want to quibble with the percentages, we would nevertheless agree whole-heartedly with the central message in Professor Chomsky's assertion: namely, students learn best when they're interested in the material. It's as simple as that. A text might contain six beautifully crafted examples of the simple past, a good spread of high frequency lexical items, and exemplify some useful functional language, but if it doesn't engage the students, if they can't relate to it, if it feels alien to them, then the most important ingredient for successful learning is missing.

In *American Inside Out Evolution*, we've drawn on our own classroom experience, and that of our colleagues around the world, to select topics, texts, and tasks that engage students both emotionally and intellectually. Students are our richest resource. They come to class with their own knowledge of the world, their own tastes, feelings, and opinions. It's up to us to exploit this rich resource by organizing learning around topics that they can relate to–topics that are part of their life experience.

Structured Support

We all know that learning a language is a messy, non-linear business. We're dismayed when there seems to be little correlation between what is taught and what is learned! However, there is plenty of evidence to suggest that "instructed" learners (those who attend classes or follow a course of study) learn faster, and ultimately attain a higher level of proficiency than "non-instructed" learners.

In *American Inside Out Evolution*, new language input is carefully controlled: we aim to maximize exposure to high frequency language appropriate to this level. Students are encouraged to notice new grammar and new vocabulary in contexts where the meaning is clear. They are then given opportunities to manipulate the new language and try it out in different situations. They discover why using one particular form rather than another one actually matters: not just because it's right or wrong, but because it does or doesn't communicate a meaning successfully. The emphasis is always on what students can do with the language rather than what they know about the language. The new language is systematically reviewed and recycled until finally the students feel confident enough to use it to make their own meanings. It becomes part of their available repertoire. It has been "learned."

Real-World Tasks

We're strong believers in the old adage: "practice makes perfect." *American Inside Out Evolution* emphasizes output, particularly speaking, and there are a huge number of tasks that are designed to develop fluency. Students practice functional language in sections entitled Language for Life. But for the most part, the speaking tasks simply encourage the students to talk about things that actually matter to them, rather than playing roles or exchanging invented information. One of our main objectives is to ensure that the language our students spend time rehearsing in the classroom is transferable to the real world. By orchestrating tasks that require the students to use grammar and vocabulary to make meaningful utterances, this objective becomes obtainable. As the linguist and academic Rod Ellis reminds us:

"It is the need to get meanings across and the pleasure experienced when this is achieved that motivates second language acquisition."

www.insideout.net

"the art of communication"

Components of the Course

Student's Components

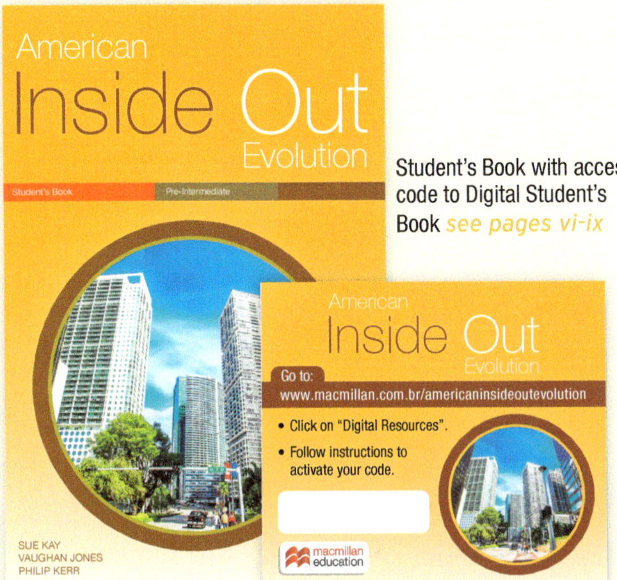

Student's Book with access code to Digital Student's Book see pages vi-ix

Workbook with access code to Digital Workbook see page ix

- Companion website: macmillan.com.br/americaninsideoutevolution
- Free app

Teacher's Components

- Teacher's Edition with access code to Teacher's Presentation Kit with Extra Resources
- Test Generator
- Class audio CDs
- Companion website: www. macmillan.com.br/americaninsideoutevolution

For the Student:
A typical Student's Book unit

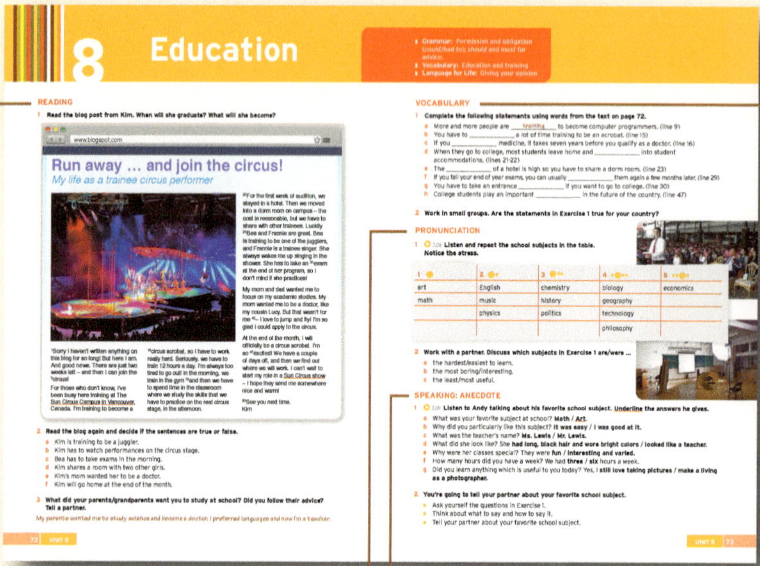

READING

Contemporary reading texts have been adapted and graded to suit each level. They have been selected not only for their language content but also for their interest and appropriacy. The texts are supported by recordings.

VOCABULARY

- Vocabulary is presented in a meaningful context and is related to the topics in the unit.
- Clear pictures help acquisition.
- There are practice activities to expand students' knowledge of particular lexical sets and that will give them opportunities to use the new vocabulary in social exchanges.
- Students will also listen and repeat the words before manipulating words in real social contexts.

PRONUNCIATION

Pronunciation work on particular areas of sound, stress, and intonation is integrated into every unit.

SPEAKING

Students will have plenty of opportunities to speak throughout the unit using language learned.

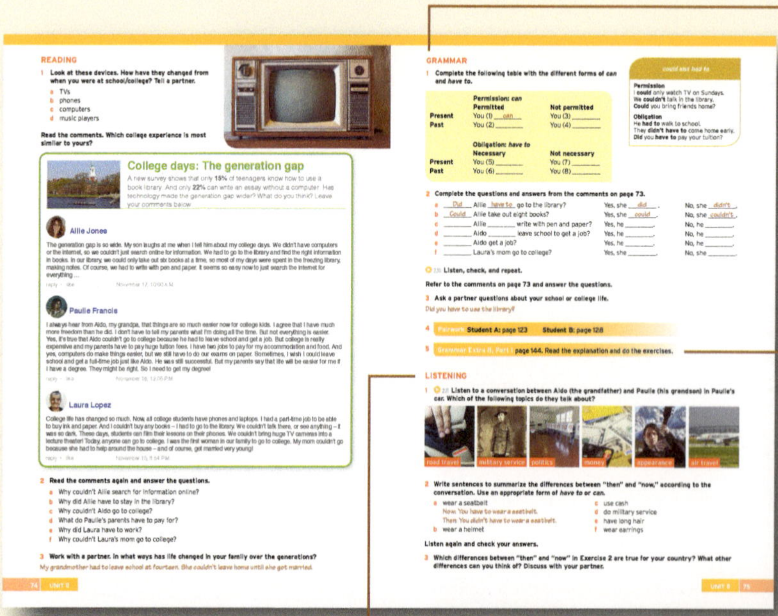

GRAMMAR

- Here students will explore new grammatical structures that have been contextualized in the reading/listening sections. Students will focus on the way language works.
- A brief summary of the grammar point is provided in the box.
- Language is explored in realistic and meaningful practice exercises.
- Students will use target language in controlled and personalized practice.

The Grammar Extra pages at the back of the Student's Book extend explanations and provide further practice.

LISTENING

The listenings include texts specially written for language learning - dialogues, conversations, monologues. They were carefulle designed to develop real-life listening skills.

LANGUAGE FOR LIFE

The Language for Life section gives students a portable toolkit of functional language. Here, they notice how language is more than just form. They will see language in fun, engaging social situations.

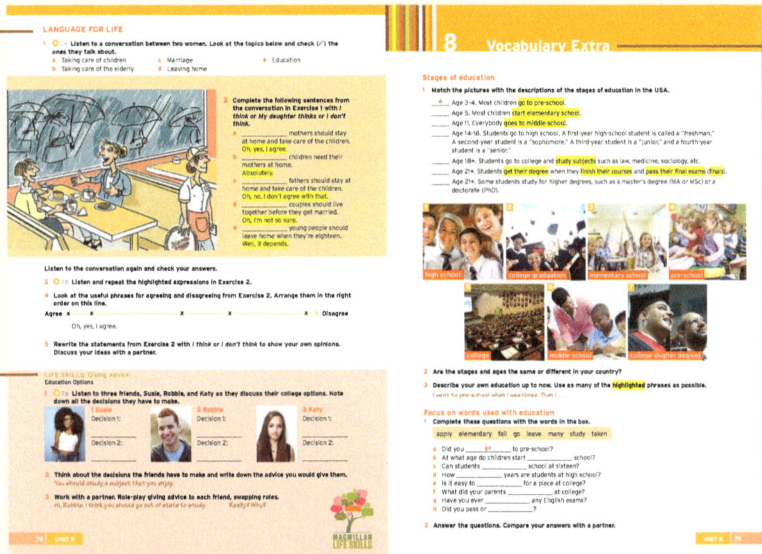

VOCABULARY EXTRA

The Vocabulary Extra pages at the end of every unit recycle the key vocabulary items taught in the unit. This provides an activated wordlist and a useful bank of vocabulary.

LIFE SKILLS

Devoping life skills alongside language skills is an essential requirement to meet the demands of the contemporary world.
American Inside Out Evolution has a Life Skills section in every unit. Life Skills present activities in order for students to reflect on and idscuss the skills necessary for social and work situations in today's world.

REVIEW

There are Review units in the Student's Book. They review new structures and vocabulary taught in the previous teaching units.

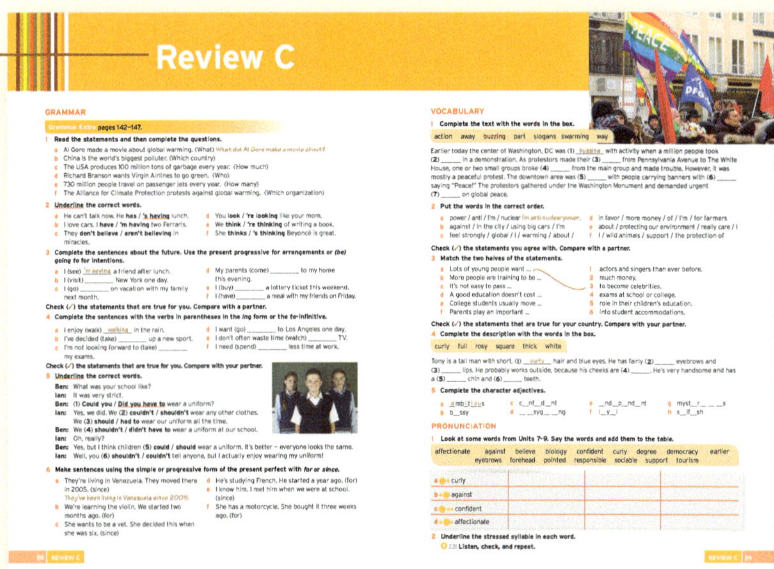

There is one pairwork for every unit which offers further speaking practice.

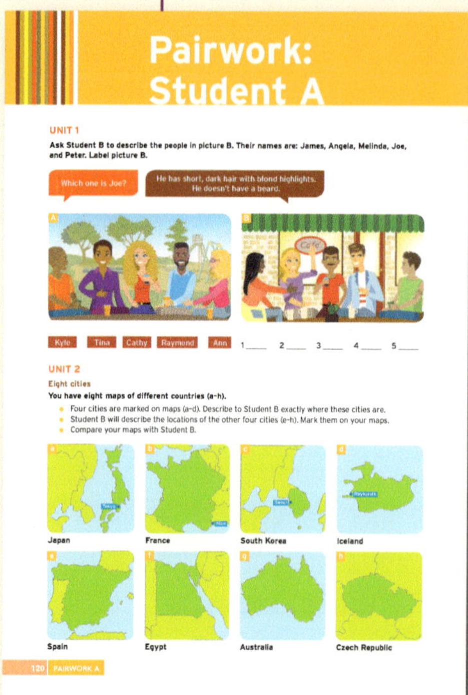
Pairwork: Student A

UNIT 1

Ask Student B to describe the people in picture B. Their names are: James, Angela, Melinda, Joe, and Peter. Label picture B.

UNIT 2

Eight cities

You have eight maps of different countries (a–h).

- Four cities are marked on maps (a–d). Describe to Student B exactly where these cities are.
- Student B will describe the locations of the other four cities (e–h). Mark them on your maps.
- Compare your maps with Student B.

Japan France South Korea Iceland Spain Egypt Australia Czech Republic

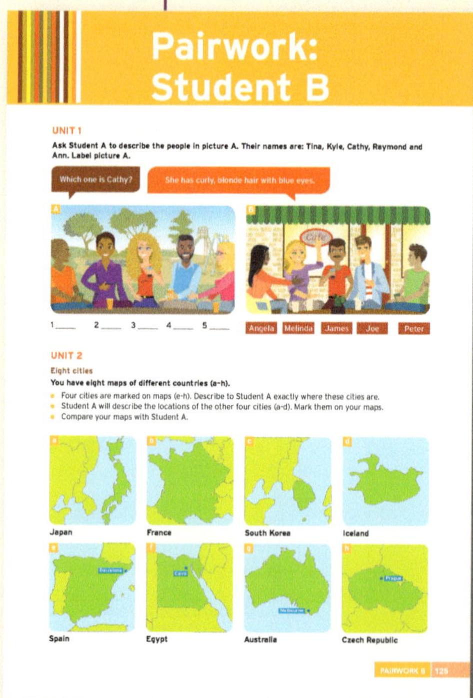
Pairwork: Student B

UNIT 1

Ask Student A to describe the people in picture A. Their names are: Tina, Kyle, Cathy, Raymond and Ann. Label picture A.

UNIT 2

Eight cities

You have eight maps of different countries (a–h).

- Four cities are marked on maps (e–h). Describe to Student A exactly where these cities are.
- Student A will describe the locations of the other four cities (a–d). Mark them on your maps.
- Compare your maps with Student A.

Japan France South Korea Iceland Spain Egypt Australia Czech Republic

GRAMMAR EXTRA

The Grammar Extra pages at the back of the Student's Book provide a summary of the new grammatical structures, as well as extra practice.

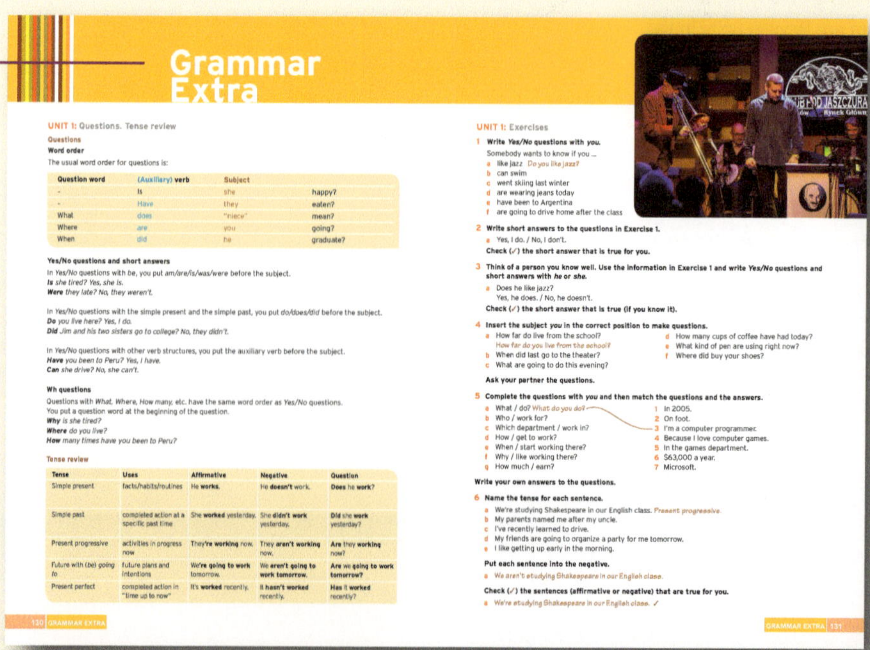
Grammar Extra

UNIT 1: Questions. Tense review

UNIT 1: Exercises

The Workbook provides a review of all the main points in the Student's Book, plus extra listening practice, pronunciation work, and a writing program.

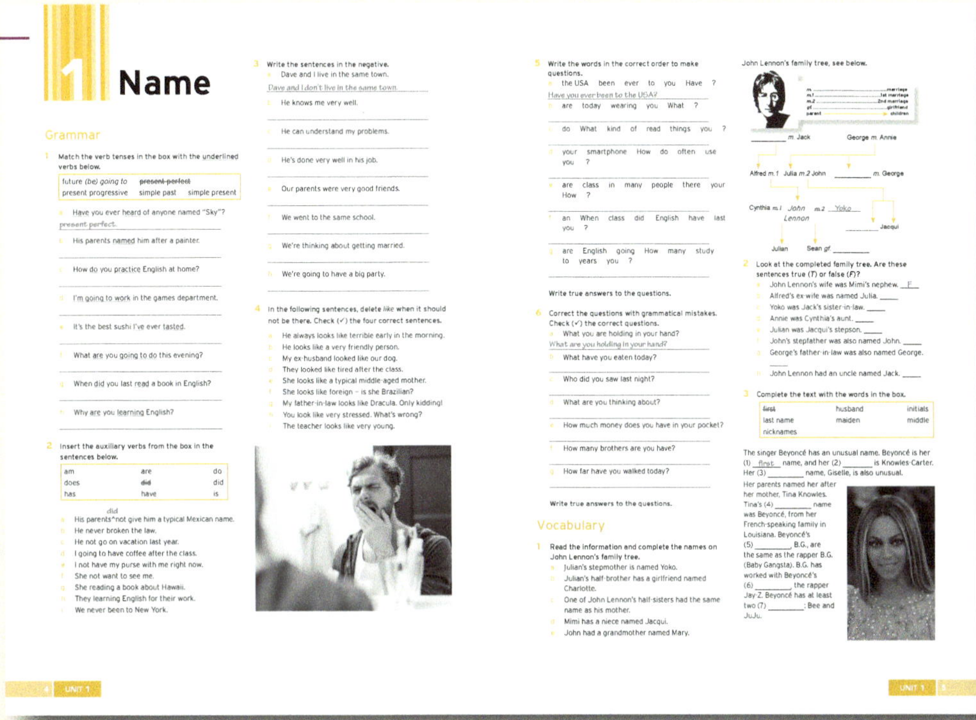

- The **Digital Student's Book** is a version of the Student's Book in digital. It includes all the student's pages plus the audio tracks for the listening activities. It can be accessed online and offline on computer and tablets.
- The **Digital Workbook** is a version of the Workbook in digital. It includes all the workbook pages plus the audio tracks for the listening activities. It can be accessed online and offline on computer and tablets.
- A free **app** gives students the opportunity for extra classroom practice on the move.
- The **companion website** www.macmillan.com.br/americaninsideoutevolution contains information about the course, its authors and access to resources.

For the Teacher

Teacher's Edition

The Teacher's Edition contains:

An Introduction

Introduction

Practical Methodology

Practical Methodology

Teaching Pre-Intermediate Students

Class CD set

The Class CDs contain:

- The dialogues and listening activities from the Student's Book
- Pronunciation activities
- Recordings of the reading texts

Common European Framework of Reference (CEFR) checklists

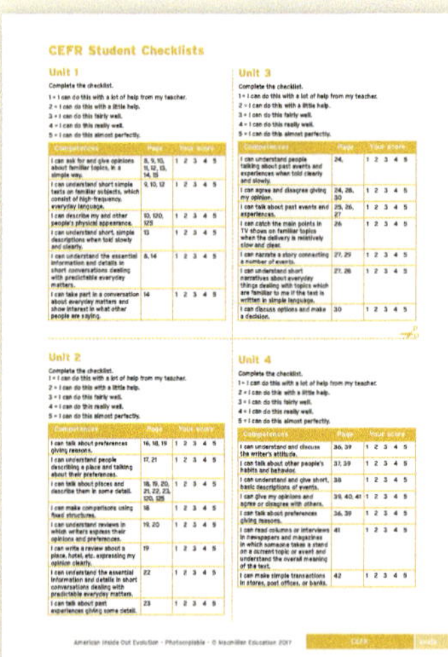
CEFR Student Checklists

Complete teaching notes with answer keys

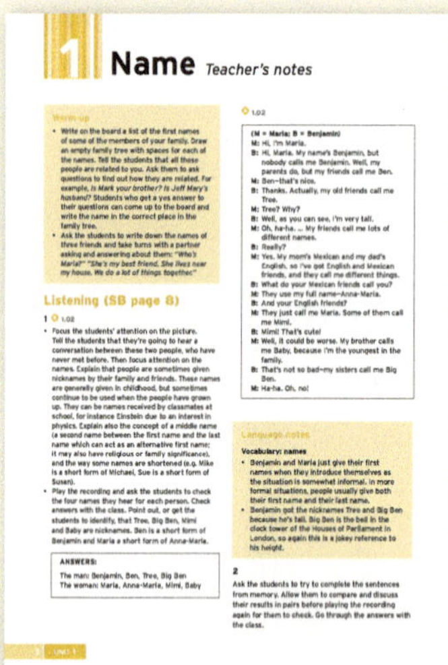
1 Name Teacher's notes

- The **Teacher's Presentation Kit** contains Student's Digital Book with audio and answers and with tools that can be used with an Interactive Whiteboard or Data Projector.
- A **Test Generator** is a tool for teachers to edit their own tests.
- The **Extra Resources** are links to tests and a bank of extra photocopiable grammar, vocabulary and communicative activities.
- The **companion website** www.macmillan.com.br/americaninsideoutevolution contains information about the course, its authors and access to resources.

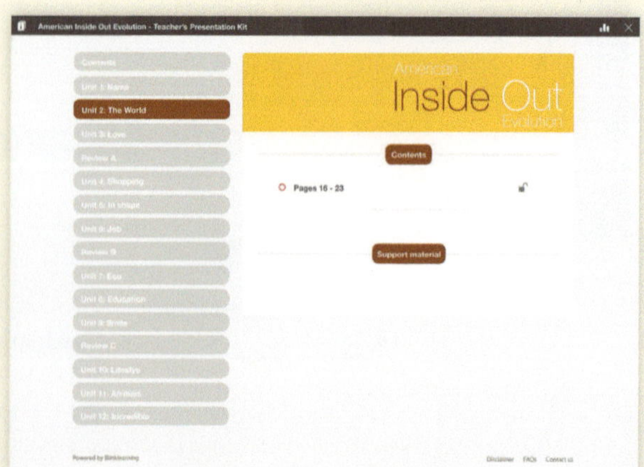

Practical Methodology

Teaching Pre-Intermediate Students

In many ways, pre-intermediate is one of the more rewarding levels to teach. Students have seen most of the basic structures and have a core vocabulary enabling them to "get by" in most situations. The teacher can therefore assume a certain amount of knowledge and this helps the pace and flow of the lesson. On the other hand, there are still plenty of new language areas to explore. The key to success at this level is how to strike the right balance between forward progress on the one hand and the consolidation of "learned" language on the other. If you go too fast, there's the risk that the students' more basic errors become permanent "fossilized" errors. If you go too slowly, the students are likely to become bored, demotivated, and disenchanted with the whole process.

In *American Inside Out Evolution Pre-intermediate* we've tried to get this balance right. Students are challenged to explore new grammar and vocabulary, but they mix this with important recycling and consolidation work in more familiar areas. A relentless focus on meaning, and in particular how students can make their own meanings with the language, is built into every stage of the learning process. It's this core feature of *American Inside Out Evolution* which helps students maintain their enthusiasm and motivation.

Right from the start

Every teacher has their own way of setting up their classroom, interacting with their students, and conducting their lessons. Here are a few things that we have found useful to bear in mind.

The right atmosphere

It's important to do everything you can to create a supportive learning environment. Start by memorizing every student's name and learn as much information as you can about them.

Make sure students learn each other's names too and that they all get to know things about each other early on in the course. Think of appropriate ways you could help foster good classroom dynamics. For example, you could nominate a "homework partner" for each student. They'd then be responsible for collecting handouts or passing on lesson notes or homework instructions when their partner is absent.

Pay attention to how you respond to students both individually and collectively. Make sure you find time to chat to individual students or small informal groups of students before or after class. More formally, it's a good idea to devote at least one lesson per term to counseling your students individually and discussing their progress.

Even at pre-intermediate level students are often shy and under-confident about speaking in class. As anyone who has learned a foreign language will know, it takes a great deal of courage to open your mouth and say something in the very early stages of a course. Yet we know that the sooner you start, the more practice you get, and the more confident you feel, the easier it becomes. For this reason, students are encouraged to work in pairs and groups so they can rehearse the language in private rather than be immediately required to speak in the more intimidating arena of the class.

Always give your students time to think. It's perfectly normal to have moments of silence while students absorb and process new information, write down new vocabulary from the board, or think about their answers. Don't be afraid of the "pregnant pause!"

The right environment

Your classroom might be the only exposure to English that students get. Make that exposure as rich as you can by decorating the walls with maps and posters. Here are some further ideas:

- Stick up useful formulaic phrases. For example, *Can you spell that please?*, *Can you repeat that please?*, or *What does XXX mean?*, etc.
- Keep a "wordbox" on your table where words or phrases that come up in the lesson are recorded on strips of paper and put in the box. Invite the students to record the words for you. They can then be used in a variety of quick revision games in subsequent lessons. Alternatively, you could

institute the "class scribe" idea. One student in the class is given the role of recording any new language that comes up during the lesson that isn't necessarily the target language of that lesson. This record is then photocopied for everyone in the class, including the teacher, who can use the data for revision activities. The role of class scribe is rotated.

- Introduce your students to simplified graded readers. Many of them now come as "talking books" with CDs. This is invaluable input. Get your students hooked on books!
- Use English in the classroom. It's very tempting to slip into the students' language—particularly if you are teaching in a monolingual situation. Try only to use L1 as an absolute last resort: an occasional quick translation or brief explanation.

The right learning skills

Students will always benefit from help with learning strategies. Here are some thoughts:

- Spend time encouraging students to experiment with how they record words and phrases from the lesson. Get them to draw the word rather than translate it. They're then associating the word with the concept rather than with another word. Make sure they note the part of speech—verb, noun, adjective, etc. Tell them to find a way of noting the pronunciation of the word, either using phonetic script or by developing their own system. Ask them to write complete personalized sentences putting the new word or phrase in a real context and thereby making it more memorable.
- A dictionary is a very important language learning tool and most students will buy one. Usually students prefer a bilingual dictionary as this provides them with a quick translation of the word they need. Spend time showing them all the other information that a dictionary can give them, in particular the phonetic symbols. Work with monolingual dictionaries in the classroom.

The right amount of practice

In our experience, the most successful lessons consist of a manageable amount of new input, and then a lot of meaningful practice. For this reason, we've tried to provide maximum practice activities in *American Inside Out Evolution*, both in the Student's Book and in the other supporting components. But there is never enough time in the lessons alone. Always give homework, even if it's just reading a chapter from a reader, and make homework feedback or correction an integral part of the lesson.

The Top 10 Activities for Pre-intermediate Students

These tried and trusted activities can be used as lead-ins, warmers, fillers, pair-forming activities, or for revision and recycling. Most of them require very little or no preparation and can be adapted to cover a wide variety of different language points. You may be familiar with some of the ideas and others may be new. In any event, we hope they provide a useful extension to your teaching repertoire. They certainly get used and re-used in our own classrooms!

It's always useful to have a stock of small white cards and access to a stock of pictures. Magazine pictures are ideal, and can be filed in alphabetical order according to topics.

1 Board Bingo

Aim

This activity is good for reviewing any type of vocabulary.

Preparation

Write down twelve to fifteen words you want to review on the board.

Procedure

- Ask the students to choose five of the words and write them down. When they've done that, tell the students that you're going to read out dictionary definitions of the words in random order and that they should cross out their words if they think they hear the definition. When they've crossed out all five words, they shout *Bingo*! Make sure you keep a record of the word definitions you call out so that you can check the students' answers.
- If you teach a monolingual class, you could read out a translation of each word rather than a definition in English. Alternatively, you could turn it into a pronunciation exercise by working on the recognition of phonetic script. Hold up cards with phonetic transcriptions of the words in random order. Students cross out their words if they think they've seen the corresponding phonetic transcription.

2 Standing in Line

Aim

This is a great way to review names after Unit 1.

Preparation

None.

Procedure

- Ask all the students to stand up and then form a line in alphabetical order according to the first letter of their first name. Show the class where the line should begin.
- Once they've lined up, check that they're in the correct order by asking them to take turns down the line saying *My name's ...*
- Here are some more criteria for different line-ups.

1 Alphabetical order according to their last names or their mother's or father's first name, or a random selection of words that you want to revise written on cards (they say the words aloud and line up according to the first letter).

2 Numerical order according to age or age of mother, or age of youngest member of their family, or number of cousins they have (most/fewest), or number of times they've been to the USA, etc.

3 Distance order (farthest/nearest) according to distance they live from the school, or distance they were born from the school, or longest distance they have ever walked, biked, or driven, etc.

4 Time order according to the time they got up this morning, or the time they went to bed last night, or the time they started work, or their favorite time of the day, etc.

5 Spelling order according to long words they know. Give each student a letter of the word you want to revise and ask them to sort themselves out into the correct order to spell the word. Here's a selection of words you might want to revise from Unit 1: *colleague*, *exercise*, *fashionable*, *neighbor*, *signature*, *technique*, etc.

6 Word order according to a sentence with at least eight words in it. Give each student a word and ask them to sort themselves out so that the sentence makes sense.

3 Battleships

Aim

To review vocabulary.

Preparation

Each student will need two grids of 10 squares across and down (see below). Squared paper is ideal for this activity.

Procedure

- Demonstrate the activity by drawing a blank grid on the board. Think of a word or words you want to revise and write them onto a different grid on a piece of paper, but do not tell the students what they are yet. You should write the words horizontally, one letter per square, as shown below.

A	p	a	j	a	m	a	s			
B										
C		g	l	o	v	e	s			
D										
E			e	a	r	r	i	n	g	s
F										
G										
H		s	u	i	t					
I										
J						p	a	n	t	s
	1	2	3	4	5	6	7	8	9	10

- Now tell the students that there are some words hidden in the grid. Explain that they need to find the squares with letters in them. Tell them to guess squares by giving letter and number references—for example, *C-2*, *F-10*, *J-4*, etc. When a student guesses a square with a letter in, write the letter in the square. They can guess a word when they think they know what it is. Continue like this until they find all the words.
- Now ask the students to work in pairs. First, they should draw two grids. One of them should remain blank, and on the other they need to write down six words, but without showing their partner. Either you can let the students choose their own words from the ones they've learned recently, or else you can give them a topic. For example, write six nationalities / jobs / classroom objects / weather conditions / animals.
- When they've written their words, tell the students to take turns naming a square on their partner's grid. If there's a letter in the square, their partner should say what the letter is and they should write it in the blank grid.
- As soon as they think they know their partner's word, they can guess. If it's wrong, they miss a turn.

4 Category Dictation

Aim

This activity can be adapted to review almost any vocabulary. It can also be used to review certain pronunciation and grammar points.

Preparation

Choose the language you want to review and devise a way of sorting it into two or more categories.

Procedure

- Write the category headings on the board and ask the students to copy them onto a piece of paper. Two simple categories are usually best. More than three can get complicated. Then dictate the words (ten to twelve maximum) slowly and clearly, and ask the students to write them down in the correct category. For example, you want to revise jobs from Unit 6, your categories might be jobs you do inside and jobs you do outside. So, write the following on the board and ask the students to copy it down.

Inside	Outside

- Then dictate the words: e.g. *a farmer*, *an archaeologist*, *a surgeon*, *a nanny*, a vet, etc. The students write down the words in the correct category. When you've dictated 10 or 12 words, ask students to compare their lists. When they've done this, ask them to call out their answers and write them on the board in the correct category, so that they can check the spelling. Alternatively, you could ask the students to take turns writing the answers on the board.
- Here are some more ideas for categories:

1 Revise family words. (Unit 1)

Suggested categories: Male or Female, *Have or Don't have* (this will obviously lead to different answers for each student).

2 Revise adjectives to describe places. (Unit 2)

Suggested categories: Positive or Negative, Can describe where we are now or Can't describe where we are now.

3 Revise past tense forms. (Unit 3)

Suggested categories: Regular or Irregular, Past form the same as the infinitive (e.g. beat/beat, hit/hit, set/set, etc.) or Past form different from the infinitive (e.g. choose/chose, forget/forgot, ride/rode, etc.)

4 Revise sports. (Unit 5)

Suggested categories: Sports with a ball and Sports without a ball; Sports you play in teams and Sports you play individually; Sports you use "go" with or Sports you use "play" with.

5 Revise parts of the body (Unit 9)

Suggested categories: Above the waist and Below the waist, or You have one of these and You have two of these.

5 Mill Drills

Aim

To provide controlled practice of new language in a drill-like way and to give students the opportunity to repeat the same language with several different partners.

Preparation

Organize your classroom so that the students can move around and speak to one another. Prepare one prompt card for each student in the class. The prompts will depend on the language you want to practice. (See below for examples of cue cards.)

Procedure

- Tell the students that they're going to spend 10 to 15 minutes practicing the new language, and that you're going to demonstrate this.
- Give one card to each student in the class, and keep one for yourself. Write a sample dialogue on the board. Point to the part of the dialogue to be supplied by the picture or word prompts on the card. For example:

side 1 | side 2 | Sample dialogue on board

Sample dialogue

expensive

A: *What are the stores like?*
B: *They're expensive.*

side 1 | side 2 | on board

Explain that the language will change according to

Mike

A: *What does Mike do?*
B: *He's a taxi driver.*

- Explain that the language will change according to the prompt on the card. Show the students how to hold their cards. This is important because cards must be held in such a way that when the students are talking to a partner, they're both able to see each other's cards.
- Choose a confident student to demonstrate the activity with you. Then ask two or three pairs of students to demonstrate the dialogue.
- Ask all the students to stand up and to go around the class or group, repeating the dialogue with as many different partners as possible, and using their cards as prompts.
- Stop the activity after a few moments and ask the students to either exchange cards with another

student, or turn their card around so that students get the opportunity to make new responses.

6 Five Favorites

Aim

This activity is good for reviewing any words learned recently.

Preparation

None

Procedure

- Students look back through their lesson notes for the last two weeks and select from the words they've recorded five words that they think are particularly useful. They compare their list with a partner and together they produce a common list of five words from the combined list of ten. To do this they'll have to argue for and against words on the combined list until they are both satisfied that they have the most useful five. If you wanted to continue the activity, you could then have each pair join up with another pair as a group of four and repeat the procedure. Depending on the size of your class, you might continue until you had established a list of "five favorites" for the whole class.
- The value of this activity lies in the students looking back through their notes, choosing the words, and then arguing for them to be part of the combined list. The whole procedure gives them valuable repeat exposure to words recently learned.
- A possible extension activity after each pair has formed their common list of five words is to collect the lists and redistribute them so that each pair has a different list. The pairs then write a dialogue or short story incorporating the five words they have on the list they've just received. You could then ask them to read out their dialogues or stories and the other students guess what the five listed words were.

7 Crosswords

Aim

This activity is good for reviewing lexical sets and can help with spelling.

Preparation

Choose a lexical set you want to review. For example, places in a city (Unit 2), office equipment (Unit 6), school subjects (Unit 8), food (Unit 10), animals (Unit 11), etc.

Procedure

- Students work in pairs. They'll need a piece of paper, preferably squared paper.
- Choose a topic, for example, *school subjects*.
- Student A writes "Across" words, and Student B writes "Down" words.
- It's a good idea to provide the first word across, and make sure that it's a long one. Student B then adds another school subject down the paper from top to bottom. This word must intersect with the school subject written across the page.
- Student A then writes another school subject across that intersects with the school subject Student B has written down. Students continue taking turns writing in their words.
- Students build up a crossword until they can't think of any more school subjects. (You could make it into a game by saying that the last person to write a school subject is a winner.) Note that students must leave one square between each word—this is why it's better and clearer to use squared paper.

8 Odd One Out

Aim

This activity can be used to review almost any language.

Preparation

Think of the vocabulary, pronunciation, or grammar point you want to review.

Procedure

- Write five words on the board and ask students which one is the odd one out. The students then explain why. This usually relates to the meaning of the word.

pink	red	dog	blue	yellow

- Here *dog* is the odd one out because it's an animal. The other words are colors.
- Note that it doesn't matter if the students can't explain in perfect English why *dog* is the odd one out. The important thing is that they're looking at and thinking about the words you want them to review.
- You can use this format to practice and review all sorts of things. Here are some examples:

1 For meaning:

sister/nephew/daughter/wife/mother

nephew is the odd one out because it's male. The other words describe females.

2 For spelling:

pen/book/bag/phone/diary

diary is the odd one out because you spell the plural *ies*. The other words you just add *s*.

3 For pronunciation: sounds

A/I/H/J/K

I is the odd one out because the vowel sound is different.

4 For pronunciation: stress

hospital/banana/potato/Italian/computer

hospital is the odd one out because the stress is on the first syllable. The other words have the stress on the second syllable.

5 For collocation: *do* or *make*

your homework / the laundry / an appointment / a training course / the grocery shopping

an appointment is the odd one out because you use *make*. For the others you use *do*.

6 For grammar:

cash / credit card / check / coin / bill

cash is the odd one out because it is uncountable– you can't say a *cash*. All the other words are countable.

- You should tell the students what the criteria are, for example "think about meaning" or "think about the sounds." To make the activity a little more challenging, instead of writing the words on the board, you can dictate them. As a follow-up, ask the students to write their own "Odd Ones Out."

9 Making Sentences

Aim

This activity is good for reviewing any type of vocabulary. It works best if the words are a fairly random selection and not part of a tight lexical set.

Preparation

Choose 12 words you want to review and write them in a circle (like a clock face) on the board.

Procedure

- Students work in pairs. They choose two or more of the words and try to make a sentence with them. Example sentences:

  My brother is doing yoga in the park.
  The snowboarder eats organic vegetables on Friday.
  I saw an ambitious puppy in the canal with a blue neck.

- The students then read out their sentences and you connect the words they have used on the board. You can correct the grammar as necessary (or you can make it more difficult for the students by only accepting grammatically correct sentences). It doesn't matter how bizarre the sentences are, the important thing is that students spend time looking at and remembering the vocabulary.
- If you write the words and draw the connecting lines on an whiteboard, you can show it to the students a few weeks later and see if they remember the sentences they wrote.

10 Random Letters

Aim

This activity is good for reviewing any type of vocabulary.

Preparation

None

Procedure

- Ask the students to call out any seven letters from the alphabet. (It doesn't have to be seven letters: anything between seven and twelve is fine.) Write the letters scattered on the board.

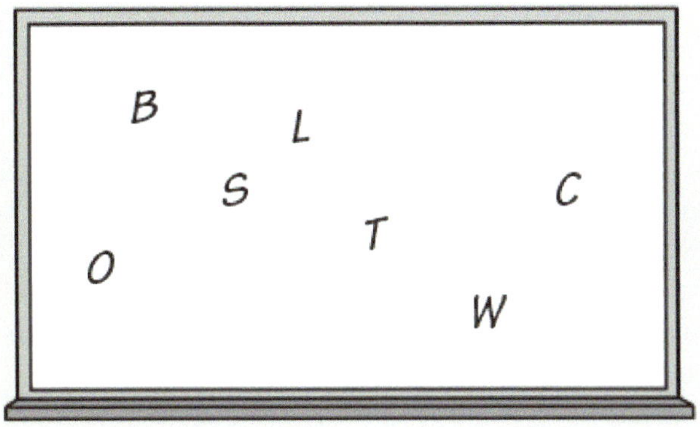

- Then ask the students in pairs to think of a word beginning with each letter on the board. The most obvious criterion is to revise words from a specific lexical set that you have taught recently, e.g. jobs, clothes, food, animals, etc. Alternatively, you could simply ask them for words they've noted down in lessons over the past two weeks.
- Another possibility would be to find the most interesting words they can from the Student's Book unit that you've just finished. If the lexical set you want them to revise is particularly rich, you could ask the students to think of as many words for each letter as they can in say three minutes: make it into a contest to find the most words.
- There are lots of possible variations using different criteria for words from the letters on the board. Here are a few:

1 Use the same criteria as above but ask the students to think of words ending with the letter on the board.

2 Ask the students to write only nouns, or adjectives or irregular verbs or some other part of speech.

3 Ask the students to write only words with three syllables or words with the same vowel sounds.

4 Ask students to write only words that start with the same letter in their own language or only words that start with a different letter.

5 Ask students to think of words that can combine to make a coherent sentence, e.g. *Ben likes selling cheap trees on weekends*. Accept only grammatically correct sentences, no matter how bizarre they might be.

Anecdote Tasks

American Inside Out Evolution Pre-intermediate includes a number of extended speaking tasks, where students tackle a longer piece of discourse. We've called these "Anecdotes." They are based on personal issues, for instance, memories, stories, people you know. When you learn a musical instrument, you can't spend all your time playing scales and exercises: you also need to learn whole pieces in order to see how music is organized. Anecdotes give students a chance to get to grips with how discourse is organized. We have found the following strategies helpful in getting our students to tell their Anecdotes.

1 Choose global topics that everybody can relate to

One of the main objectives of an Anecdote is to encourage students to experiment with, and hopefully grow more competent at, using language at the more demanding end of their range. It therefore seems only fair to ask them to talk about subjects they know something about. With familiar subject matter students can concentrate on how they're speaking, as well as what they're speaking about. The nine Anecdote topics in *American Inside Out Evolution Pre-intermediate* have been carefully selected to appeal to the widest range of students, while at the same time, fitting into the context of the unit.

Unit 1 Somebody who is important to you

Unit 2 The best place you ever visited

Unit 4 A gift you bought for somebody

Unit 5 Your experiences of sports at school

Unit 6 A person you know with a good job

Unit 8 Your favorite subject at school

Unit 10 The healthiest person you know

Unit 11 Your pet or a pet you know

Unit 12 The most incredible building you've ever seen

As soon as you have got to know your students well enough, you'll be able to choose other Anecdote topics suited to their particular interests and experiences.

2 Allow sufficient preparation time

Students need time to assemble their thoughts and think about the language they'll need. The Anecdotes are set up through evocative questions. Students read or listen to a planned series of questions and choose what specifically they'll talk about; shyer students can avoid matters they feel are too personal. This student preparation is a key stage and should not be rushed. Research, by Peter Skehan and Pauline Foster among others, has shown that learners who plan for tasks attempt more ambitious and complex language, hesitate less, and make fewer basic errors.

The simplest way to prepare students for an Anecdote is to ask them to read the list of questions in the book and decide which they want to talk about. This could be done during class time or as homework preparation for the following lesson. Ask them to think about the language they'll need. Sentence beginnings are provided in the Student's Book to give the students some extra help. Encourage them to use dictionaries and make notes—but not to write out what they'll actually say. Finally, put them into pairs to exchange Anecdotes.

A variation is to ask the students to read the questions in the book while, at the same time, listening to you read them aloud. Then ask them to prepare in detail for the task, as above. Alternatively, ask the students to close their books—and then to close their eyes. Ask them to listen to the questions as you read them aloud and think about what they evoke. Some classes will find this a more involving process. It also allows you to adapt the questions to your class: adding new ones or leaving out ones you think are inappropriate. After the reading, give them enough time to finalize their preparation before starting the speaking task.

3 Monitor students and give feedback

It's important for students to feel that their efforts are being monitored by the teacher. Realistically, it's probably only possible for a teacher to monitor and give feedback to one or two pairs of students during each Anecdote activity. It's therefore vital that the teacher adopts a strict rota system, and makes sure that everyone in the class is monitored over the course of a semester. Constructive feedback helps students improve their delivery.

4 Provide a "model anecdote"

It's always useful for the students to hear a model Anecdote at some stage during the Anecdote task cycle. The most obvious model is you, the teacher.

Alternatively, you might ask another teacher or a friend to talk to the students. For every Anecdote activity in *American Inside Out Evolution Pre-intermediate* there's a model listening on the CD with an accompanying task in the Student's Book.

5 Repeat the same anecdote with a new partner at regular intervals

Consider going back to Anecdotes and repeating them in later classes. Let the students know that you're going to do this. This will reassure them that you're doing it on purpose, but more importantly, it will mean that they'll be more motivated to dedicate some time and thought to preparation. When you repeat the task, mix the class so that each student works with a new partner, i.e. one who has not previously heard the Anecdote.

In our experience, most students are happy to listen to their partner's Anecdotes. If, however, any of your students are reluctant listeners, you might think about giving them some sort of "listening task." Here are three examples:

- Ask the listener to check the prompt questions that the "Anecdote teller" answers while telling the Anecdote.
- Ask the listener to time the "Anecdote teller." In Teaching Collocations (page 91), Michael Lewis suggests reducing the time allowed to deliver the Anecdote each time it's repeated: for example, in the first instance the student has five minutes; for the second telling they have four minutes; and the third three minutes.
- Ask the listener to take brief notes about the Anecdote and write them up as a summary for homework. Then give the summary to the "Anecdote teller" to check.

The pedagogic value of getting students to re-tell Anecdotes—repeat a "big chunk" of spoken discourse—cannot be overstated. Repeating complex tasks reflects real interactions. We all have our set pieces: jokes, stories, and we tend to refine and improve them as we retell them. Many students will appreciate the opportunity to do the same thing in their second language. Research by Martin Bygate among others has shown that given this opportunity students become more adventurous and at the same time more precise in the language they use.

You can also use the Anecdotes to test oral proficiency and thereby add a speaking component to accompany the tests in the Teacher's Edition.

KEY CONCEPTS

The following excerpts are from *An A-Z of ELT* by Scott Thornbury (Macmillan Books for Teachers, 2006). They give clear authoritive definitions and explanations of some of the most important concepts in this textbook.

Contents

- classroom interaction
- collocation
- communicative activity
- context
- drill
- dynamics: group, classroom
- fluency
- focus on form
- function
- grammar teaching
- learner-centered instruction, learner-centeredness
- learning style
- listening
- motivation
- noticing
- personalization
- practice
- pronunciation teaching
- reading
- speaking
- task
- vocabulary teaching
- writing

Note: SLA = Second Language Acquisition

classroom interaction

methodology

Classroom interaction is the general term for what goes on between the people in the classroom, particularly when it involves language. In traditional classrooms, most interaction is initiated by the teacher, and learners either respond individually, or in unison. Teacher-centered interaction of this kind is associated with transmissive teaching, such as a lecture or presentation, where the teacher transmits the content of the lesson to the learners.

In order to increase the amount of student involvement and interaction, teacher-learner interaction is often combined with **pairwork** and **groupwork**, where learners interact among themselves in pairs or small groups. Other kinds of interaction include mingling or milling. Pairwork and groupwork are associated with a more **learner-centered** approach. Rather than passively receiving the lesson content, the learners are actively engaged in using language and discovering things for themselves. The value of pairwork and groupwork has been reinforced by the belief that **interaction** facilitates language learning. Some would go as far as to say that it is all that is required.

The potential for classroom interaction is obviously constrained by such factors as the number of students, the size of the room, the furniture, and the purpose or type of activity. Not all activities lend themselves to pairwork or groupwork. Some activities, such as reading, are best done as individual work. On the other hand, listening activities (such as listening to an audio recording, or to the teacher) favor a whole class format, as do grammar presentations. The whole class is also an appropriate form of organization when reviewing the results of an activity, as, for example, when spokespersons from each group are reporting on the results of a discussion or survey.

The success of any classroom interaction will also depend on the extent to which the learners know what they are meant to be doing and why, which in turn depends on how clearly and efficiently the interaction has been set up. Pairwork and groupwork can be a complete waste of time if learners are neither properly prepared for it, nor sure of its purpose or outcome.

Finally, the success of pairwork and groupwork will depend on the kind of group **dynamics** that have been established. Do the students know one another? Are they happy working together? Do they mind working without constant teacher supervision? Establishing a productive classroom dynamic may involve making decisions as to who works with whom. It may also mean deliberately staging the introduction of different kinds of interactions, starting off with the more controlled, teacher-led interactions before, over time, allowing learners to work in pairs and finally in groups.

collocation

vocabulary

If two words *collocate*, they frequently occur together. The relation between the words may be grammatical, as when certain verbs collocate with particular prepositions, such as *depend on*, *account for*, *abstain from*, or when a verb, like *make*, *take*, or *do*, collocates with a noun, as in *make an arrangement*, *take advantage*, *do the shopping*. The collocation may also be lexical, as when two **content words** regularly co-occur, as in a *broad hint*, *a narrow escape* (but not *a *wide hint* or *a *tight escape*). The strength of the collocation can vary: *a broad street* or a *narrow path* are weak collocations, since both elements can co-occur with lots of other words: *a broad river*, *a busy street*, etc. *Broad hint* and *narrow escape* are stronger. Stronger still are combinations where one element rarely occurs without the other, as in *moot point*, *slim pickings* and *scot-free*. Strongest of all are those where both elements never or rarely occur without the other, such as *dire straits* and *spick and span*. These have acquired the frozen status of *fixed expressions*.

Unsurprisingly, learners lack intuitions as to which words go with which, and this accounts for many errors, such as *You can <u>completely</u> enjoy it* (instead of *thoroughly*), *On Saturday we made shopping* (instead of *went*), and *We went the <u>incorrect</u> way* (for wrong). Using texts to highlight particular collocations and teaching new words in association with their most frequent collocations are two ways of approaching the problem. Nowadays learners' dictionaries also include useful collocational information.

communicative activity

methodology

A communicative activity is one in which real communication occurs. Communicative activities belong to that generation of classroom **activities** that emerged in response to the need for a more **communicative approach** in the teaching of second languages. (In their more evolved form as **tasks**, communicative activities are central to **task-based learning**). They attempt to import into a practice activity the key features of "reallife" communication. These are:

- *purposefulness:* speakers are motivated by a communicative goal (such as getting information, making a request, giving instructions) and not simply by the need to display the correct use of language for its own sake
- *reciprocity:* to achieve a purpose, speakers need to interact, and there is as much need to listen as to speak
- *negotiation:* following from the above, they may need to check and **repair** the communication in order to be understood by each other
- *unpredictability:* neither the process, nor the outcome, nor the language used in the exchange, is entirely predictable
- *heterogeneity:* participants can use any communicative means at their disposal; in other words, they are not restricted to the use of a pre-specified grammar item.

And, in the case of spoken language in particular:

- *synchronicity*: the exchange takes place in real time.

The best known communicative activity is the *information gap* activity. Here, the information necessary to complete the task is either in the possession of just one of the participants, or distributed among them.

In order to achieve the goal of the task, therefore, the learners have to share the information that they have. For example, in a *describe-and-draw* activity, one student has a picture which is hidden from his or her partner. The task is for that student to describe the picture so that the partner can accurately draw it. In a *find-the-difference task*, both students of a pair have pictures (or texts) that are the same apart from some minor details. The goal is to identify these differences. In a *jigsaw activity*, each member of a group has different information. One might have a bus timetable, another a map, and another a list of hotels. They have to share this information in order to plan a weekend break together.

Information gap activities have been criticized on the grounds that they lack **authenticity.** Nor are information gap activities always as productive as might be wished: unsupervised, learners may resort to **communication strategies** in order to simplify the task. A more exploitable information gap, arguably, is the one that exists between the learners themselves, i.e., what they don't know—but might like to know—about one another (➜ **personalization**).

context

linguistics

The context of a language item is its adjacent language items. In the absence of context, it is often impossible to assign exact meaning to an item. A sentence like *Ben takes the bus to work*, for example, could have past, present, or future reference, depending on the context:

> I know this guy called Ben. One day Ben takes the *bus to work*, and just as ...
>
> Most days Ben *takes the bus to work*, but sometimes he rides his bike ...
>
> If Ben takes the bus to work tomorrow, he'll be late, because there's a strike ...

Likewise, a sentence like *You use it like this* is meaningless in the absence of a context. By the same token, a word or sentence in one context can have a very different meaning in another. The sign *NO BICYCLES* in a public park means something different to *NO BICYCLES* outside a bicycle rental shop. It is sometimes necessary to distinguish between different kinds of context. On the one hand, there is the context of the accompanying text, sometimes called the *co-text*. The context of this sentence, for example, includes the sentences that precede and follow it, as well as the paragraph of which it forms a part. It is the co-text that offers clues as to the meaning of unfamiliar vocabulary in a text.

The situational context (also context of situation, context of use), on the other hand, is the physical and temporal setting in which an instance of language use occurs. The typical context for the spoken question *Are you being served?* is in a shop, for example. Both co-text and context influence the production and interpretation of language. **Discourse analysis** studies the relationship between language and co-text, including the way that sentences or utterances are connected. **Pragmatics** studies the relationship between language and its contexts of use, including the way meaning can be inferred by reference to context factors. Various theories have been proposed in order to account for the ways that language choices are determined by contextual factors. One of the best known of these is Michael Halliday's **systemic functional linguistics.** Halliday distinguishes three variables in any context that systematically impact on language choices and which, together, determine a text's **register**:

- the field: what the language is being used to talk about, and for what purposes
- the tenor: the participants in the language event, and their relationship
- the mode: how language is being used in the exchange, e.g. is it written or spoken?

For example, this short text shows the influence of all three factors:

> Do u fancy film either 2nite or 2moro? Call me.

The field is "making arrangements about leisure activities", hence the use of words like *film*, *2nite* (*tonight*), *2moro* (*tomorrow*). The tenor is one of familiarity and equality (accounting for the informal fancy and the imperative: *call me*); and the mode is that of a written text message, which explains its brevity, its use of abbreviated forms (*u*, *2nite*) and the absence of salutations. A change in any of these contextual factors is likely to have a significant effect on the text.

Language learners, it is argued, need to know how these contextual factors correlate with language choices in order to produce language that is appropriate to the context. One way of doing this is to ask them to make changes to a text (such as the text message above) that take into account adjustments to the field, tenor, or mode.

drill

methodology

A drill is repetitive oral practice of a language item, whether a sound, a word, a phrase, or a sentence structure. Drills that are targeted at sentence structures are sometimes called pattern practice drills. Drills follow a prompt-response sequence, where the prompt usually comes from the teacher, and the students respond, either in chorus (a choral drill), or individually. An imitation drill simply involves repeating the prompt, as in:

Teacher: They have been watching TV.
Student: They have been watching TV.

A *substitution drill* requires the students to substitute one element of the pattern with the prompt, making any necessary adjustments:

Teacher: They have been watching TV.
Student: They have been watching TV.
Teacher: She

Student:	She has been watching TV.
Teacher:	I
Student:	I have been watching TV.

A *variable substitution* drill is the same, but the prompts are not restricted to one element of the pattern:

Teacher:	They have been watching TV.
Student:	They have been watching TV.
Teacher:	She
Student:	She has been watching TV.
Teacher:	radio
Student:	She has been listening to the radio.
Teacher:	We
Student:	We have been listening to the radio.

Drills were a defining feature of the **audiolingual** method, and were designed to reinforce good language "habits." The invention of language laboratories allowed sustained drilling without the need for a teacher to supply the prompts. With the demise of audiolingualism, drilling fell from favor. However, many teachers—even those who subscribe to a **communicative approach**—feel the need for some form of repetition practice of the kind that drills provide. This may be for the purpose of developing **accuracy**, or as a form of **fluency** training, i.e. in order to develop **automaticity**.

Hence, communicative drills were developed. A communicative drill is still essentially repetitive, and focuses on a particular structure or pattern but it has an *information gap* element built in. Learners can perform the drill in pairs, or as a *milling activity* (**classroom interaction**) and they are required to attend to what they hear as much as what they say. The milling activity popularly known as *Find someone who ...* is one such activity. Students are set the task of finding other students in the class who, for example, can ride a horse, can speak French, can play the guitar, etc. They mill around, asking questions of the type *Can you ...?* until they have asked all the other students their questions, and then they report their findings.

dynamics: group, classroom

methodology

Dynamics are the actions and interactions, both conscious and unconscious, that take place between members of a group, whether the whole class or subgroups. Group dynamics are instrumental in forging a productive and motivating classroom environment. They are determined by such factors as: the composition of the group (including the age, sex, and relative status of the members, as well as their different attitudes, beliefs, learning styles and abilities); the patterns of relationships between members of the group, including how well they know each other, and the roles they each assume, such as group leader, spokesperson, etc; physical factors such as the size of the group and the way it is seated; and the tasks that the group are set, e.g.: Does the task require everyone to contribute? Does it encourage co-operation or competition? Are the goals of the task clear to the group members?

Ways that the teacher can promote a positive group (and class) dynamic include:

- ensuring all class or group members can see and hear one another, and that they know (and use) each other's names
- keeping groups from getting too big—three to six members is optimal
- setting—or negotiating—clear rules for groupwork, such as using only the target language, giving everyone a turn to speak, allowing individuals to "pass" if they don't want to say anything too personal
- using "ice-breaking" activities to encourage interaction, laughter, and relaxation
- ensuring that group tasks are purposeful, interactive, and collaborative
- personalizing tasks, i.e., setting tasks that involve the sharing of personal experiences and opinions
- defining the roles and responsibilities within the group, and varying these regularly, e.g. by appointing a different spokesperson each time
- monitoring groupwork in progress, and being alert to any possible conflicts or tensions between members, and reconstituting groups, if necessary
- discussing the importance of groupwork with learners, and getting feedback on group processes.

fluency

SLA

If someone is said to be fluent in a language, or to speak a language fluently, it is generally understood that they are able to speak the language idiomatically and accurately, without undue pausing, without an intrusive accent, and in a manner appropriate to the context. In fact, research into listeners' perceptions of fluency suggests that fluency is primarily the ability to produce and maintain speech in real time.

To do this, fluent speakers are capable of:

- appropriate pausing, i.e.:
  - their pauses may be long but are not frequent
  - their pauses are usually filled, e.g. with **pause fillers** like *erm*, you know, sort of

    - their pauses occur at meaningful transition points, e.g. at the intersections of clauses or phrases, rather than midway in a phrase
- long runs, i.e., there are many syllables and words between pauses

All of the above factors depend on the speaker having a well-developed grammar, an extensive vocabulary, and, crucially, a store of memorized chunks. Being able to draw on this store of chunks means not having to depend on grammar to construct each utterance from scratch. This allows the speaker to devote **attention** to other aspects of the interaction, such as planning ahead. Speakers also use a number of "tricks" or *production* strategies to convey the illusion of fluency. One such strategy is disguising pauses by filling them, or by repeating a word or phrase.

Some proponents of the **communicative approach** redefined fluency so as to distinguish it from **accuracy**. Fluency came to mean "communicative effectiveness", regardless of formal accuracy or speed of delivery. Activities that are communicative, such as information-gap activities, are said to be *fluency-focused*. This is the case even for activities that produce short, halting utterances. Separating accuracy and fluency, and defining the latter as *communicative* language use, is misleading, though. There are many speech events whose communicativeness depends on their accuracy. Air traffic control talk is just one. Moreover, many learners aspire to being more than merely communicative.

Classroom activities that target fluency need to prepare the learner for real-time speech production. Learning and memorizing lexical chunks, including useful conversational gambits, is one approach. **Drills** may help here, as will some types of **communicative activity** that involve repetition. Research has also shown that fluency improves the more times a **task** is repeated. Fluency may also benefit from activities that manage to distract learners' attention away from formal accuracy so that they are not tempted to slow down. (This has been called "parking their attention"). Some interactive and competitive language **games** have this effect. **Drama** activities, such as role-plays, recreate conditions of real-time language use, and are therefore good for developing fluency. Finally, learners can achieve greater fluency from learning a repertoire of **communication strategies**, i.e., techniques for getting around potential problems caused by a lack of the relevant words or structures.

focus on form

SLA

When learners focus on form, they direct conscious attention to some formal feature of the language **input**. The feature may be the fact that the past of *has* is *had*, or that *enjoy* is followed by verb forms ending in *-ing*, or that adjectives do not have plural forms in English. The learners' attention may be self-directed, or it may be directed by the teacher or by another learner. Either way, it has been argued that a focus on form is a necessary condition for language learning. Simply focusing on the **meaning** of the input is not enough. Focusing on form is, of course, not a new idea: most teaching methods devote a great deal of time to the forms of the language, e.g. when new grammar items are presented. But the term focus on form captures the fact that this focus can, theoretically, occur at any stage in classroom instruction. Thus, **correction**, especially in the form of negative **feedback**, is a kind of focus on form. In fact, some researchers argue that the most effective form focus is that which arises incidentally, in the context of communication, as when the teacher quickly elicits a correction during a classroom discussion. This incidental approach contrasts with the more traditional and deliberate approach, where teaching is based on a **syllabus** of graded structures (*or forms*), and these are pre-taught in advance of activities designed to practice them. This traditional approach is called—by some researchers—*a focus on forms*.

function

linguistics

The function of a language item is its communicative purpose. Language is more than simply forms and their associated meanings (i.e., **usage**). It is also the communicative **uses** to which these forms and meanings are put. These two sentences, for example, share the same forms, but function quite differently:

[in an email]	Thank you for sending me the disk.
[a notice in a taxi]	Thank you for not smoking.

The function of the first is expressing thanks, while the second is more like a prohibition. Likewise, the same function can be expressed by different forms:

[a notice in a taxi]	Thank you for not smoking.
[a sign in a classroom]	No smoking.

Thus, there is no one-to-one match between form and function. Assigning a function to a text or an utterance usually requires knowledge of the **context** in which the text is used. The study of how context and function are interrelated is called **pragmatics**.

Communicative functions can be categorized very broadly and also at increasing levels of detail. The "big" functions, or macrofunctions, describe the way language is used in very general terms. These include the use of language for *expressive purposes* (e.g. poetry), for *regulatory purposes* (e.g. for getting people to do things), for *interpersonal purposes* (e.g. for socializing), and for *representational purposes* (e.g. to inform). More useful, from the point of view of designing language syllabuses, are microfunctions. These are usually expressed as **speech acts**, such as *agreeing* and *disagreeing*, *reporting*, *warning*, *apologizing*, *thanking*, *greeting*, etc. Such categories form the basis of **functional syllabuses**, a development associated with the **communicative approach**. They often appear as one strand of a coursebook **syllabus**. Functions differ from notions in that the latter describe areas of meaning such as *ability*, *duration*, *quantity*, *frequency*, etc.–rather than the uses to which these meanings are put.

One way to teach functions is to adopt a "phrasebook" approach, and teach useful ways of expressing common functions (what are called functional exponents), such as *Would you like ...?* (*inviting*) and *Could you ..., please?* (*requesting*). More memorable, though, is to teach these expressions in the contexts of **dialogues**, so that the functional exponents are associated not only with common situations in which they are used, but with related functions (such as *accepting* and *refusing*). The term *function*, in contrast to **form**, is also used in linguistics, specifically with regard to the functions of the different elements of a **clause** (such as subject and object).

grammar teaching

methodology

Like the word **grammar** itself, the topic of grammar teaching is a controversial one, and teachers often take opposing views. Historically, language teaching methods have positioned themselves along a scale from "zero grammar" to "total grammar", according to their approach to grammar teaching. Proponents of *natural methods*, who model their approach to teaching second languages on the way that first languages are acquired, reject any explicit teaching of grammar at all. (They may, however, teach according to a grammar **syllabus**, even if no mention of grammar as such is made in the classroom.) This implicit approach is common both to the **direct method** and to **audiolingualism**. Through exposure to demonstrations, situations or examples, learners are expected to pick up the rules of grammar by **inductive learning**. At the other end of the spectrum, there are approaches, such as **grammar-translation**, that adopt an explicit and **deductive learning** approach. From the outset, learners are presented with rules which they study and then practice. Occupying a midway point between zero grammar and total grammar is the approach called **consciousness-raising**. Instead of being given rules, learners are presented with language data which challenge them to rethink (and *restructure*) their existing mental grammar. This data might take the form of **input** that has been manipulated in some way. For example, pairs of sentences, such as the following, have to be matched to pictures, forcing learners to discriminate between them, and, in theory, **notice** the difference (**→ noticing**):

> The Queen drove to the airport.
> The Queen was driven to the airport.

(This is sometimes called a *grammar interpretation* task, or structured input.) In order to do the task, learners have to process not just the individual words, but also their grammatical form. That is why this approach to teaching grammar is sometimes called *processing instruction*. There are other researchers who argue that it is by means of manipulating the learner's output, e.g. through productive practice, that mental restructuring is best effected.

The **communicative approach** accommodates different approaches to grammar teaching. Proponents of **taskbased learning**, for example, argue that if the learner is engaged in solving problems using language, then the mental grammar will develop of its own accord. However, advocates of the weaker version of the communicative approach (and the version that is most widespread) justify a role for the pre-teaching of grammar in advance of production. This view finds support in **cognitive learning theory**, which suggests that conscious attention to grammatical form (called **focus on form**) speeds up language learning, and is a necessary corrective against premature **fossilization**. There is some debate, though, as to whether this form focus should be planned or incidental. Incidental grammar teaching occurs when the teacher deals with grammar issues as and when they come up, e.g. in the form of **correction**, or task **feedback**.

In this way (it is argued) grammar teaching follows the learner's own "syllabus." Such an approach attempts to address one of the dilemmas of grammar teaching: the fact that the learner's mental grammar, and the way it develops, bears only an accidental relation to a formal grammar syllabus.

Nevertheless, the research into these different choices is still inconclusive. It may be the case that some items of grammar respond better to explicit teaching, while others are more easily picked up through exposure. There are also different learner types: some prefer learning and applying rules, while others are happier with a more "deep-end" approach (→ **learning style**). Most current teaching materials hedge their bets on these issues. They offer both deductive and inductive grammar presentations, and opportunities for incidental as well as for planned learning.

learner-centered instruction, learner-centeredness

methodology

Learner-centered instruction aims to give learners more say in areas that are traditionally considered the domain of the teacher or of the institution. Learner-centered instruction is true to the spirit of progressive education, including the movement towards providing learners with greater **autonomy**. For example, a learner-centered **curriculum** would involve learners in negotiating decisions relating to the choice of syllabus content, of materials, of activity-types, and of assessment procedures. Learner-centeredness also describes ways of organizing **classroom interaction** so that the focus is directed away from the teacher, and on to the learners, who perform tasks in pairs or small groups. This contrasts with traditional, teacher-centered, classroom interaction. Some writers believe that the dichotomy between learner-centered (= good) and teacher-centered (= bad) is a false one. It might be more useful to talk about *learning-centered instruction*, i.e., instruction which prioritizes sound learning principles. In a learning-centered approach there would be room for both learner-centered and teacher-centered interactions.

learning style

psychology

Your learning style is your preferred way of learning. This style may be influenced by biographical factors (such as how you were taught as a child) or by innately endowed factors (such as whether you have a "good ear" for different sounds). Types of learning style are often presented in the form of polarities (some of which may overlap), such as:

- analytic versus global (or holistic) thinkers, i.e., learners who tend to focus on the details, versus learners who tend to see "the big picture"
- rule-users versus data-gatherers, i.e., learners who learn and apply rules, versus those who prefer exposure to lots of examples
- reflective versus impulsive learners
- group-oriented versus solitary learners
- extrovert versus introverted learners
- verbal versus visual learners
- passive versus active learners.

Attempts have been made to group these polarities and relate them to brain lateralization. So, a bias towards left-brain processing correlates with analytic, rule forming and verbal learners, while a bias towards right-brain processing correlates with their opposite. A less binary view of learning style is that proposed by the psychologist Howard Gardner. He identified at least seven distinct intelligences that all individuals possess but to different degrees. These include the *logical/mathematical*, the *verbal/linguistic*, and the *visual/spatial*. Similarly, proponents of **neuro-linguistic programming** distinguish between different sensory orientations, including the *visual*, *aural*, and *kinesthetic* (i.e., related to movement, touch). So far, though, there is no convincing evidence that any of these dispositions correlates with specific learning behaviors. Nor has it been shown that a preference in one area predicts success in language learning. In fact, it is very difficult to separate learning style from other potentially influential factors, such as personality, intelligence, and previous learning experience. Nor is it clear to what extent learning style can be manipulated, e.g. through **learner training**. The best that can be said is that, if the learner's preferred learning style is out of synch with the type of instruction on offer, then success is much less likely than if the two are well matched. This supports the case for an **eclectic** approach, on the one hand, and the individualization of learning, on the other.

listening

methodology

Listening is the skill of understanding spoken language. It is also the name given to classroom activities that are designed to develop this skill—what are also called *listening comprehension activities*—as in "today we're going to do a listening." Listening is one of the four language **skills**, and, along with **reading**, was once thought of as being a "passive" skill. In fact, although receptive, listening is anything but passive. It is a goal-oriented activity, involving not only processing of the incoming speech signals (called *bottom-up processing*) but also the use of prior knowledge, contextual clues, and expectations (*top-down processing*) in order to create meaning. Among the sub-skills of listening are:

- perceiving and discriminating individual sounds

- segmenting the stream of speech into recognizable units such as words and phrases
- using **stress** and **intonation** cues to distinguish given information from new information
- attending to **discourse markers** and using these to predict changes in the direction of the talk
- guessing the meaning of unfamiliar words
- using clues in the text (such as vocabulary) and context clues to predict what is coming
- making inferences about what is not stated
- selecting key information relevant to the purpose for listening
- integrating incoming information into the mental "picture" (or **schema**) of the speech event so far

Also, since listening is normally interactive, listeners need to be capable of:

- recognizing when speakers have finished their turns, or when it is appropriate to interrupt
- providing ongoing signals of understanding, interest, etc. (*backchanneling*)
- asking for clarification, asking someone to
- repeat what they have just said, and repairing misunderstandings

These sub-skills exist across languages, so, in theory, learners should be able to transfer them from their first language into their second. In fact, there are a number of reasons why this does not always happen. One is that speakers of different languages process speech signals differently, depending on the phonetic characteristics of the language they are used to. This means that speakers of some languages will find it harder than others to match the spoken word to the way that the word is represented in their mind. They simply do not recognize the word. Another problem is lack of sufficient L2 knowledge, such as vocabulary or grammar. A third problem is that learners may lack the means (and the confidence) to negotiate breakdowns in understanding. Finally, many learners simply lack exposure to spoken language, and therefore have not had sufficient opportunities to experience listening. These problems can be compounded in classrooms because:

- Listening to audio recordings deprives the learners of useful visual information, and allows the learners no opportunity to interact and repair misunderstandings.
- Classroom acoustics are seldom ideal.
- If learners do not know what they are listening for (in the absence, for example, of some pre-set listening task) they may try to process as much information as possible, rather than being selective in their listening. This can lead to listening overload, which in turn can cause inhibiting anxiety.
- Listening texts that have been specially written for classroom use are often simplified. But if this simplification means eliminating a lot of redundant language, such as speaker repetitions, pause fillers and vague language, the density of information that results may make it harder—not easier—to process.

For this reason, the use of audio recordings to develop listening skills needs to be balanced against the advantages of using other media, such as video and face-to-face interaction with the teacher or another speaker.

Nevertheless, the use of audio recordings is an established part of classroom practice, so it is important to know how to use them to best advantage. The following approach is one that is often recommended:

- Provide some minimum contextual information, e.g. who is talking to whom about what, and why. This helps to compensate for lack of visual information, and allows learners to activate the relevant mental **schema**, which in turn helps top-down processing, including the sub-skill of prediction.
- Pre-teach key vocabulary: this helps with bottom-up processing, although too much help may mean that learners don't get sufficient practice in guessing from context.
- Set some "while-listening" questions. Initially, these should focus on the overall gist of the text. For example: true/false questions, selecting, ordering or matching pictures, ticking items on a list, following a map.
- Play a small section of the recording first, to give learners an opportunity to familiarize themselves with the different voices, and to trigger accurate expectations as to what they will hear.
- Play the recording right through, and then allow learners to consult on the answers to the pre-set task. Check these answers. If necessary, re-play the recording until satisfied that learners have "got the gist."
- Set a more demanding task, requiring more intensive listening, such as listening for detail, or inferring speakers' attitudes, intentions, etc. If the recording is a long one, it may pay to stage the intensive listening in sections. Again, allow learners to consult in pairs, before checking the task in open class.
- On the basis of the learners' success with these tasks, identify problem sections of the recording and return to these, playing and replaying them, and perhaps eliciting a word-by-word transcription and writing this on the board.
- Distribute copies of the transcript of the recording (if available) and replay the recording while learners read the transcript. This allows the

learners to clear up any remaining problems, and also to match what they hear to what they see.

The above approach can be adapted to suit different kinds of recorded texts and different classroom needs. For higher-level learners, for example, it may be counterproductive to make listening too easy. The approach can also be adapted to the use of video, and even to live listenings, such as listening to the teacher or a guest.

motivation

psychology

Motivation is what drives learners to achieve a goal, and is a key factor determining success or failure in language learning. The learner's goal may be a short-term one, such as successfully performing a classroom task, or a long-term one, such as achieving native-like proficiency in the language. With regard to long-term goals, a distinction is often made between *instrumental motivation* and *integrative motivation*. Instrumental motivation is when the learner has a functional objective, such as passing an exam or getting a job. Integrative motivation, on the other hand, is when the learner wants to be identified with the target language community. Intersecting with these two motivational *orientations* are two different *sources* of motivation: *intrinsic* (e.g. the pleasure of doing a task for its own sake) and *extrinsic* (e.g. the "carrot and stick" approach). Another motivational source that has been identified is success: experience of succeeding can result in increased motivation (called *resultative motivation*), which raises the question as to whether motivation is as much a result as a cause of learning.

Various theories of motivation have been proposed. Most of these identify a variety of factors that, in combination, contribute to overall motivation, such as:

- *attitudes*, e.g. to the target language and to speakers of the language
- *goals*, both long-term and short-term, and the learners' *orientation* to these goals
- how much *value* the learner attaches to achieving the goals, especially as weighed against *expectancy of success*; expectancy of success may come from the learners' assessment of their own abilities, and how they account for previous successes or failures
- *self-esteem*, and the need to achieve and maintain it through *intrinsic interest*, *pleasure*, *relevance* or *challenge* of the task
- *group dynamic:* is it competitive, collaborative, or individualistic?
- *teacher's attitudes*, e.g. what expectations does the teacher project about the learners' likelihood of success?

As the last point suggests, teachers can play a key role in motivating learners, not just in terms of choosing activities that are intrinsically motivating, but in the attitudes they project. Two researchers on motivation offer the following advice for teachers:

Ten commandments for motivating language learners:

1. Set a personal example with your own behavior.
2. Create a pleasant, relaxed atmosphere in the classroom.
3. Present the tasks properly.
4. Develop a good relationship with the learners.
5. Increase the learners' linguistic self-confidence.
6. Make the language classes interesting.
7. Promote learner autonomy.
8. Personalize the learning process.
9. Increase the learners' goal-orientedness.
10. Familiarize learners with the target language culture.

noticing

SLA

If you notice a feature of the language that you are exposed to, it attracts your attention and you make a mental note of it. For example, a learner might notice (without necessarily understanding) the sign *Mind the gap*, repeated several times on a railroad station platform. That same day, the learner hears the teacher say *would you mind* in the context of making a request in class. A day or two later, the same learner hears someone else say *I don't mind*. Each successive "noticing" both primes the learner to notice new occurrences of mind, and at the same time contributes to a growing understanding of the use and meaning of *mind*. Proponents of **cognitive learning theory** believe that noticing is a prerequisite for learning: without it input would remain as mere "noise." The *noticing hypothesis*, then, claims that noticing is a necessary condition for acquisition, although not the only one. Some kind of mental processing of what has been noticed is also necessary before the **input** becomes *intake*, i.e., before it is moved into long-term **memory**.

Teachers obviously play an important role in helping learners to notice features of the language. They do this when they repeat words or structures, write them on the board, or even drill them. One way of increasing the chance of learners' noticing an item is to include it lots of times in a text, a technique called *input flood*. For example, learners read a text with the word *mind* included several times. They then categorize these examples according to their meaning. A set of **concordance** lines for a particular word can be used in the same way.

There is another type of noticing, called *noticing the gap*. This is when learners are made aware of a gap in their language knowledge. This might happen when they do a **dictation**, for example. When they compare their version with the correct version, they may notice certain differences, such as the lack of past tense endings, which represent a gap in their **interlanguage**. It has been argued that noticing the gap can trigger the **restructuring** of interlanguage. That is, "minding the gap" leads learners to "fill the gap."

personalization

methodology

When you personalize language you use it to talk about your knowledge, experience, and feelings. Personalization of the type *Now write five true sentences about yourself using "used to"* is often motivated by the need to provide further practice of pre-taught grammar structures. But it is also good preparation for the kinds of situations of genuine language use that learners might encounter outside the classroom. These advantages are lost, though, if the teacher's response is to treat the exercise as *only* an exercise, and correct the learners' errors without responding to the content.

The influence of **humanistic approaches** has given a fresh impetus to personalization, both in terms of providing a more coherent rationale and suggesting a broader range of activity types. For a start (it is argued), personalization creates better classroom **dynamics**. This is because groups are more likely to form and bond if the individuals in them know more about one another. And the mental and emotional effort that is involved in finding personal associations with a language item is likely to make that item more memorable. This quality is called cognitive and affective *depth*. Finally, lessons are likely to be more interesting, and hence more motivating, if at least some of the content concerns the people in the room, rather than the characters in course books. On these grounds, some writers have suggested that personalization should not be considered simply as an "add-on," but should be the principle on which most, if not all, classroom content should be based. One teaching approach that is committed to this view is **community language learning**. In this approach, all the content of the lesson comes from the learners themselves. Personalization is not without risks, though. Teachers need to be sensitive to learner resistance: learners should have the right to "pass" on questions that they consider too intrusive. And teachers should be authentic in the way that they respond to learners' personalizations. This means that they should respond to what their learners are saying, not just how they say it.

practice

methodology

If you practice a skill, you experience doing it a number of times in order to gain control of it. The idea that "practice makes perfect" is fundamental to **cognitive learning theory**. It is through practice that the skill becomes automatic. **Sociocultural learning theory** finds room for practice too. Performing a skill with the assistance of someone who is good at it can help in the **appropriation** of the skill. At issue, then, is not so much whether practice is beneficial, but what form it should take, when, and how much of it is necessary. In addressing these questions, it is customary to distinguish between different kinds of practice, such as *controlled practice vs. free practice*, *mechanical practice vs. meaningful/communicative practice*, and *receptive practice vs. productive practice*.

Controlled practice is associated with the second P of the PPP instructional model. Practice can be controlled in at least two senses: *language control* and *interactional control*. In the first, the language that is being practiced is restricted to what has just been presented (hence it is also called *restricted practice*). For example, if the first **conditional** has been presented, learners practice this, and only this, structure, and in a repetitive way, e.g. through a sequence of **drills**. Practice is also said to be controlled if the learners' participation is overtly managed and monitored by the teacher, such as in open-class work, as opposed to closed **pairwork** or **groupwork**. One reason for this degree of control is that it maintains a focus on accuracy, and pre-empts, or corrects errors. *Free practice*, on the other hand, allows learners a measure of creativity, and the opportunity to integrate the new item into their existing language "pool." It is also less controlled in terms of the interactions, with pairwork and groupwork being favored. Typical free practice activities might be **games**, **discussions**, or **drama**-based activities.

Mechanical practice is a form of controlled practice, where the focus is less on the meaning of an item than on manipulating its component parts. Mechanical practice can be either oral or written: many traditional **exercises** are mechanical in this sense, such as when learners transform sentences from active into passive, or from direct speech into reported speech. The arguments in favor of controlled and mechanical practice have lost their force since the decline of **behaviorism** and its belief that learning is simply habit-formation.

Meaningful practice requires learners to display some understanding of what the item that they are practicing actually means. One way of doing this is through **personalization.** *Communicative practice* involves the learners interacting in order to complete some kind of task, such as in an *information gap activity* (➜ **communicative activity**). Proponents of a communicative approach argue that it is only this kind of practice that is truly effective. This is because learners are not simply practicing language, but are practicing the behaviors associated with the language, and this is a pre-condition for long-term behavioral change.

Finally, some practice activities are purely *receptive*. They involve the learners in identifying, selecting, or discriminating between language items, but not actually producing them. Many **consciousness-raising** activities are receptive, on the grounds that learners first need to understand a new structure before they can properly internalize it. Receptive practice is also associated with comprehension-based approaches to teaching. Productive practice, on the other hand, requires learners to produce the targeted items (either orally or in writing), and is associated with output-based models of learning.

There is fairly general agreement nowadays that the most effective practice activity combines at least some of the following features:

- It is meaningful, which may mean that it is personalized.
- It is communicative, thus it will require learners to interact.
- It involves a degree of repetition—not of the mindless type associated with imitation drills, but of the type associated with many games.
- It is language-rich, i.e., learners have to interpret or produce a lot of language.
- Learners can be creative and take risks, but support is at hand if they need it.
- Learners are pushed, at least some of the time, to the limits of their competence.
- Learners get **feedback**.

pronunciation teaching

phonology

Pronunciation is the general term for that part of language classes and courses that deals with aspects of the **phonology** of English. This includes the individual sounds (**phonemes**) of English, sounds in **connected speech**, word and sentence **stress**, **rhythm**, and **intonation**. These components are customarily divided into two groups: the *segmental* features of pronunciation, i.e., the individual sounds and the way they combine, and the *suprasegmental* features, i.e., stress, rhythm, and intonation. **Paralinguistic** features of speech production such as voice quality, tempo and loudness, are also classed as suprasegmental.

Effective pronunciation teaching needs to consider what goals, course design, and methodology are most appropriate for the learners in question. The goal of acquiring a native-like **accent** is generally thought to be unachievable for most learners (and perhaps even undesirable). Instead, the goal of **intelligibility** is nowadays considered more realistic, if less easily measurable. It is often claimed that suprasegmental features play a greater role in intelligibility than do segmental ones. Unfortunately, however, some of these suprasegmental features, such as intonation, are considered by many teachers to be unteachable. Moreover, learners intending to interact with native speakers may need to set different goals from those learners whose purpose is to learn **English as an international language** (**EIL**). For this latter group, the so-called phonological core is a checklist of those pronunciation features considered critical for intelligibility in EIL.

In terms of the design of course content, a basic choice is whether the pronunciation focus is *integrated* or *segregated*. In an integrated approach, pronunciation is dealt with as part of the teaching of grammar and vocabulary, or of speaking and listening. In a segregated approach it is treated in isolation. A classical segregated exercise is the **minimal pairs** task, in which learners are taught to discriminate and produce two contrasted phonemes (as in *hit* and *heat*). There are doubts as to whether this item-by-item approach to pronunciation reflects the way that the features of pronunciation are interconnected. Nor does it reflect the way that they jointly emerge over time ("as a photo emerges in the darkroom"). A related issue is whether pronunciation teaching should be *pre-emptive* or *reactive*. That is to say, should pronunciation teaching be planned around a syllabus of pre-selected items, or should the focus on pronunciation emerge out of practice activities, in the form, for example, of **correction**? There is evidence that the latter approach is more effective than the former.

In 1964, the writer (and former language teacher) Anthony Burgess wrote, "Nothing is more important than to acquire a set of foreign phonemes that shall be entirely acceptable to your hosts." However, there is generally less emphasis given to pronunciation teaching nowadays. Indeed, some teachers are skeptical as to the value of teaching pronunciation at all. This view is reinforced by research that suggests that the best predictors of intelligible pronunciation are "having a good ear", and prolonged residence in an English-speaking country. On the other hand, faulty pronunciation is one of the most common causes of misunderstandings. This is an argument for demanding higher standards than the learners can realistically achieve, in the hope that they will meet you "halfway."

reading

methodology

Reading is a receptive **skill**. But the fact that it is receptive does not mean that it is passive: reading is an active, even interactive, process. Readers bring their own questions to the text, which are based on their background knowledge, and they use these to interrogate the text, modifying their questions and coming up with new ones according to the answers they get. In order to do this, they draw on a range of knowledge bases. They need to be able to decode the letters, words, and grammatical structures of the individual sentences—what is called *bottom-up processing*. But they also enlist top-down processes, such as drawing on **discourse** and schematic knowledge, as well as on immediate contextual information. Discourse knowledge is knowing how different text-types—such as news reports, recipes, or academic papers—are organized. Schematic knowledge is the reader's existing knowledge of the topic. Reading involves an interaction between these different "levels" of knowledge, where knowledge at one "level" can compensate for lack of knowledge at another.

Readers also bring their own *purposes* to texts, and these in turn determine the way they go about reading a text. The two main purposes for reading are for *information* (such as when consulting a directory), and for *pleasure* (such as when reading a novel), although these purposes may overlap. Different ways of reading include:

- *skimming* (*skim-reading, reading for gist*): rapidly reading a text in order to get the gist, or the main ideas or sense of a text. For example, a reader might skim a film review in order to see if the reviewer liked the film or not.
- *scanning*: reading a text in search of specific information, and ignoring everything else, such as when consulting a bus timetable for a particular time and destination.
- *detailed reading*: reading a text in order to extract the maximum detail from it, such as when following the instructions for installing a household appliance.
- *reading aloud*: such as when reading a prepared speech or lecture, or reading a story aloud, or an extract from the newspaper.

A reader's purpose usually matches the writer's intentions for the text. Readers seldom read telephone books from cover to cover, for example. Nor do they normally skim through a novel looking for names beginning with *Vron*.... In classrooms, however, texts are frequently used for purposes other than those for which they were originally intended. They are often used not so much as vehicles of information or of pleasure, but as "linguistic objects," that is, as contexts for the study of features of the language. A distinction needs to be made, therefore, between two types of classroom reading: reading as *skills development*, and reading as *language study*. There is no reason why the same text cannot be used for both purposes.

Another distinction that is often made is between *intensive reading* and *extensive reading*. The former applies to the way short texts are subject to close and detailed classroom study. Extensive reading, on the other hand, means the more leisurely reading of longer texts, primarily for pleasure, or in order to accumulate vocabulary, or simply to develop sound habits of reading. This is typically done outside class, using graded **readers**, authentic texts, or literary texts.

A third important distinction is between testing reading and teaching reading. Traditional reading tasks usually involve reading a text and then answering **comprehension questions** about it. This is the testing approach. A teaching approach, on the other hand, aims to help learners to become more effective readers by training them in the *sub-skills* of reading, and by teaching them *reading strategies*. Some of the sub-skills of reading are:

- understanding words and identifying their grammatical function
- recognizing grammar features, such as word endings, and "unpacking" (or **parsing**) the syntax of sentences
- identifying the topic of the text, and recognizing topic changes
- identifying text type, text purpose, and text organization, and identifying and understanding **discourse markers** and other cohesive devices
- distinguishing key information from less important information
- identifying and understanding the gist
- inferring the writer's attitude
- following the development of an argument
- following the sequence of a narrative
- paraphrasing the text.

Activities designed to develop these sub-skills include: underlining topic-related words; contrasting different text-types; comparing different examples of the same text type and identifying *generic* features; circling and categorizing discourse markers; identifying what the pronouns refer to; predicting the direction the text will take at each discourse marker; choosing the best summary of a text; putting a set of pictures in order; extracting key information on to a grid, writing a summary of the text, etc. *Strategy training* involves training learners in ways of overcoming problems when they are reading. Some useful strategies include:

- using contextual and extra-linguistic information (such as pictures, layout, headlines) to make predictions regarding what the text is about
- brainstorming background (or schematic) knowledge in advance of reading
- skimming a text in advance of a more detailed reading
- keeping the purpose of the text in mind
- guessing the meaning of words from context
- using the dictionary.

There is some argument, however, as to the value of a "skills and strategies" approach to teaching reading. Most adult learners of English come to English texts with already well-developed reading skills in their own language. They already know how to skim, scan, use context clues, enlist background knowledge, and so on. Theoretically, at least, these skills are transferable. What makes reading difficult is not so much lack of reading skills as lack of *language knowledge*. That is, learners lack sufficient vocabulary and grammar to unpack sentences, and they cannot easily identify the ways that sentences are connected. This can result in "tunnel vision," with readers becoming distracted by unfamiliar words, at the expense of working out meaning from context. On the other hand, it can also result in an over-reliance on guesswork, and on superficial "text attack" strategies such as skimming. This suggests that the texts need to be chosen in a way that does not overstretch learners' ability to read them fluently. At the same time, texts should not be so easy that learners can process them simply by skimming. It also means that tasks need to be chosen so that they both match the original purpose of the text, and encourage learners to transfer their first language reading skills. Such tasks are likely to be those that motivate learners to want to read the text. This might mean activating interest in the topic of the text through, for example, a pre-reading quiz. At the same time, classroom reading texts should be exploited, not just for their potential in developing reading skills, but as sources of language input. This will involve, at some point, detailed study of the text's formal features, such as its linking devices, its collocations, or its grammar.

speaking

methodology

Speaking is generally thought to be the most important of the four **skills.** The ability to speak a second language is often equated with proficiency in the language, as in *She speaks excellent French.* Indeed, one frustration commonly voiced by learners is that they have spent years studying English, but still can't speak it. One of the main difficulties, of course, is that speaking usually takes place spontaneously and in real time, which means that planning and production overlap. If too much **attention** is paid to planning, production suffers, and the effect is a loss of **fluency**. On the other hand, if the speaker's attention is directed solely on production, it is likely that accuracy will suffer, which could prejudice **intelligibility**. In order to free up attention, therefore, the speaker needs to have achieved a degree of **automaticity** in both planning and production. One way of doing this is to use memorized routines, such as **formulaic language**. Another is to use *production strategies*, such as the use of **pause fillers**, in order to "buy" planning time. The situation is complicated by the fact that most speaking is interactive. Speakers are jointly having to manage the flow of talk. The management of interaction involves *turn-taking skills*, such as knowing how and when to take, keep, and relinquish speaker turns, and also knowing how to repair misunderstandings.

For language learners these processing demands are magnified through lack of basic knowledge of grammar and vocabulary. For the purposes of most day-to-day talk, however, the grammar that is required is not as complex nor need be as accurate as the grammar that is required for writing. Nor do speakers need an enormous vocabulary, especially if they have developed some **communication strategies** for getting round gaps in their knowledge. A core vocabulary of 1000-1500 high frequency words and expressions will provide most learners with a solid basis for speaking.

Activating this knowledge, though, requires practice. This in turn suggests that the more speaking practice opportunities that learners are given, and the sooner, the easier speaking will become. Speaking practice means more than simply answering the teacher's questions, or repeating sentences, as in grammar practice activities. It means interacting with other speakers, sustaining long turns of talk, speaking spontaneously, and speaking about topics of the learners' choice.

Approaches to teaching speaking vary. Traditionally, speaking was considered to be a by-product of teaching grammar and vocabulary, reinforced with work on **pronunciation**. This view has been replaced by approaches that treat speaking as a skill in its own right. One such approach is to break down the speaking skill into a number of discrete sub-skills, such as *opening* and *closing conversations*, *turn-taking*, *repairing*, *paraphrasing*, *interrupting*, etc. Another approach is to focus on the different *purposes* of speaking and their associated **genres**, such as *narrating*, *obtaining service*, *giving a presentation*, *making small talk*, etc. This approach is particularly well suited to learners who have a specific purpose for learning English. A third is to adopt a topic-based approach, where learners are encouraged to speak freely on a range of topics, at least some of which they have chosen themselves. This is the format used in many conversation classes. Typical activity types for the teaching of speaking include: **dialogues**, **drama** activities (including *role-plays* and *simulations*), **games**, **discussions**, and debates, as well as informal classroom chat.

task

methodology

A task is a classroom activity whose focus is on communicating meaning. The objective of a task may be to reach some consensus on an issue, to solve a problem, to draft a plan, to design something, or to persuade someone to do something. In contrast, practicing a preselected item of language (such as the present perfect) for its own sake would not be a valid task objective. In the performance of the task, learners are expected to make use of their own language resources. In theory, tasks may be receptive or productive, and may be done individually, or in pairs, or small groups. However, in practice, most activities that are labeled "tasks" in coursebooks involve production (either speaking or writing, or both) and require learners to interact with one another.

Tasks are the organizing principle in **task-based learning.** In order to devise a syllabus of tasks it is necessary both to classify tasks, and to identify the factors that make one task more difficult than another. Different criteria for classifying tasks have been suggested. For example, tasks can be *open-ended* or *closed*. An open-ended task is one in which learners know there is no predetermined solution. It might be planning an excursion, or debating a topical issue. A closed task, on the other hand, requires learners to discover the solution to a problem, such as identifying the differences in a spot-the-difference task (→ communicative activity). Tasks can also be classified according to the kinds of operations they involve, such as *ranking*, *selecting*, *sorting*, *comparing*, *surveying*, and *problem-solving*.

Factors which influence the degree of difficulty of the task, and hence which affect the grading of tasks, include:

- *linguistic factors*: How complex is the language that learners will need to draw on, in order to do the task? How much help, either before, or during the task, will they get with their language needs?
- *cognitive factors*: Does the task require the processing of complex data? Is the task type familiar to learners?
- *performance factors*: Do the learners have to interact in real time in order to do the task? Do they have time to rehearse? Do they have to "go public?"

The term *task* is now widely accepted as a useful way of labeling certain types of classroom activity, including many which have a thinly disguised grammar agenda. But the concept of task is not without its critics. Some writers feel that the associations of task with "work" undervalues the more playful—and possibly less authentic or communicative—types of classroom activity, such as games, songs, and drama.

vocabulary teaching

methodology

Vocabulary describes that area of language learning that is concerned with word knowledge. Vocabulary learning is a major goal in most teaching programs. It hasn't always been so. In methods such as **audiolingualism**, vocabulary was subordinated to the teaching of grammar structures. Words were simply there to fill the slots in the sentence patterns. The move towards *semantic* (i.e., meaning-based) **syllabuses** in the 1970s, along with the use of **authentic** materials, saw a revival of interest in vocabulary teaching. Subsequently, developments in **corpus** linguistics and **discourse analysis** started to blur the distinction between vocabulary and grammar. In the 1990s, the **lexical approach** ushered in a major re-think regarding the role of vocabulary. This concerned both the *selection* of items (**frequency** being a deciding factor) and the type of items: **formulaic language** (or lexical chunks) were recognized as being essential for both **fluency** and **idiomaticity**. These developments have influenced the design of teaching materials. Most contemporary course books incorporate a lexical syllabus alongside the grammar one. Recent developments in lexicography have complemented this trend. There is now a wide range of **dictionaries** available for learners, many of which come with sophisticated software for accessing databases of examples and collocations.

It is now generally agreed that, in terms of goals, learners need a receptive vocabulary of around 3,000 high-frequency words (or, better, **word families**) in order to achieve independent user status. This will give them around ninety per cent coverage of normal text. For a productive vocabulary, especially for speaking, they may only need half this number.

Classroom approaches to achieving these goals include dedicated vocabulary lessons. Typically these take the form of teaching lexical sets of words (i.e., groups of thematically linked words) using a variety of means, including visual **aids**, demonstration, situations, texts, and dictionary work. As well as the **meaning** of the items, **the form**, both spoken (i.e., **pronunciation**) and written (i.e., **spelling**), needs to be dealt with, especially if the words are being taught for productive use. Other aspects of word knowledge that may need to be highlighted include **connotation** and **style**, **collocation**, derived forms, and grammatical features, such as the word's **word class**. Vocabulary is also taught as preparation for listening or reading (*pre-teaching vocabulary*) or as a by-product of these skills.

It would be impossible, in class, to teach all the words that learners need. Learners therefore need opportunities for *incidental* learning, e.g. through *extensive reading*. They may also benefit from training in how to make the most of these opportunities, e.g. by means of dictionary use, note-keeping, etc. Some strategies for deducing the meaning of unfamiliar words will also help.

Amassing a fully functioning vocabulary is essentially a **memory** task, and techniques to help in the memorizing of words can be usefully taught, too. It also helps to provide learners with repeated encounters with new words, e.g. through the re-reading of texts, or by reading several texts about the same topic. Constant recycling of newly learned words is essential. One simple way of doing this is to have a *word box* (or word bag) in the classroom. New words are written on to small cards and added to the word box. At the beginning of the next lesson, these words can be used as the basis for a review activity. For example, the teacher can take words out of the box and ask learners to define them, provide a translation, or put them into a sentence. The words can also form the basis for peer-testing activities, in which learners take a number of word cards and test each other in pairs or small groups.

writing

methodology

Like speaking, writing is a productive skill, and, like other skills, writing involves a hierarchy of subskills. These range from the most mechanical (such as handwriting or typing legibly) through to the ability to organize the written text and lay it out according to the conventions of the particular text type. Along the way, writers also need to be able to:

- produce grammatically accurate sentences
- connect and punctuate these sentences
- select and maintain an appropriate style
- signal the direction that the message is taking
- anticipate the reader's likely questions so as to be able to structure the message accordingly

In order to enable these skills, writers need an extensive knowledge base, not only at the level of vocabulary and grammar, but at the level of connected discourse. This includes familiarity with a range of different text types, such as informal letters, instructions, product descriptions, etc. It follows that if classroom writing is mainly spelling- or grammar-focused, many of the sub-skills of writing will be neglected.

Nevertheless, the teaching of writing has tended to focus on the "lower-level" features of the skill, such as being able to write sentences that are both accurate and complex, that demonstrate internal cohesion, and that are connected to the sentences next to them. This language-based approach is justified on the grounds that stricter standards of accuracy are usually required in writing than in speaking. Also, writing demands a greater degree of explicitness than speaking, since writers and their readers are separated in time and space. They therefore can't rely on immediate feedback in order to clear up misunderstandings.

By contrast, a text-based approach to teaching writing takes a more "top-down" view. This approach finds support in **discourse analysis**, which shows that a **text** is more than a series of sentences, however neatly linked. Instead, texts are organized according to larger *macrostructures*, such as problem-solution, or definition examples. Hence, learners need explicit guidance in how texts are structured. This typically involves analyzing and imitating models of particular text types. For example, a business letter might be analyzed in terms of its overall layout, the purpose of each of its paragraphs, the grammatical and lexical choices within each paragraph, and the punctuation. Each of these features is then practiced in isolation. They are then recombined in tasks aimed first at reproducing the original text, and then at producing similar texts incorporating different content.

This approach is called a *product approach* to the teaching of writing, since the focus is exclusively on producing a text (the product) that reproduces the model. By contrast, a *process approach* argues that writers do not in fact start with a clear idea of the finished product. Rather, the text emerges out of a creative process. This process includes: *planning* (*generating ideas*, *goal setting*, and *organizing*), *drafting* and *re-drafting*; *reviewing*, including *editing* and *proofreading*, and, finally, "*publishing*." Advocates of a process approach argue for a more organic sequence of classroom activities, beginning with the brainstorming of ideas, writing preliminary drafts, comparing drafts, re-drafting, and *conferencing*, that is, talking through their draft with the teacher, in order to fine-tune their ideas.

The process approach to writing has a lot in common with the **communicative approach** to language teaching, and each has drawn support from the other. The communicative approach views writing as an act of communication in which the writer interacts with a reader or readers for a particular purpose. The purpose might be to ask for information about a language course, to relay personal news, to complain about being overcharged at a hotel, or simply to entertain and amuse. Thus, advocates of a communicative approach argue that classroom writing tasks should be motivated by a clear purpose and that writers should have their reader(s) in mind at all stages of the writing process. Such principles are now reflected in the design of writing tasks in public examinations, such as this one, from the Cambridge ESOL First Certificate in English (FCE) paper:

> The school where you learn English has decided to buy some videos in English. You have been asked to write a report to the Principal, suggesting what kinds of videos the school should buy. In your report you should also explain why students at the school will like these videos. Write your report.

The social purposes of writing are also foregrounded by proponents of a *genre-based approach*. **Genre** analysis attempts to show how the structures of particular text types are shaped by the purposes they serve in specific social and cultural contexts. Put simply, a business letter is the way it is because of what it does. Advocates of genre-based teaching reject a process approach to teaching writing. They argue that to emphasize self-expression at the expense of teaching the generic structures of texts may in fact disempower learners. Many learners, especially those who are learning English as a second language, need a command of those genres—such as writing a resume, or requesting a bank loan—that permit access to the host community. A genre approach to teaching writing is not unlike a product approach, therefore. It starts with model texts that are subjected to analysis and replication. The difference is that these models are closely associated with their contexts of use, and they are analyzed in functional terms as much as in linguistic ones. The genre approach has been particularly influential in the teaching of academic writing.

In reality, none of these approaches is entirely incompatible with any other. Resourceful teachers tend to blend elements of each. For example, they may encourage learners to "discover" what they want to write, using a process approach. They may then give them a model text, both as a source of useful language items, and as a template for the final product. They may also provide exercises in specific sub-skills, such as linking sentences, or using a formal style.

Life Skills

What are Life Skills?

Life skills are the skills students need to deal effectively with the challenges in everyday life, whether at school, at work, or in their personal lives. Students who are able to understand and use these skills, along with their educational qualifications, will be better placed to take advantage of educational and employment opportunities. In a constantly changing environment, having life skills is an essential part of being able to meet the challenges of everyday life.

The dramatic changes in global economies over the past five years have been matched with the transformation in technology and these are all impacting on education, the workplace, and our home life. To cope with the increasing pace and change of modern life, students need new life skills such as the ability to deal with stress and frustration. Today's students will have many new jobs over the course of their lives, with associated pressures and the need for flexibility. As medical science advances, home life and the community will place additional demands on future generations.

Topics:

Social Skills
People Management
Critical Thinking
Time Management
Cultural Awareness
Networking
Career and Work
Study Skills
Creativity
Self-awareness
Getting Organized
www.macmillanenglish.com/life-skills/classroom-resources/

How do we approach Life Skills in this book?

In every unit of *American Inside Out Evolution* one of these topics will be discussed, according to the theme of the unit, and students will have the opportunity to reflect and discuss based on simple activities.

MACMILLAN LIFE SKILLS

The Common European Framework of Reference for Language Learning

Introduction

The Common European Framework of Reference (CEFR) is a widely used standard created by the Council of Europe. In the classroom, familiarity with the CEFR can be of great help to any teacher in identifying students' actual progress and helping them to set their learning priorities.

Students can use the descriptors (description of competences) at any point to get a detailed, articulated, and personal picture of their own individual progress. This is important, as no two language learners progress in the same way, and consequently it is always rather artificial to apply a "framework level" to a class as a whole, or to a course or course book.

The European Language Portfolio is another Council of Europe project, designed to give every learner a structure for keeping a record of their language learning experiences and their progress as described in the CEFR. Up-to-date information about developments with the CEFR and Portfolio can be found on www.coe.int/portfolio.

The Swiss-based Eurocentres Foundation played a major role in the development of the levels and the descriptors for the CEFR and the prototype Portfolio. The CEFR descriptors, developed in a Swiss National Research Foundation project, were presented in clearer, simpler, self-assessment form in the prototype (Swiss) Portfolio. There are now dozens of different national versions of the Portfolio for different educational sectors, but the only version for adults is that developed from the Swiss version[1] by EAQUALS[2] (European Association for Quality Language Services) in collaboration with ALTE[3] (Association of Language Testers in Europe). The descriptors used in this guide are taken from the EAQUALS/ALTE Portfolio. An electronic version that can be completed online can be downloaded in English or French from www.eelp.org. The EAQUALS/ALTE Portfolio descriptors have been used in this guide, as they are more concrete and practical than the original CEFR descriptors.

CEFR Checklists

American Inside Out Evolution Pre-intermediate is appropriate for students who have seen most of the basic structures of the language and have enough vocabulary to cope in most situations. By the end of *American Inside Out Evolution Pre-intermediate*, if the students have had access to English outside the classroom, and have had the opportunity to practice, they should be able to do the things described at the A2 level quite comfortably, and should sometimes be able to accomplish things described at the B1 level, although these will still be somewhat challenging.

In order to help the teacher and student assess their progress, we have provided a list of A2 and B1 descriptors for each unit of *American Inside Out Evolution Pre-Intermediate*. A basic level of confidence with the A2 descriptors is presupposed at the start of the book. Students will first consolidate their A2 abilities, and as the course proceeds they'll gradually start to work on B1 descriptors. Many of the B1 descriptors talk of greater confidence with the same kinds of ability already described at A2: others only emerge for the first time at B1. The descriptors in these charts allow the teacher to see a typical pattern of language acquisition, but it is important always to remember that every student learns differently, and that the various abilities will be acquired in a different sequence and at a different pace by each individual.

At pre-intermediate level, students might begin to be able to make some sense of the descriptors for purposes of self-assessment, but it will still be more useful to them to work with descriptors in their first language. The descriptors given here will be of more use to the teacher in gauging the students' progress through the course across the whole range of language abilities. This will help clarify for the teacher which students are making quicker or slower progress in the different areas, and will assist them in planning the focus of future lessons. *American Inside Out Evolution* offers a wide range of teaching materials in its various components, which together give teachers the opportunity to develop all aspects of their students' language ability. The CEF can be used to follow their progress. By checking whether the students' confidence is at an appropriate level across the whole range of language skills at any point in the course, the teacher can decide if there is an area that requires more practice. Suggested targets for the checklist are provided on the website www.insideout.net and on the Test CD at the back of the Teacher's Edition.

---

1 Schneider, Gunther, & North, Brian (2000): "Fremdsprachen können – was heisst das?»
Zürich, Ruegger; North, Brian (2000): «The Development of a Common Framework Scale of Language Proficiency», New York, Peter Lang.

2 EAQUALS is a pan-European language school accreditation body with over 100 full members.

3 ALTE is an association dedicated to raising standards in language testing and encompasses the major European examination providers. Eurocentres provides high-quality language teaching in countries where the language concerned is spoken. EAQUALS, ALTE, and Eurocentres are the three NGOS advisers for language learning to the Council of Europe and all three implement the CEFR.

CEFR Student Checklists

Unit 1

Complete the checklist.

1 = I can do this with a lot of help from my teacher.
2 = I can do this with a little help.
3 = I can do this fairly well.
4 = I can do this really well.
5 = I can do this almost perfectly.

Competences	Page	Your score
I can ask for and give opinions about familiar topics, in a simple way.	8, 9, 10, 11, 12, 13, 14, 15	1 2 3 4 5
I can understand short simple texts on familiar subjects, which consist of high-frequency, everyday language.	9, 10, 12	1 2 3 4 5
I can describe my and other people's physical appearance.	10, 120, 125	1 2 3 4 5
I can understand short, simple descriptions when told slowly and clearly.	13	1 2 3 4 5
I can understand the essential information and details in short conversations dealing with predictable everyday matters.	8, 14	1 2 3 4 5
I can take part in a conversation about everyday matters and show interest in what other people are saying.	14	1 2 3 4 5

Unit 2

Complete the checklist.
1 = I can do this with a lot of help from my teacher.
2 = I can do this with a little help.
3 = I can do this fairly well.
4 = I can do this really well.
5 = I can do this almost perfectly.

Competences	Page	Your score
I can talk about preferences giving reasons.	16, 18, 19	1 2 3 4 5
I can understand people describing a place and talking about their preferences.	17, 21	1 2 3 4 5
I can talk about places and describe them in some detail.	18, 19, 20, 21, 22, 23, 120, 125	1 2 3 4 5
I can make comparisons using fixed structures.	18	1 2 3 4 5
I can understand reviews in which writers express their opinions and preferences.	19, 20	1 2 3 4 5
I can write a review about a place, hotel, etc. expressing my opinion clearly.	19	1 2 3 4 5
I can understand the essential information and details in short conversations dealing with predictable everyday matters.	22	1 2 3 4 5
I can talk about past experiences giving some detail.	23	1 2 3 4 5

Unit 3

Complete the checklist.
1 = I can do this with a lot of help from my teacher.
2 = I can do this with a little help.
3 = I can do this fairly well.
4 = I can do this really well.
5 = I can do this almost perfectly.

Competences	Page	Your score
I can understand people talking about past events and experiences when told clearly and slowly.	24,	1 2 3 4 5
I can agree and disagree giving my opinion.	24, 28, 30	1 2 3 4 5
I can talk about past events and experiences.	25, 26, 27	1 2 3 4 5
I can catch the main points in TV shows on familiar topics when the delivery is relatively slow and clear.	26	1 2 3 4 5
I can narrate a story connecting a number of events.	27, 29	1 2 3 4 5
I can understand short narratives about everyday things dealing with topics which are familiar to me if the text is written in simple language.	27, 28	1 2 3 4 5
I can discuss options and make a decision.	30	1 2 3 4 5

Unit 4

Complete the checklist.
1 = I can do this with a lot of help from my teacher.
2 = I can do this with a little help.
3 = I can do this fairly well.
4 = I can do this really well.
5 = I can do this almost perfectly.

Competences	Page	Your score
I can understand and discuss the writer's attitude.	36, 39	1 2 3 4 5
I can talk about other people's habits and behavior.	37, 39	1 2 3 4 5
I can understand and give short, basic descriptions of events.	38	1 2 3 4 5
I can give my opinions and agree or disagree with others.	39, 40, 41	1 2 3 4 5
I can talk about preferences giving reasons.	36, 39	1 2 3 4 5
I can read columns or interviews in newspapers and magazines in which someone takes a stand on a current topic or event and understand the overall meaning of the text.	41	1 2 3 4 5
I can make simple transactions in stores, post offices, or banks.	42	1 2 3 4 5

Unit 5

Complete the checklist.

1 = I can do this with a lot of help from my teacher.

2 = I can do this with a little help.

3 = I can do this fairly well.

4 = I can do this really well.

5 = I can do this almost perfectly.

Competences	Page	Your score
I can understand the main ideas and details in a variety of texts, e.g. articles, interviews, blog posts, etc.	44, 48	1 2 3 4 5
I can talk about the frequency and length of activities.	45	1 2 3 4 5
I can make comparisons using a variety of fixed structures.	46, 47	1 2 3 4 5
I can understand and use a variety of long numbers, fractions, and decimals.	47, 121, 126	1 2 3 4 5
I can understand the main points of radio news bulletins and simpler recorded material on topics of personal interest delivered relatively slowly and clearly.	46, 49	1 2 3 4 5
I can understand and give instructions.	50	1 2 3 4 5

Unit 7

Complete the checklist.

1 = I can do this with a lot of help from my teacher.

2 = I can do this with a little help.

3 = I can do this fairly well.

4 = I can do this really well.

5 = I can do this almost perfectly.

Competences	Page	Your score
I can understand the main points in short newspaper articles about current and familiar topics.	64	1 2 3 4 5
I can guess the meaning of single unknown words from the context thus deducing the meaning of expressions if the topic is familiar.	64	1 2 3 4 5
I can understand the speaker's attitude and opinion.	65, 68, 69	1 2 3 4 5
I can express myself reasonably accurately in familiar, predictable situations.	65, 66, 67, 68, 69, 70, 71	1 2 3 4 5
I can understand and write a survey report.	67	1 2 3 4 5
I can compare and discuss information in fact files.	68	1 2 3 4 5
I can talk about future plans and intentions in some detail.	68, 69, 70, 122, 127	1 2 3 4 5
I can understand and use specific expressions used in formal phone conversations.	70	1 2 3 4 5

Unit 6

Complete the checklist.

1 = I can do this with a lot of help from my teacher.

2 = I can do this with a little help.

3 = I can do this fairly well.

4 = I can do this really well.

5 = I can do this almost perfectly.

Competences	Page	Your score
I can describe what people do at work.	52, 57, 58	1 2 3 4 5
I can ask for and give opinions, agree and disagree about familiar topics giving reasons.	52, 53, 56	1 2 3 4 5
I can understand the main ideas and details in a variety of texts, e.g. articles, short messages, etc.	53, 54	1 2 3 4 5
I can talk about what is and isn't permitted at school, work, etc.	53	1 2 3 4 5
I can ask and talk about past experiences in detail.	54, 55, 59, 122, 126	1 2 3 4 5
I can understand the main points and details in interview about current and familiar topics.	52, 56, 57, 58	1 2 3 4 5
I can understand and write a job application using appropriate language.	57	1 2 3 4 5
I can negotiate and reach an agreement on everyday topics.	58	1 2 3 4 5

Unit 8

Complete the checklist.

1 = I can do this with a lot of help from my teacher.

2 = I can do this with a little help.

3 = I can do this fairly well.

4 = I can do this really well.

5 = I can do this almost perfectly.

Competences	Page	Your score
I can understand the main ideas and details in a variety of texts, e.g. articles, blog posts, short messages, etc.	72, 74, 76, 77	1 2 3 4 5
I can ask for and give opinions, agree and disagree about familiar topics giving reasons.	73, 74, 76, 77, 78, 79	1 2 3 4 5
I can understand the speaker's attitude and opinion.	73, 78	1 2 3 4 5
I can talk about permission and obligation now and in the past.	75, 123, 128	1 2 3 4 5
I can generally follow the main points of extended discussion around me, provided speech is clearly articulated in standard dialect.	75, 76	1 2 3 4 5
I can discuss and give advice on familiar everyday topics.	77, 78	1 2 3 4 5

Unit 9

Complete the checklist.

1 = I can do this with a lot of help from my teacher.

2 = I can do this with a little help.

3 = I can do this fairly well.

4 = I can do this really well.

5 = I can do this almost perfectly.

Competences	Page	Your score
I can understand the main ideas and details in a variety of texts, e.g. articles, blog posts, surveys, etc.	80, 81, 82, 83	1 2 3 4 5
I can talk about preferences giving reasons.	80, 82, 83, 84	1 2 3 4 5
I can understand and give descriptions of people's physical appearance and personality.	80, 81, 123, 128	1 2 3 4 5
I can understand the speaker's attitude and opinion.	83, 84	1 2 3 4 5
I can talk about the duration of activities and situations.	84, 85	1 2 3 4 5
I can use everyday expressions and idioms in the right context.	86	1 2 3 4 5
I can prepare and carry out a survey.	86	1 2 3 4 5

Unit 10

Complete the checklist.

1 = I can do this with a lot of help from my teacher.

2 = I can do this with a little help.

3 = I can do this fairly well.

4 = I can do this really well.

5 = I can do this almost perfectly.

Competences	Page	Your score
I can understand the main information and details in a variety of texts, e.g. descriptions, recipes, etc.	92, 95, 96	1 2 3 4 5
I can talk on a variety of everyday topics, e.g. my lifestyle, work, hobbies, family, etc.	92, 93, 94, 96, 98, 99	1 2 3 4 5
I can understand straightforward information about everyday topics identifying both general messages and specific details, provided people speak clearly.	93, 95, 97	1 2 3 4 5
I can describe dreams, hopes, and ambitions.	93, 97, 98	1 2 3 4 5
I can give an extended description of a person and talk about their lifestyle in detail.	95	1 2 3 4 5
I can understand and talk about past situations or habits.	97, 124, 129	1 2 3 4 5

Unit 11

Complete the checklist.

1 = I can do this with a lot of help from my teacher.

2 = I can do this with a little help.

3 = I can do this fairly well.

4 = I can do this really well.

5 = I can do this almost perfectly.

Competences	Page	Your score
I can understand and discuss the writer's attitude and opinions in short, descriptive texts.	100, 102	1 2 3 4 5
I can maintain a conversation or discussion but may have problems trying to say exactly what I would like to.	100, 104, 106	1 2 3 4 5
I can understand the main ideas and details in informal conversations or monologues about everyday topics, e.g. preferences, past experiences, etc.	101, 104, 105, 106	1 2 3 4 5
I can give short definitions of people and animals.	103, 124, 129	1 2 3 4 5
I can discuss unreal or imaginary situations.	105	1 2 3 4 5
I can give detailed descriptions on everyday topics, e.g. pets.	105	1 2 3 4 5
I can ask a favor and refuse or accept politely.	106	1 2 3 4 5

Unit 12

Complete the checklist.

1 = I can do this with a lot of help from my teacher.

2 = I can do this with a little help.

3 = I can do this fairly well.

4 = I can do this really well.

5 = I can do this almost perfectly.

Competences	Page	Your score
I can skim short, descriptive texts and find relevant facts and information, e.g. who has done what and where, dates, etc.	108, 110, 124, 129	1 2 3 4 5
I can understand and talk about past experiences, expressing attitude and opinions.	108, 109, 110, 111	1 2 3 4 5
I can make predictions about the future, e.g. the weather, personal predictions, etc. and express likelihood.	112, 113, 114	1 2 3 4 5
I can understand the main ideas and details in informal conversations or monologues about everyday topics and understand speakers' attitude and opinions.	114	1 2 3 4 5

CEFR Student Checklists: Suggested targets

Unit 1

Competences	Page	Your score
I can ask for and give opinions about familiar topics, in a simple way.	8, 9, 10, 11, 12, 13, 14, 15	1 ② 3 4 5
I can understand short simple texts on familiar subjects, which consist of high-frequency, everyday language.	9, 11, 12	1 2 ③ 4 5
I can describe my and other people's physical appearance.	10, 120, 125	1 2 ③ 4 5
I can understand short, simple descriptions when told slowly and clearly.	13	1 ② 3 4 5
I can understand the essential information and details in short conversations dealing with predictable everyday matters.	8, 14	1 ② 3 4 5
I can take part in a conversation about everyday matters and show interest in what other people are saying.	14	1 ② 3 4 5

Unit 2

Competences	Page	Your score
I can talk about preferences, giving reasons.	16, 18, 19	1 ② 3 4 5
I can understand people describing a place and talking about their preferences.	17, 21	1 2 ③ 4 5
I can understand people describing a place and talking about their preferences.	18, 19, 20, 21, 22, 23, 120, 125	1 ② 3 4 5
I can understand people describing a place and talking about their preferences.	18	1 ② 3 4 5
I can understand reviews in which writers express their opinions and preferences.	19, 20	1 2 ③ 4 5
I can write a review about a place, hotel, etc. expressing my opinion clearly.	19	1 ② 3 4 5
I can understand the essential information and details in short conversations dealing with predictable, everyday matters.	22	1 2 ③ 4 5
I can talk about past experiences giving some detail.	23	1 2 ③ 4 5

Unit 3

Competences		Your score
I can understand people talking about past events and experiences when told clearly and slowly.	24	1 2 ③ 4 5
I can agree and disagree giving my opinion.	24, 28, 30	1 2 ③ 4 5
I can talk about past events and experiences.	25, 26, 27	1 2 ③ 4 5
I can catch the main points in TV shows on familiar topics when the delivery is relatively slow and clear.	25, 26, 27	1 2 ③ 4 5
I can talk about actions taking place at specific times in the past.	27, 121, 125	1 ② 3 4 5
I can narrate a story connecting a number of events.	27, 29	1 ② 3 4 5
I can understand short narratives about everyday things dealing with topics which are familiar to me if the text is written in simple language.	27, 28	1 2 ③ 4 5
I can discuss options and make a decision.	30	1 ② 3 4 5

Unit 4

Competences	Page	Your score
I can understand and discuss the writer's attitude.	36, 39	1 2 ③ 4 5
I can talk about other people's habits and behavior.	37, 39	1 2 ③ 4 5
I can understand and give short, basic descriptions of events.	38	1 2 ③ 4 5
I can give my opinions and agree or disagree with others.	39, 40, 41	1 2 3 ④ 5
I can talk about preferences giving reasons.	36, 39	1 2 ③ 4 5
I can read columns or interviews in newspapers and magazines in which someone takes a stand on a current topic or event and understand the overall meaning of the text.	41	1 2 3 ④ 5
I can talk about what's happening at the moment of speaking.	41, 121, 126	1 2 3 ④ 5
I can make simple transactions in stores, post offices, or banks.	42	1 2 ③ 4 5

Unit 5

Competences	Page	Your score
I can understand the main ideas and details in a variety of texts, e.g. articles, interviews, blog posts, etc.	44, 48	1 2 3 (4) 5
I can talk about the frequency and length of activities.	45	1 2 (3) 4 5
I can understand people talking about past events and experiences when told clearly and slowly.	45	1 2 (3) 4 5
I can make comparisons using a variety of fixed structures.	46, 47	1 2 (3) 4 5
I can understand and use a variety of long numbers, fractions, and decimals.	47, 121, 126	1 (2) 3 4 5
I can understand the main points of radio news bulletins and simpler recorded material on topics of personal interest delivered relatively slowly and clearly.	46, 49	1 2 3 (4) 5
I can understand and give instructions.	50	1 2 (3) 4 5

Unit 6

Competences	Page	Your score
I can describe what people do at work.	52, 57, 58	1 2 (3) 4 5
I can ask for and give opinions, agree and disagree about familiar topics giving reasons.	52, 53, 56	1 2 3 (4) 5
I can understand the main ideas and details in a variety of texts, e.g. articles, short messages, etc.	53, 54	1 2 3 (4) 5
I can talk about what is and isn't permitted at school, work, etc.	53	1 2 (3) 4 5
I can talk about what is and isn't permitted at school, work, etc.	54, 55, 59, 122, 126	1 2 (3) 4 5
I can understand the main points and details in interview about current and familiar topics.	52, 56, 57, 58	1 2 (3) 4 5
I can understand and write a job application using appropriate language.	57	1 2 3 (4) 5
I can understand and write a job application using appropriate language.	58	1 2 (3) 4 5

Unit 7

Competences	Page	Your score
I can understand the main points in short newspaper articles about current and familiar topics.	64	1 2 (3) 4 5
I can understand the main points in short newspaper articles about current and familiar topics.	64	1 (2) 3 4 5
I can understand the speaker's attitude and opinion.	65, 68, 69	1 2 (3) 4 5
I can express myself reasonably accurately in familiar, predictable situations.	65, 66, 67, 68, 69, 70, 71	1 (2) 3 4 5
I can understand and write a survey report.	67	1 (2) 3 4 5
I can compare and discuss information in fact files.	68, 69, 122, 127	1 (2) 3 4 5
I can understand and use specific expressions used in formal phone conversations.	70	1 2 (3) 4 5

Unit 8

Competences	Page	Your score
I can understand the main ideas and details in a variety of texts, e.g. articles, blog posts, short messages, etc.	72, 74, 76, 77	1 2 3 (4) 5
I can ask for and give opinions, agree and disagree about familiar topics giving reasons.	73, 74, 76, 77, 78, 79	1 2 (3) 4 5
I can understand the speaker's attitude and opinion.	73, 78	1 2 (3) 4 5
I can talk about permission and obligation now and in the past.	75, 123, 128	1 (2) 3 4 5
I can generally follow the main points of extended discussion around me, provided speech is clearly articulated in standard dialect.	75, 76	1 2 (3) 4 5
I can discuss and give advice on familiar everyday topics.	77, 78	1 (2) 3 4 5

Unit 9

Competences	Page	Your score
I can understand the main ideas and details in a variety of texts, e.g. articles, blog posts, surveys, etc.	80, 81, 82, 83	1 2 3 ④ 5
I can talk about preferences giving reasons.	80, 81, 123, 128	1 ② 3 4 5
I can understand the speaker's attitude and opinion.	83, 84	1 2 3 ④ 5
I can talk about the duration of activities and situations.	84, 85	1 ② 3 4 5
I can use everyday expressions and idioms in the right context.	86	1 ② 3 4 5
I can prepare and carry out a survey.	86	1 ② 3 4 5

Unit 10

Competences	Page	Your score
I can understand the main information and details in a variety of texts, e.g. descriptions, recipes, etc.	92, 95, 95, 96	1 2 3 ④ 5
I can talk on a variety of everyday topics, e.g. my lifestyle, work, hobbies, family, etc.	92, 93, 94, 96, 98, 99	1 2 ③ 4 5
I can understand straightforward information about everyday topics identifying both general messages and specific details, provided people speak clearly.	93, 95, 97	1 2 ③ 4 5
I can describe dreams, hopes, and ambitions.	93, 97	1 2 ③ 4 5
I can give an extended description of a person and talk about their lifestyle in detail.	95	1 2 ③ 4 5
I can understand and talk about past situations or habits.	97, 124, 129	1 2 ③ 4 5

Unit 11

Competences	Page	Your score
I can understand and discuss the writer's attitude and opinions in short, descriptive texts.	100, 102	1 2 3 4 ⑤
I can maintain a conversation or discussion but may have problems trying to say exactly what I would like to.	100, 104, 106	1 ② 3 4 5
I can understand the main ideas and details in informal conversations or monologues about everyday topics, e.g. preferences, past experiences, etc.	101, 104, 105, 106	1 2 3 ④ 5
I can give short definitions of people and animals.	103, 124, 129	1 ② 3 4 5
I can discuss unreal or imaginary situations.	105	1 ② 3 4 5
I can give detailed descriptions on everyday topics, e.g. pets.	105	1 2 ③ 4 5
I can ask a favor and refuse or accept politely.	106	1 ② 3 4 5

Unit 12

Competences	Page	Your score
I can skim short, descriptive texts and find relevant facts and information, e.g. who has done what and where, dates, etc.	108, 110, 124, 129	1 2 3 4 ⑤
I can understand and talk about past experiences, expressing attitude and opinions.	108, 109, 110, 111	1 ② 3 4 5
I can ask and talk about past experiences in detail.	111	1 2 3 ④ 5
I can make predictions about the future, e.g. the weather, personal predictions, etc. and express likelihood.	112, 113, 114	1 2 ③ 4 5
I can understand the main ideas and details in informal conversations or monologues about everyday topics and understand speakers' attitude and opinions.	114	1 2 3 ④ 5

1 Name *Overview*

Section	Aims	What the students are doing
Listening SB page 8	Listening for specific information	Listening to people talking about names. Underlining the names and nicknames they hear. Completing sentences with words for family and friends.
Vocabulary SB page 8	Family	Listening and repeating words for family members. Identifying male and female family words and completing a table. Talking about names.
Reading SB page 9	Reading for specific information	Reading an article and finding out the reasons for choosing a name. Talking about choosing names.
Grammar SB page 9	Tenses and auxiliary verbs	Matching verb phrases with tense names. Writing negative forms of sentences and naming tenses. Turning sentences into questions with short answers.
Pronunciation SB page 10	*Vowel sounds* /u/, /i/, /ɑ/, /ɜr/, /ɔ/	Listening and repeating names which contain vowel sounds /u/, /i/, /ɑ/, /ɜr/, /ɔ/. Labeling groups of names with the correct vowel sound.
Listening SB page 10	Listening and remembering	Listening to the names of people in pictures and remembering them. Discussing techniques for remembering names.
Vocabulary SB page 10	Words and phrases for describing people	Completing descriptions of people. Completing a table with words and phrases for describing people.
Speaking SB page 10	Fluency practice	Describing people in the class, then guessing their identities. Writing short descriptions of people they know and telling their partners about them.
Reading SB page 11	Reading for gist	Matching headings to sections of a text. Discussing advice in a text on improving your memory.
Grammar SB page 11	*look(s) / look(s) like*	Identifying parts of speech and using *look(s)* and *look(s)* like with adjectives and nouns. Writing sentences describing people using *look(s)* and *look(s)* like.
Reading SB page 12	Reading for specific information	Discussing language learning tips. Reading about language learning tips from an English expert. Writing a list of their own language learning tips.
Speaking SB page 12	Fluency practice	Making changes to questions and asking a partner the questions.
Grammar SB page 13	Question forms	Matching questions and answers. Rewriting questions and discussing the acceptability of them.
Speaking: Anecdote SB page 13	Fluency practice	Listening to somebody talking about a person who is important to him. Talking about a person who is important to them.
Language for Life SB page 14	Useful conversational phrases: showing you're interested	Matching conversations with pictures. Listening and repeating useful phrases for showing interest. Completing a conversation and practicing it. Writing a new conversation about last weekend.
Life Skills SB page 14	Cultural awareness: What's in a name?	Explaining what their names mean. Matching names, meanings, and nationalities. Completing a table and discussing which names suit which people.
Vocabulary Extra SB page 15	Review of words from the unit: family and relationship words; names	Completing a table with family words. Answering questions about family and relationships. Underlining the correct words in sentences. Completing a form about names.
Writing WB page 7		Filling out a form with personal information.

1 Name *Teacher's notes*

Warm-up

- Write on the board a list of the first names of some of the members of your family. Draw an empty family tree with spaces for each of the names. Tell the students that all these people are related to you. Ask them to ask questions to find out how they are related. For example, *Is Mark your brother? Is Jeff Mary's husband?* Students who get a yes answer to their questions can come up to the board and write the name in the correct place in the family tree.
- Ask the students to write down the names of three friends and take turns with a partner asking and answering about them: *"Who's Maria?" "She's my best friend. She lives near my house. We do a lot of things together."*

Listening (SB page 8)

1 1.02

- Focus the students' attention on the picture. Tell the students that they're going to hear a conversation between these two people, who have never met before. Then focus attention on the names. Explain that people are sometimes given nicknames by their family and friends. These names are generally given in childhood, but sometimes continue to be used when the people have grown up. They can be names received by classmates at school, for instance Einstein due to an interest in physics. Explain also the concept of a middle name (a second name between the first name and the last name which can act as an alternative first name; it may also have religious or family significance), and the way some names are shortened (e.g. Mike is a short form of Michael, Sue is a short form of Susan).
- Play the recording and ask the students to check the four names they hear for each person. Check answers with the class. Point out, or get the students to identify, that Tree, Big Ben, Mimi and Baby are nicknames. Ben is a short form of Benjamin and Maria a short form of Anna-Maria.

ANSWERS:

The man: Benjamin, Ben, Tree, Big Ben
The woman: Maria, Anna-Maria, Mimi, Baby

1.02

(M = Maria; B = Benjamin)
M: Hi, I'm Maria.
B: Hi, Maria. My name's Benjamin, but nobody calls me Benjamin. Well, my parents do, but my friends call me Ben.
M: Ben—that's nice.
B: Thanks. Actually, my old friends call me Tree.
M: Tree? Why?
B: Well, as you can see, I'm very tall.
M: Oh, ha-ha. ... My friends call me lots of different names.
B: Really?
M: Yes. My mom's Mexican and my dad's English, so I've got English and Mexican friends, and they call me different things.
B: What do your Mexican friends call you?
M: They use my full name—Anna-Maria.
B: And your English friends?
M: They just call me Maria. Some of them call me Mimi.
B: Mimi! That's cute!
M: Well, it could be worse. My brother calls me Baby, because I'm the youngest in the family.
B: That's not so bad—my sisters call me Big Ben.
M: Ha-ha. Oh, no!

Language notes

Vocabulary: names

- Benjamin and Maria just give their first names when they introduce themselves as the situation is somewhat informal. In more formal situations, people usually give both their first name and their last name.
- Benjamin got the nicknames Tree and Big Ben because he's tall. Big Ben is the bell in the clock tower of the Houses of Parliament in London, so again this is a jokey reference to his height.

2

Ask the students to try to complete the sentences from memory. Allow them to compare and discuss their results in pairs before playing the recording again for them to check. Go through the answers with the class.

ANSWERS:

a parents
b old friends
c sisters
d Mexican friends
e English friends
f brother

Vocabulary (SB page 8)

1 1.03

- Focus the students' attention on the box. Point out that the underlining indicates the syllable of the word that has the strongest stress. Play the recording for the students to listen and repeat the words.
- Ask several students to repeat the words individually and check that they're putting the stress on the correct syllables.

2

- Focus the students' attention on the table. Point out that most relationship words describe either male or female family members. Ask the students to complete the table with the words in the box in Exercise 1, adding the names of their own family members where appropriate. (If you wish, you could turn this into a competition, with the winner being the person in the class who can match a name from their family to as many different words as possible.)
- When the students have completed the table, ask them if any of the words could go in both columns *(cousin)*. Check answers with the class. Then read out the example and put the students into pairs to tell each other about some of the members of their families.
- Go around, monitoring and giving help. Make sure the students are pronouncing all the words for family members correctly.

ANSWERS:

Male: boyfriend, brother, brother-in-law, cousin, father, grandfather, half-brother, nephew, son, stepfather, uncle
Female: aunt, cousin, daughter, girlfriend, grandmother, half-sister, mother, niece, sister, sister-in-law, stepmother
(Note that cousin can be both male and female.)

Language notes

Vocabulary: *sister-in-law*

Your sister-in-law could be any of the following: the wife of your brother; the sister of your husband; the sister of your wife.

Vocabulary: *stepsister*

If one of your parents marries again, the children of the person they marry become your stepbrothers and/or stepsisters.

Vocabulary: *half-sister*

Your half-sister shares either the same mother or the same father as you, but not both.

3 Pairwork

Focus the students' attention on the table again. Go through the questions with the class and elicit a couple of answers to the first question. You could give some examples from your own country, if appropriate. Ask the students to discuss the questions in pairs. Go around, monitoring and giving help, and encourage some pairs to report back to the class on their discussions.

Reading (SB page 9)

1 Pairwork

Explain to the class how your own parents chose your own name (or give an example of someone you know). Then go through the reasons with the class. Put the students into pairs to discuss how their parents chose their names. Go around, monitoring and giving help if necessary. Take note of any interesting discussions and ask the students to report these back to the class.

2

- Focus the students' attention on the post. Give them enough time to read it, and answer any questions they may have about vocabulary. Ask them which of the reasons listed in Exercise 1 is not mentioned.

ANSWER:

Reason g is not mentioned.

Cultural notes

Leonardo DiCaprio (born 1974)

Leonardo DiCaprio was named after Leonardo da Vinci. He started acting when he was fourteen, appearing in TV commercials and educational movies. He's starred in a number of successful movies, such as *Romeo and Juliet* (1995), *Titanic* (1996), *Gangs of New York* (2002), and *The Aviator* (2005). He's also heavily involved in environmental work in the US.

Taylor Swift (born 1989)

An American singer and songwriter, Taylor Swift has sold 40 million records and won multiple Grammy awards. Like Justin Bieber, she was discovered as a fourteen-year-old, when she moved to Nashville to pursue a career as a country singer. She later moved into pop music with records like *Red* (2012) and *1989* (2014).

Caia Caecilia

In Roman mythology, Caia Caecilia (also called Gaia Caecilia) was the goddess of fire and women. She was often associated with wedding rituals and domestic life.

3

Ask the students to think about the question for a moment or two and then discuss in pairs which names they would choose. Ask them to report back to the class.

Grammar (SB page 9)

Tenses and auxiliary verbs

1

- This exercise offers a quick review of some of the tenses the students should already have encountered. Focus the students' attention on the information in the margin which gives them the names of the tenses they'll need and the auxiliary verbs that these tenses use. Explain that the simple present and simple past only use auxiliary verbs in negatives and questions. (You can use do in affirmative sentences for emphasis, but this is not taught at this level.)
- Ask the students to look at the highlighted verb phrases in the article in the previous section and ask them to match them to the tense names. Allow them to work in pairs or small groups. Then check answers with the class.

ANSWERS:

We brought – simple past
we haven't chosen – present perfect
we're having – present progressive
it is going to be – future *(be) going to*
Noah likes Japan – simple present

Extra activity

To give further practice of the link between auxiliary verbs and tenses, put this matching activity on the board:

Match each tense with its auxiliary verb.

a	Simple present	am/am not are/aren't is/isn't
b	Present progressive	has/hasn't have/haven't
c	Present perfect	do/don't does/doesn't
d	Simple past	am/am not are/aren't is/isn't did/didn't
e	Future	(be) going to

Language notes

Grammar: tense review

- The simple present is used to talk about facts, habits, or routines: *I live in a small house in Mexico City.*
- The present progressive is used to talk about activities in progress now or around now: *He's wearing an old pair of jeans.*
- The present perfect is used to talk about completed past actions in "time up to now." There is no past time marker: *They've visited fourteen different countries.*
- The simple past is used to talk about completed past actions, where a past time marker is mentioned or implied: *She met him a long time ago.*
- The future (*be*) *going to* is used to talk about future plans and intentions–things you've decided to do: *I'm going to see him on Thursday.*

Grammar: auxiliary verbs

- *Do/does/did* are used with the simple present and simple past to help form questions, negatives and short answers: *Do you come here every day? / Yes, I do. I didn't see you yesterday.*

- *Am/are/is* are used to form the present progressive: *I'm studying art and design.* / *She's staying with her friend.* They're usually used in contracted form (*'m, 're, 's*) except in formal writing. *Am/are/is* are also used to form going to sentences for the future and are usually used in contracted form: *I'm going to see two old friends this weekend.* When *am/are/is* are used in questions and short answers, they aren't contracted. *Are you listening to me? Yes, I am* (not ~~Yes, I'm~~).
- *Have/has* are used to form the present perfect: *I've been to New York.* / *My brother's been to most US cities.* They're usually used in contracted form (*'ve, 's*) except in formal writing. When *have/has* are used in questions and short answers, they aren't contracted. *Have you been to Miami? Yes, I have* (not ~~Yes, I've~~).

2

- Go through the example with the class and then ask the students to write the negative forms of the remaining sentences. Allow them to compare in pairs before checking answers with the class.
- Ask them to go through the negative sentences and tick the ones that are true for them.

ANSWERS:

a I don't like rock music. (Simple present)
b I'm not reading a good book right now. (Present progressive)
c I'm not going to have some coffee after the class. (Future (*be*) *going to*)
d I didn't go out last night. (Simple past)
e I haven't been to Peru. (Present perfect)
f I can't play the piano. (Simple present)

3

Students write the question forms. As they do this, go around checking that they're forming the questions correctly. With weaker classes, check the questions with the class before putting the students into pairs to practice asking and answering them.

ANSWERS:

a Do you like rock music? Yes, I do. / No, I don't.
b Are you reading a good book right now? Yes, I am. / No, I'm not.
c Are you going to have some coffee after the class? Yes, I am. / No, I'm not.
d Did you go out last night? Yes, I did. / No, I didn't
e Have you been to Peru? Yes, I have. / No, I haven't.
f Can you play the piano? Yes, I can. / No, I can't.

Pronunciation (SB page 10)

1 1.04

- Focus the students' attention on the vowel sounds /u/, /i/, /ɑ/, /ɜr/, and /ɔ/. Play the recording and ask them to repeat the vowel sounds. After they've done this chorally, ask several students to repeat the words individually, and check that everyone is producing the sounds correctly.
- If the students are unfamiliar with phonetic symbols, you may want to do a bit more work on this. Write the symbols on the board and point to them at random, asking the students (at first chorally and then individually) to say the sounds. Choose the names of some of the students in the class whose names exemplify the different sounds and write them on the board next to the appropriate phonemes.

2 1.05

- Focus the students' attention on the table. Read the names in the first column aloud, exaggerating the vowel sound. Then play the recording and ask the students to listen and repeat.
- Give the students a minute or two to write in the correct phonetic symbols. Remind them that they are all listed in Exercise 1. Encourage them to say the sounds as they write them to reinforce the link between the sounds and the symbols. Check answers with the class. Then ask different students to read out the different columns of names.

ANSWERS:

a /u/
b /ɜr/
c /ɑ/
d /i/
e /ɔ/

Listening (SB page 10)

1 1.06

- Ask the students whether or not they find it easy to remember people's names when they are first introduced. Then focus their attention on the pictures and ask them to look at the people for a couple of minutes. Explain that they're going to hear the names of all these people on the recording and that they should try to remember them, without writing anything down. Play the recording once.
- Ask the students to work individually to write down as many of the names as they can remember, either next to the pictures in the book, or with the numbers 1 to 9 in their notebooks. When they've finished, allow them to compare with a partner.

ANSWERS:

Frank
Tina
Bobby
Margaret
Toby
Anita
Todd
Georgina
Karen

2

Play the recording for the students to check their answers. Find out who remembered the most names correctly. Ask this person if they have any special techniques for remembering names.

Vocabulary (SB page 10)

1 1.07

- Focus the students' attention on the pictures of the nine people on page 10. Write on the board: *What does he look like?* Underneath write some descriptions for one of the people (but don't tell students which one). For example, *He has short hair. He has a beard. His hair is gray.* Ask students to say which of the people you described (the man in picture 1).
- Ask students to complete the descriptions with the names and the numbers of the pictures. Point out that the first one has been done for them. Play the recording for students to check their answers, then play it a second time for them to repeat.

ANSWERS:

a Toby (5) has a shaved head. He's very good-looking.
b Georgina (8) has short, straight hair with blond highlights.
c Todd (7) has dark hair and green eyes.
d Bobby (3) has short, gray hair.
e Anita (6) has dark brown eyes and long hair.
f Margaret (4) has long, blonde hair. She's very cute.
g Tina (2) has long, red hair. She has a beautiful smile.
h Karen (9) has dark, curly hair.
i Frank (1) has gray hair and a gray beard.

2

- Focus the students' attention on the table. Go through the headings and the examples with them, and make sure they understand what they should put under "Opinion" (descriptions that aren't facts, but rather the speaker's own) and "Other". Then give them some time to complete the table with the words and phrases from the previous exercise. While they work, go around and help them with any vocabulary they have trouble with. Allow them to check their answers in pairs before checking as a class.

ANSWERS:

Hair length: a shaved head, short, long hair, medium-length
Hair color: dark, blond highlights, gray, blonde
Hair style: straight, curly, wavy
Eyes: green, dark brown
Opinion: very good-looking, very cute, beautiful smile
Other: a beard, a mustache

3 1.08

- Focus the students' attention on the box. Point out that the underlining indicates the syllable of the word that has the strongest stress. Play the recording for the students to listen and repeat the words.
- Ask several students to repeat the words individually and check that they're putting the stress on the correct syllables.

Language notes

Vocabulary: mustache

A *mustache* is the facial hair between the nose and the upper lip, sometimes grown with a beard.

4 Pairwork

- The pairwork exercise for this unit is on pages 120 and 125 of the Student's Book. Put the students into pairs and tell them who will be Student A, and who will be Student B.
- While they're doing the exercise, go around, monitoring and giving help. Take note of any errors which may need particular attention later, and also any examples of good language use which you can praise.

Speaking (SB page 10)

1 Pairwork

Describe one of the students in the class (but don't tell the students who it is.) Ask them to guess the identity of the student you're describing. Then go through the speech bubbles with the class, before putting them into pairs to play the game.

2

- Students choose three people they know—they can be family members, friends, neighbors, etc. Ask them to write short descriptions, like the ones in the previous sections, about each of the three people.
- Pairwork. Students share their descriptions with a partner. Encourage them to make eye contact with each other, and to not simply read the sentences they wrote.

Reading (SB page 11)

1

- Tell the students they're going to read about some ways of improving their memory for names. Go through the headings with them first, since this will give them a general idea of what the text is about. Then ask them to read the text and match the headings to the appropriate sections. Allow them to compare results in pairs or small groups before checking with the class. Give the students a chance to read the text again, and answer any questions they may have about vocabulary.
- Ask them if they know of any other techniques for trying to remember other people's names. One method is to connect a person's name with a common word. For example, for the name Cathy, imagine her holding a cat. For Robert, imagine him as a robber.

ANSWERS:

5 - a	Looks like ...
4 - d	On repeat!
3 - b	How do you spell it?
2 - c	Draw a picture!
1 - e	Ask!

2

- Go through the questions with the whole class and make sure the students understand them before putting them into pairs to discuss them. Go around, monitoring and giving help.
- Ask the pairs to report back to the whole class on their discussions. Write any suggestions they make for remembering and learning new English words on the board. Encourage the students to make a note of these and try them out.

Grammar (SB page 11)

look(s) / look(s) like

1

- Focus the students' attention on the box of words. Point out the two examples: the adjective *friendly* and the noun phrase *a banker*. Ask the class for two or three more examples of adjectives and nouns or noun phrases. Then ask them to go through the box and write *N* or *A* for the remaining words and phrases. You may need to explain that a noun phrase or an adjective phrase is just a noun or adjective in combination with two or more words. As they do this go around, monitoring and giving help. Check answers with the class before moving on to the second part of the exercise.
- Ask the students to look at the information about the use of *look(s)* and *look(s) like* in the margin. Ask them what type of word you use after *look(s)* (adjective / adjective phrase) and what type of word you use after *look(s) like* (noun / noun phrase). Ask the students to give some examples using both structures.

ANSWERS:

A friendly
N a banker
A intelligent
A shy
N a doctor
A very young
A middle-aged
A stressed
A about sixty
A Mexican
N a waiter
N a student
N a retired police officer
A rich

After *look(s)* you use adjectives or adjective phrases.
After *look(s) like* you use nouns or noun phrases.

2

- Choose one of the pictures on page 10 and ask the whole class to suggest sentences using *looks* and *looks like* to describe him or her.
- Then ask the students to work individually to write sentences about the other people on page 10. Go through the example with the class and point out that they should leave spaces for the people's names.
- Put the students into pairs and ask them to exchange their descriptions and try to complete their partner's sentences with the correct names.

Extra activity

If appropriate, repeat the activity using people in the class. Ask the students to choose three classmates and write sentences using *looks* and *looks like* to describe them. As they do this, go around, helping and making sure that no one writes anything hurtful or offensive. Put them into pairs to complete the sentences.

Reading (SB page 12)

1

- Go through the language learning tips with the class, and ask them to tick the ones that they follow. Then put them into pairs to compare answers.

2

- Tell students that they are going to read an interview with an English expert, Dr. Sally Haines. Make sure they understand what Q&A stands for (Questions and Answers).
- Give students a chance to read the text, and to make a note of which of the language tips from the previous section Dr. Haines mentions.
- Ask the students to suggest other tips for learning English. Give them some time to write their own list before comparing their tips with a partner. Get some students to share their tips with the class, and write their suggestions on the board. Encourage the class to try them out.

ANSWER:

She mentions b, c, f, and g

Speaking (SB page 12)

1

- Demonstrate the activity by using some of the alternatives to form new questions and ask various students around the class to answer them. If you don't want to pre-empt the questions the students will ask and answer in the exercise, write the following on the board and use it to demonstrate:

  How many languages can you speak? (musical instruments – play / people in the class – name / phone numbers – remember)
- Ask the students to work individually to make five new questions. As they do this, go around, monitoring and making sure they're forming the questions correctly. The alternatives are all correctly formed to slot into the questions, so the students shouldn't make any changes to the verb forms.

2

- Put the students into pairs and ask them to take turns asking and answering their questions. Tell them that they should try to remember any interesting answers which they can report back to the class.
- In a feedback session, ask the students to tell the class what they found out about their partners.

Grammar (SB page 13)

Question forms

1

- Focus the students' attention on the table. Read out each statement, followed by the corresponding question. Ask the students what they notice about statements and questions (the word order changes).
- Go through the questions one by one with the class, asking them to match them with the correct answers. Make sure they can identify the auxiliary verbs correctly and point out that auxiliary verbs are not used in questions with *be*. Explain also that you use *do/does/did* to form questions when there's no auxiliary verb in the corresponding statement.
- Put the students into pairs and tell them to take turns asking and answering the questions in the table.

ANSWERS:

a 2
b 3
c 4
d 1

Language notes

Grammar: word order

When making questions ...

... the auxiliary comes before the subject, not after it (as in statements).

... if there is no other auxiliary verb, use *do*.

... if there is another auxiliary verb, don't use *do* (~~*Do you can swim?*~~).

... *What*, *Who*, *Where*, *How*, etc. (question words) come at the beginning.

2

- Ask the students to look carefully at the six questions and decide which ones are incorrect and need *do*, *does*, or *did* to make them correct. Remind them that *do*, *does*, and *did* are used when there's no auxiliary verb in the corresponding statement which can be used to form the question.
- Ask the students to work individually to write correct questions. Go around, monitoring and giving help.
- Put the students into pairs and ask them to take turns asking and answering their questions.

ANSWERS:

a Do you play the guitar?
b Did you sleep well last night?
c Can you drive?
d Where does your mother come from?
e Have you been to California?
f What's your favorite color?

3

- Go through the example with the class and then ask the students to work individually to rewrite the questions in the correct order, but tell them not to ask their partners the questions. Allow them to compare their results in pairs before checking with the class.
- Ask the students to work in small groups and discuss in which situations it is OK to ask these questions. Ask them to make notes of their answers. In multinational groups, the answers may differ according to the nationalities of the students, so ask groups to note any differences and report these back to the class.
- Finally, find out what conclusions the groups came to. Ask if they think age, nationality, or cultural background are factors in whether or not questions are acceptable.

ANSWERS:

a How old are you?
b Do you believe in life after death?
c How much do you earn?
d Have you ever broken the law?
e Which political party do you vote for?
f How many boyfriends or girlfriends have you had?

Cultural notes

It's difficult to give hard and fast rules about which questions are or are not acceptable. Generally, in the USA, question a) would probably only be used with children. Adults might feel uncomfortable to be asked their age. Question b) might be acceptable amongst friends if the conversation had turned to such a topic. It would be unacceptable to ask this of a stranger. Questions c), d), e), and f) could make most people very embarrassed and wouldn't normally be asked, even by close friends.

4 Grammar Extra 1

Ask the students to turn to Grammar Extra 1 on page 130 of the Student's Book. Here they'll find an explanation of the grammar they've been studying and further exercises to practice it.

ANSWERS:

1
a Do you like jazz?
b Can you swim?
c Did you go skiing last winter?
d Are you wearing jeans today?
e Have you been to Argentina?
f Are you going to drive home after the class?

2
a Yes, I do. / No, I don't.
b Yes, I can. / No, I can't.
c Yes, I did. / No, I didn't.
d Yes, I am. / No, I'm not.
e Yes, I have. / No, I haven't.
f Yes, I am. / No, I'm not.

3
a Does he like jazz? Yes, he does. / No, he doesn't.
b Can he swim? Yes, he can. / No, he can't.
c Did he go skiing last winter? Yes, he did. / No, he didn't.
d Is he wearing jeans today? Yes, he is. / No, he isn't.
e Has he been to Argentina? Yes, he has. / No, he hasn't.
f Is he going to drive home after the class? Yes, he is. / No, he isn't.

4
a How far do you live from the school?
b When did you last go to the theater?
c What are you going to do this evening?
d How many cups of coffee have you had today?
e What kind of pen are you using right now?
f Where did you buy your shoes?

5
a What do you do? - 3
b Who do you work for? - 7
c Which department do you work in? - 5
d How do you get to work? - 2
e When did you start working there? - 1
f Why do you like working there? - 4
g How much do you earn? - 6

6
a Present progressive.
b Simple past.
c Present perfect.
d Future (*be*) *going to*.
e Simple present.
a We aren't studying Shakespeare in our English class.
b My parents didn't name me after my uncle.
c I haven't recently learned to drive.
d My friends aren't going to organize a party for me tomorrow.
e I don't like getting up early in the morning.

Speaking: anecdote (SB page 13)

Anecdotes are features that occur regularly in this series. They're extended speaking tasks, where the students tackle a longer piece of discourse on a personal topic. There are questions to guide them and a model to listen to. For more information about how to set up, monitor and repeat Anecdotes, see page xviii-xx in the Introduction.

1 1.09

- Focus the students' attention on the picture of John. Explain that they're going to hear his friend Brad talking about somebody who is important to him.
- Go through the sentences and the choices with the class. Explain any unknown vocabulary. Then play the recording and ask the students to listen and decide which is the correct information. They should underline it in their books.

ANSWERS:

a John Carter.
b When we were five years old.
c In Los Angeles.
d He's a teacher.
e In the summer.
f He knows me so well.
g He's a really good listener.
h He's always late.
i On my birthday.

1.09

John Carter is my best friend. We met when we were five years old, because our parents were friends and we went to the same school. He lives in Los Angeles now - he's a teacher at a high school there. So I only see him in the summer when he comes home to visit his family. Of course, we stay in touch by email and phone. He's important to me because he knows me so well. When I'm feeling down or when I need to talk to somebody, I can always call him. Recently, I had girlfriend problems and he was great. I'd say his best quality is that he's a really good listener. He just lets you talk and he listens. But he isn't perfect! He's always late for everything and he never says sorry. Never! One day last summer, we arranged to meet at seven o'clock to play baseball, and he arrived at nine thirty! It was almost dark! Oh well, nobody's perfect, are they? Last time I saw him was on my birthday, and we had a great time. We always have a great time.

2

- Give the students a minute or two to decide who they're going to talk about. Then ask them to look at the questions in Exercise 1 again. Allow them to make notes of what they're going to say about the person and how they're going to say it, but discourage them from writing a paragraph that they can simply read out. Go around, monitoring and giving help.
- **Pairwork.** Put the students into pairs and ask them to take turns to tell their partner about their important person. Encourage them to ask each other follow-up questions to get further information. Then ask some pairs to report back to the class about what they found out.

Language for Life (SB page 14)

1 1.10

Focus the students' attention on the illustrations which show two friends discussing the weekend. Ask them what the difference is between the two pictures (in the first Beth looks bored; in the second she looks interested). Play the recording and ask the students to say which picture best illustrates the conversation.

ANSWER:

The conversation matches picture 1.

1.10

(A = Adam; B = Beth)
A: Did you have a good weekend?
B: Not bad. How about you?
A: I had a really good dinner on Saturday night.
B: Oh.
A: Yes, we went to a new place in town– Edamame.
B: Ah.
A: They have a Japanese chef from Tokyo.
B: Uh-huh.
A: And the food is fantastic–they make their own sushi.
B: Oh.
A: Yes. It's the best sushi I've ever tasted.
B: Mm.
A: And it wasn't expensive. We had appetizers, an entrée, dessert, and wine, and it only cost $25 each.
B: Ah.
A: I know. Unfortunately, when we got back to the car, we had a parking ticket.
B: Oh.

2 ▶ 1.11

Tell the students they're going to listen to another version of the same conversation. Play the recording and ask them to say if Beth sounds more interested this time. Ask them to give reasons. (She doesn't just say *Oh*, she uses other expressions to convey interest, she asks questions and reacts to what Adam says.)

ANSWER:

Yes, she does.

▶ 1.11

(A = Adam; B = Beth)
A: Did you have a good weekend?
B: Not bad. How about you?
A: I had a really good dinner on Saturday night.
B: Really?
A: Yes, we went to a new place in town – Edamame.
B: I've never heard of it.
A: They have a Japanese chef from Tokyo.
B: That sounds interesting.
A: And the food is fantastic – they make their own sushi.
B: Do they?
A: Yes. It's the best sushi I've ever tasted.
B: That sounds great.
A: And it wasn't expensive. We had appetizers, an entrée, dessert, and wine, and it only cost $25 each.
B: Wow! That's great.
A: I know. Unfortunately, when we got back to the car, we had a parking ticket.
B: Oh, no! That's terrible.

3 ▶ 1.12

Play the recording. The students repeat the phrases after the speaker. Make sure that they match the speaker's intonation.

4

- Ask the students to complete the conversation with the phrases from Exercise 3. Allow them to work in pairs if they wish.
- After checking answers with the class, put the students into pairs and ask them to practice the conversation, taking turns to be Adam and Beth. Go around, monitoring and giving help. Tell the student playing Beth to use slightly exaggerated intonation in order to convey real interest. Ask any particularly good pairs to perform their conversations for the class.

ANSWERS:

1 Really?
2 I've never heard of it. (*also possible* That sounds interesting. That sounds great.)
3 That sounds interesting. (*also possible* Do they? That sounds great.)
4 Do they? (*also possible* That sounds interesting. That sounds great. Wow! That's great.)
5 That sounds great. (*also possible* Wow! That's great.)
6 Wow! That's great. (*also possible* That sounds great.)
7 Oh, no! That's terrible.

5 Pairwork

Give the students a few minutes to write their conversations. Go around, monitoring and giving help. Encourage them to use as many of the useful phrases as possible. Then ask several pairs to perform their conversations for the class.

Life Skills: Cultural awareness (SB page 14)

What's in a name?

1 Pairwork

- Explain that in certain cultures people's names have a meaning. In this lesson, we are looking at the meaning of some of these names. Ask the students to work in pairs and explain the meaning of their names to each other. Go around, monitoring and giving help.
- In a whole class feedback session, ask several pairs to report back to the rest of the class on what their partners have told them about their names.

2 ▶ 1.13

Ask students to guess the meanings and nationalities of the names before playing the recording—they aren't expected to know the meanings, so this can be turned into a fun game with points for the right answers. Play the recording and go through the answers as a whole class, and see which name guesses were right.

ANSWERS:

a Rei = 6 "beautiful" = vii Japanese
b Virat = 3 "brilliant" = iv Indian
c Abeda = 8 "flower" = i Ethiopian
d Ana = 5 "grace" = vi Mexican
e Bjorn = 4 "bear" = ii Swedish
f Fabrice = 1 "craftsman" = v French
g Hai = 7 "ocean" = iii Chinese
h Dieter = 2 "warrior" = viii German

1.13

a I'm Rei. I'm Japanese. My name means "beautiful".
b I'm Virat. My name means "brilliant". I'm from India.
c I'm Abeda from Ethiopia. My name means "flower".
d I'm from Mexico and my name is Ana, which means "grace".
e I'm Bjorn from Sweden. My name means "bear".
f I'm French. I'm Fabrice. My name means "craftsman".
g I'm Hai from China. My name means "ocean".
h I'm Dieter. My name means "warrior". I'm from Germany.

3

Focus the students' attention on the table and demonstrate the task by referring to the speech bubble. For example, "I think Brad is a good name for an actor because it's short and easy to remember." Allow students some time to complete the table individually. Go around, monitoring and helping with vocabulary.

4 Pairwork

Put students into pairs and have them explain their choices to each other. Time allowing, ask pairs to compare their answers with other pairs and/or lead a whole class discussion on the most suitable names.

Vocabulary Extra (SB page 15)

Family and other relationships

1

Focus the students' attention on the table and point out that they're all family words. Then ask them to complete the table with the correct family words. Point out that the first one has been done for them. Check that the students can pronounce the words correctly.

ANSWERS:

a granddaughter
b sister
c grandfather
d parents
e brother
f cousin
g sister
h father-in-law
i stepmother
j half-brother
k ex-husband
l twin

2 Pairwork

Demonstrate first with a confident student by getting them to ask you the first two questions. Then ask the students to work in pairs and take turns asking and answering the questions.

Focus on names

1

- Ask the students to work individually and underline the correct words. Then allow them to compare answers in pairs before checking with the class.
- Ask the students to check the sentences that are true for them and compare with a partner.

ANSWERS:

a call
b meaning
c named
d maiden
e initials
f signature

2

Ask the students to complete the form for themselves. Go around, monitoring and giving help.

Writing

Workbook page 7

Filling out a form with personal information.

Further Practice Material

Need more classroom practice activities?
Photocopiable resource materials in the Teacher's Presentation Kit / Extra Resources

Need more tests?
Test Generator
Teacher's Presentation Kit / Extra Resources / Tests

Need more on important teaching concepts?
Key concepts in *American Inside Out Evolution* pages xxi-xxxvii

Need student self-study practice?
Workbook pages 4-7

Need more information and ideas?
American Inside Out Evolution website www.macmillan.com.br/americaninsideoutevolution

Need to check what your students can do by the end of this unit?
Self-evaluation checklists on pages xxix-xliii

2 The World *Overview*

Section	Aims	What the students are doing
Vocabulary SB page 16	Places in a city	Finding features of a place in pictures. Ordering the features near their school from nearest to farthest away.
Listening SB page 17	Listening for gist	Listening to people talking about the places where they live and matching them to pictures. Completing descriptions with adjectives.
Grammar & Vocabulary SB page 17	*so/such, very/too*; adjectives to describe places	Identifying the uses of *so* and *such*. Completing an email. Then changing the email to sound negative. Identifying the uses of *very* and *too*. Completing sentences with *very* or *too*.
Grammar SB page 18	Countable and uncountable nouns	Matching questions and responses. Completing a table with nouns and discussing the plurals of nouns. Asking questions about cities and villages.
Vocabulary & Pronunciation SB page 18	Country and nationality words; word stress	Completing a table with country and nationality words and marking the stress. Talking about countries they would like to visit.
Speaking SB page 18	Fluency practice	Comparing things from different countries.
Reading & Writing SB page 19	Reading for detail Writing a review	Reading about vacation resorts and discussing where they would like to stay. Explaining their choices to a partner. Writing a review of the best hotel they have stayed in.
Reading SB page 20	Reading for detail Words and phrases	Reading and completing the description of a country. Discussing which country it is and whether it could be their own.
Grammar SB page 20	Quantity expressions	Matching quantity expressions with countable and uncountable nouns. Underlining the correct quantity expressions. Rewriting sentences to make them true for them. Asking and answering questions about where they live.
Vocabulary SB page 21	Location	Labeling the points of a compass. Matching location descriptions to cities.
Speaking: anecdote SB page 21	Fluency practice	Listening to somebody talking about the best place they have ever visited. Talking about the best place they have ever visited.
Language for Life SB page 22	Useful conversational phrases for talking about where you are from	Reading and listening to a conversation to identify nationalities. Matching people with maps. Completing useful expressions, then listening and repeating them. Writing a conversation about where they are from and where they live now.
Life Skills SB page 22	Prioritizing: What to do ...?	Completing a table about their city/town. Prioritizing places to visit in their city/town.
Vocabulary Extra SB page 23	Review of words from unit: Places, adjectives, furniture, *like*	Matching places in a picture with words. Talking about the last time they visited places. Categorizing adjectives, then using them to the describe their cities. Matching pictures of furniture with words. Matching the uses of *like* with example sentences and writing their own sentences.

2 The World *Teacher's notes*

Warm-up

Think of a city that you and your students know well, or which is so famous that they're likely to know a lot about it. Tell them that you are thinking of a city and that they must ask you questions to find out where it is. Encourage them to ask about buildings and other features in the city as well as what country it's in. A student who identifies the city correctly can then think of a new city and answer questions from the class.

Vocabulary (SB page 16)

1

- Focus the students' attention on the pictures. Ask them to look closely at the pictures and to decide whether they would like to live in any of the places shown.
- **Pairwork.** Ask the students to discuss with a partner whether they would like to live in any of the places. Encourage them to give reasons why or why not.
- Go around, monitoring and giving help with vocabulary. Ask some students to report back on their discussion to the whole class.

Cultural notes

Venice

A city in the north east of Italy, built on 118 small islands and separated by 150 canals. The main square is St. Mark's Square (Piazza San Marco), which features St. Mark's Basilica and The Doge's Palace (Palazzo Ducale). The city has a long association with the arts. The Venice Biennale has taken place there every other year since 1895, and the annual Venice Carnival is held in February, during which people dress up in costumes and wear masks.

Rio de Janeiro

The second largest city in, and former capital of, Brazil. With a population of 5.6 million, Rio contains many world famous sites. These include Copacabana and Ipanema Beaches, Sugarloaf Mountain, and the statue of Christ the Redeemer. Rio de Janeiro is also the venue of the famous carnival parade, which usually takes place in February.

La Bastide

This is a fictional village, created for the purposes of this exercise.

2 1.14

- Focus the students' attention on the words in the box. Point out that the underlining indicates the syllable of the word that has the strongest stress. Play the recording and ask the students to listen and repeat the words in the box. When they've done this chorally, ask several students to repeat the words individually. Check that the students can pronounce the words correctly.
- Give the students a few minutes to find as many of the items as they can in the pictures. Check answers with the class and make sure that they can understand and pronounce all the items.

ANSWERS:

Venice: a bridge, a canal, a cathedral
La Bastide: a church, a park
Rio de Janeiro: a beach, high-rise buildings, a hill, the ocean, a statue

Language note

Vocabulary: places of worship

Traditionally a church or a cathedral is a place of worship associated with Christians, while a mosque is a place of worship associated with Muslims.

3

Ask the students first to check the things that they can find near their school. They can then put them in order along the line. You may need to establish a distance for "near," such as within two kilometers or within five kilometers. Point out the superlative forms *nearest* from *near* and *farthest* from *far*.

Listening (SB page 17)

1 1.15

- Focus the students' attention on the pictures in the margin. Tell them that they're going to listen to Paulo, Armelle, and Luigi talking about the three places in the pictures on page 16. Ask them to listen and match each person with one of the pictures. Check answers before moving on to the next part of the exercise.
- See if the students can remember who does and who doesn't like living where they live without listening to the recording again. Encourage them to say what they can remember. Then play the recording again for them to check their answers.

ANSWERS:

Paulo:	c) Rio de Janeiro. He likes it apart from the summer.
Armelle:	b) La Bastide. She doesn't like it.
Luigi:	a) Venice. He hates living there.

1.15

Paulo
(I = Interviewer; P = Paulo)
I: Do you like your city?
P Oh, yes, I feel lucky to be living in a city that's so big and exciting.
I: What's the architecture like?
P: A mixture of old and new. There are too many high-rise buildings in some parts of the city. But there are plenty of cheap restaurants and interesting cafés and bars. And the nightlife is great. We also have the most famous beach in the world–Copacabana Beach.
I: Ah. What's the weather like?
P: It's great most of the time. The only time I don't like Rio very much is in the summer: it's too hot and humid.

Armelle
(I = Interviewer; A = Armelle)
I: Where do you live?
A: Well, I live in a small village with my parents. My grandparents live here too, and my aunts and uncles. In fact, I think I'm related to about fifty percent of the people in my village.
I: What's your village like?
A: It's very pretty. The countryside is beautiful, and the air is fresh and clean. But at night it's too quiet. I find it so dull and boring here–there aren't any discos or movie theaters.
I: What are the people like?
A: Oh, they're nice and really friendly, but there aren't many young people. I want to go and live in the city. Soon.

Luigi
(I = Interviewer; L = Luigi)
I: What do you think of your city?
L: It's a very special place. It's such a romantic city.
I: What's it like downtown?
L: The buildings are beautiful, and we have San Marco, one of the most famous churches in the world. The Piazza San Marco is wonderful, and during carnival in February, Venice is the best place in the world to be.
I: Do you like living here?
L: No, I really hate living here. It's horrible. There are too many tourists everywhere. It gets very noisy and crowded.
I: Oh, no. What are the stores like?
L: Well, because of the tourists the stores are too expensive, and the canals are so dirty and polluted. My city is too small for all these people. Why don't they leave us in peace?

2

- Go through the adjectives with the class and make sure that everyone understands them. Then ask them to work individually to complete the descriptions using the adjectives. Allow them to compare in pairs before checking with the class.
- Ask the students to say which of these adjectives they would use to describe the places where they live.

ANSWERS:

a	exciting	**e**	romantic
b	humid	**f**	crowded
c	clean	**g**	polluted
d	boring	**h**	small

Language note

Vocabulary: humid

Humid describes a climate that is hot and wet in a way that makes you feel uncomfortable. Damp describes a climate that is wet and slightly cold.

Grammar & Vocabulary (SB page 17)

so/such and *very/too*

1

- Ask the students to find and underline the instances of *so* and *such a/an* in Exercise 2 of the Listening section. Ask several students to read out the sentences containing these words.
- Focus the students' attention on the rules and ask them to complete them using information from the sentences in Listening Exercise 2. Check answers with the class and go through the example sentences in the margin. Then ask the students to produce one or two more sentences using so or such to describe where they live.

ANSWERS:

a so **b** such

2

Ask the students to complete the email. Check answers with the class and then ask if they think the person is happy or unhappy.

> **ANSWERS:**
>
> | | |
> |---|---|
> | **1** such | **5** so |
> | **2** so | **6** such an |
> | **3** so | **7** so |
> | **4** such a | **8** such a |
>
> They're happy.

3

- Tell the students that they're going to rewrite the email in Exercise 2 to make it sound negative. Go through the example with the class and point out that *ugly* is the opposite of the adjective *beautiful*. Ask them what the adjective in the next sentence of the email is (*lucky*) and what its opposite is (*unlucky*). Then give them a few minutes to rewrite the rest of the email. Go around, monitoring and giving help.
- Allow them to compare their results in pairs before checking with the class. Accept any alternative versions that make sense. For example, the students may put *terrible* instead of *awful*, etc.

> **MODEL ANSWER:**
>
> This is such an ugly place. We're so unlucky with our hotel. It's really far from downtown and the staff are so unfriendly. Our room is dirty, and we have such a terrible view of the city. There aren't many good restaurants and bars, and they're so expensive. It's such a boring city. The museums and art galleries are awful, and we aren't going to visit the royal palace because it's closed. It's so boring. We're having such a bad time—we want to come home now.

4

- Ask the students to look back again at Exercise 2 in the Listening section. This time ask them to highlight the instances of *very* and *too*. Ask several students to read out the sentences containing these words.
- Focus attention on the rules and ask the students to complete them using information from the sentences in Listening Exercise 2. Then go through the information and example sentences in the margin. Ask the students to produce one or two more sentences using *very* or *too* to describe where they live.

> **ANSWERS:**
>
> **a** very **b** too

5

- Ask the students to work individually to complete the sentences.
- Ask the students to read their sentences again and check any that are true for them. Then let them compare with a partner.

> **ANSWERS:**
>
> **a** very
> **b** too
> **c** very
> **d** very
> **e** too
> **f** too

Grammar (SB page 18)

Nouns: countable/uncountable

1

- Focus the students' attention on the information in the margin. Point out that countable nouns have plural forms, but uncountable nouns don't.
- Ask the students to match the questions with the responses.
- Check answers with the class by getting one student to read out a question and another to read out the correct response. Then ask them to identify which of the nouns in the questions are countable (*stores, people*) and uncountable (*weather, architecture*).

> **ANSWERS:**
>
> **a** 4
> **b** 3
> **c** 2
> **d** 1

Language notes

Vocabulary: irregular plurals

There are a number of irregular plural forms in English. Here are some of the most common:

- Words ending in *-f* or *-fe* in the singular change to *-ves*.
  For example: half - halves, loaf - loaves, wife - wives, life - lives
- Words ending in -o in the singular change to *-oes*.
  For example: potato - potatoes, tomato - tomatoes
- Words ending in -y in the singular change to *-ies*.
  For example: city - cities, activity - activities
- Irregular plural nouns: woman - women, person - people, mouse - mice, child - children

Vocabulary: countable/uncountable

- Countable nouns are the names of individual objects, people or ideas which can be counted, e.g. *a man, two women, five chairs*. With countable nouns you can use numbers and the indefinite article *a/an* (*two movie theaters, a church*). Countable nouns have plurals (store, stores). You can use some with plural countable nouns: *some restaurants*.
- Uncountable or mass nouns are the names of materials, liquids, and collections without clear boundaries, which aren't seen as separate objects, e.g. *water, weather, air*. Uncountable nouns don't have plurals (~~*weathers*~~). You can use *some* with uncountable nouns: *some water*.
- The distinction between countable and uncountable objects can seem a little difficult to determine in some cases. For example, you say *two chairs* and *three tables* (as both *chair* and *table* are countable), but you say *some furniture* (because *furniture* is uncountable in English). However, *furniture* is countable in some languages and this may confuse some students.

2

- Focus the students' attention on the table and point out that *movie theater* is countable and has a plural form (*movie theaters*), but *nightlife* is uncountable and doesn't have a plural form. Ask them to complete the table with the nouns in the box, in each case indicating what the plural form is, if it has one, and marking it countable or uncountable.
- Check answers with the class before asking the students to work in pairs and discuss the questions.

ANSWERS:

Singular form	Plural form	Countable or uncountable?
movie theater	movie theaters	countable
nightlife	-	uncountable
park	parks	countable
person	people	countable
public transportation	-	uncountable
restaurant	restaurants	countable
traffic	-	uncountable

a stores, buses, churches, cities, countries, leaves
b person
c men, women, children, feet, teeth

3 Pairwork

- Ask the students to choose two cities, villages, or towns they know well and to write down their names. Give them time to prepare the questions that they will ask each other.
- As they ask and answer their questions, go around, monitoring and giving help where necessary.

Vocabulary & Pronunciation (SB page 18)

1 1.16

- Write *Mexico* and *Mexican* on the board. Explain or elicit that *Mexico* is a noun and the name of a country, and *Mexican* is an adjective which describes the nationality of someone from Mexico.
- Focus attention on the table and point out that in each column, the country word is on the left and the corresponding nationality word on the right.

Ask the students to complete the table. Check answers.

- Point out that the underlining indicates the syllable of the word that has the strongest stress. Ask them to look at the words they've written in the table and to underline the stressed syllables in these words.
- Play the recording for the students, check their answers and repeat the words. Ask them what they notice about the word stress in each set (A, B, and C).

ANSWERS:

A
Cuba - Cuban
Mexico - Mexican
Brazil - Brazilian
Argentina - Argentinian
Same stress.

B
Egypt - Egyptian
Italy - Italian
Hungary - Hungarian
Canada - Canadian
Stress different—moves to second syllable in nationality word.

C
China - Chinese
Vietnam - Vietnamese
Portugal - Portuguese
Japan - Japanese
Stress different—moves to last syllable in nationality word.

Language note

Pronunciation: nationalities

As a general rule, nationalities ending in *-(i)an*, *-ican*, and *-ish* are stressed on the preceding syllable sound, whereas countries ending in *-(u) ese* are stressed on the final syllable sound.

2

- Give the students a minute or two to write down six more countries and their nationalities. Go around, monitoring and giving help. Ask the students to mark the stress on their words. Check answers with the class, asking individual students to write their words and mark the stresses on the board.
- Ask the students to think about which countries they'd most like to visit. Put them into pairs to discuss with a partner.

Speaking (SB page 18)

1 Groupwork

Put the students into groups and ask them to discuss whether or not they agree with the two statements. If they disagree, ask them to substitute another nationality adjective for *Argentinian* or *Japanese* to make the statements into something they would agree with.

2

- Staying in their groups, the students discuss the nouns in the box and try to combine them with a nationality to produce statements with which they can all agree. As they do this, go around, monitoring and giving help.
- Ask a representative from each group to report back to the class on the statements they've agreed on and see if there is any consensus within the class as a whole.

Reading & Vocabulary (SB page 19)

1

- Go through the reviews as a class, and ask students to take note of the kind of information they include, for example its location, features or interesting spots close to the hotel, types of rooms, etc. Point out that the reviews use adjectives to describe the hotels and locations.
- **Pairwork.** Students read the reviews and discuss which of the places they would choose to stay in on vacation. Ask them explain their choices to a partner.

2

- Ask students about any good hotels they would recommend.
- Refer the students to the headings in the table and the examples and brainstorm possible items for each heading. Then ask the students to read the reviews and complete the table individually before comparing their answers in pairs. Go around, helping with vocabulary.
- Check the answers by asking several students to share their answers with the whole class.

ANSWERS:

Hotel rooms: deluxe room, presidential suite, suite, standard room
Rooms: bedroom, bathroom, hallway, dining room, kitchen, living room
Furniture: bed, TV, desk, chairs, couch, bathtub, shower, lamps, double bed, flat screen TV, toilet, sink, table

3

- Tell them to write a short review for their hotel—about 50-80 words long. Remind them to use adjectives (positive or negative).
- You can ask some of the students to share their reviews with the class. Did any of the students write about the same hotel? How are their reviews similar/different?

Reading (SB page 20)

1

Ask the students to read the text and to complete it with the words in the box. Allow them to work in pairs if they wish. Go around, monitoring and giving help. Check answers with the class and answer any questions on vocabulary.

> **ANSWERS:**
>
> **1** meat
> **2** cigarettes
> **3** coffee
> **4** wine
> **5** hours
> **6** sleep
> **7** people
> **8** cars
> **9** noise

2

Ask the students to discuss in pairs or groups which country they think the text describes. Ask them to give reasons why it could or couldn't be their own country.

Grammar (SB page 20)

Quantity expressions with countable and uncountable nouns

1

- Focus the students' attention on the information in the margin. Point out the two question forms *How many?* and *How much?* and ask the students to suggest nouns which could be used with each one. For example, *How many people? How much water?*
- Focus the students' attention on categories in the table. Ask them to use the information in the margin to help them complete the headings.

> **ANSWERS:**
>
> **A:** countable
> **B:** uncountable
> **C:** countable, uncountable

2

- Ask the students to work individually to choose the correct alternatives. Then allow them to compare their results in pairs. When checking answers, ask the students to read out the complete sentences so that they get a feel for what sounds right.
- Ask the students to check the sentences that are true for them and then to rewrite the others to make them true.
- When they've compared their sentences with a partner, ask them to report back to the class.

> **ANSWERS:**
>
> **a** much
> **b** lots of
> **c** way too much
> **d** enough
> **e** a lot of
> **f** enough

Language note

Vocabulary: *little*

Generally speaking, if a student makes a mistake with a quantity expression, they'll still be understood. If, for example, one of your students says *Bill Gates has many money*, although the sentence is grammatically incorrect, the meaning is clear.

The word *little* presents a bigger problem: if used with a countable noun, *little* refers to the size of the noun; if used with an uncountable noun, it refers to the quantity. This can produce problems with meaning. It's therefore important that the teacher is aware that sentences like *There were little people at the party* are probably grammatically rather than politically incorrect, the desired sentence being *There were few people at the party*, or, more naturally, *There weren't many people at the party*.

3 Pairwork

Go through the example questions and answers with the class. Then elicit a few more questions using words from the box.

4 Grammar Extra 2

Ask the students to turn to Grammar Extra 2 on page 132 of the Student's Book. Here they'll find an explanation of the grammar they've been studying and further exercises to practice it.

> **ANSWERS:**
>
> **1**
> **a** names **b** places **c** menus **d** buses
> **e** families **f** wives **g** people **h** feet **i** days
> **j** mice **k** cameras **l** watches
>
> **2**
> Countable nouns: child, city, office, problem, tooth, woman
> Uncountable nouns: advice, homework, information, money, news, weather
>
> **3**
> **a** some **b** a **c** some **d** some **e** some **f** a
> **g** some **h** some
>
> **4**
> **a** is **b** was **c** are **d** is **e** were **f** was
>
> **5**
> **a** are a lot of
> **b** is a lot of
> **c** are a lot of
> **d** is a lot of
> **e** is a lot of
> **f** are a lot of
>
> **a** There aren't many parks.
> **b** There isn't much nightlife.
> **c** There aren't many good restaurants.
> **d** There isn't much traffic.

- **e** There isn't much pollution.
- **f** There aren't many bookstores.

6

- **a** He drinks too much beer.
- **b** He eats too many pizzas.
- **c** He doesn't eat enough fruit and vegetables.
- **d** He smokes too many cigarettes.
- **e** He doesn't do enough exercise.
- **f** He watches too much TV.
- **g** He doesn't get enough fresh air.

Vocabulary (SB page 21)

1

Focus the students' attention on the compass. Ask them to complete the labels.

ANSWERS:

a North	**d** South-West
b East	**e** West
c South	**f** North-West

2

Focus the students' attention on the maps. Ask them to find each of the cities (Los Angeles, Bogotá, London, and Philadelphia) and match them with the descriptions. Remind them to refer to the compass they completed in Exercise 1 if they aren't sure of the direction words. Then check answers with the class.

ANSWERS:

a 2	**c** 1
b 4	**d** 3

3 Pairwork

- The pairwork exercise for this unit is on pages 120 and 125 of the Student's Book. Put the students into pairs and tell them who will be Student A, and who will be Student B.
- While they're doing the exercise, go around, monitoring and giving help. Take note of any errors which may need particular attention later, and also any examples of good language use which you can praise in a feedback session.

Speaking: anecdote (SB page 21)

For more information about how to set up, monitor and repeat Anecdotes, see pages xviii–xx in the Introduction.

1 1.17

- Explain to students that they're going to hear Emma talking about the best place she's ever visited. Go through the questions with the class.
- Play the recording and ask the students to listen and check the questions.

ANSWERS:

She talks about: a, b, c, d, f, g, h, i

1.17

The best place I've ever visited is Buenos Aires, the capital of Argentina. It's a crazy city, but I really love it. The first time I went there was on my summer vacation. It was the year before I went to college. So I was young and excited, and it was my first time in South America. I flew there on my own, but I went to stay with friends. Of course I visited all the tourist places – the Colón Theater, the Plaza de Mayo, La Boca, and my friends took me to watch a tango show. That was great. I even took some tango lessons, but I'm not very good. I also went out dancing a lot – Buenos Aires' nightlife is fantastic. The streets are crowded at three o'clock in the morning with people going to restaurants and discos. The discos are open until six or seven o'clock in the morning – in fact, Buenos Aires never sleeps! Now I go back to Buenos Aires as often as possible. I've been there three times, and last year I went there for New Year's. What I particularly like about Buenos Aires is the people. Argentinian people are very special. They're loud, energetic, and a lot of fun. I love them!

2

- Give the students a minute or two to decide on the place they're going to talk about. Then ask them to look at the questions in Exercise 1 again and decide how they'd answer them about their place. Allow them to make notes of what they're going to say and how they're going to say it, but discourage them from writing a paragraph that they can simply read out. Go around, monitoring and giving help.
- **Pairwork**. Put the students into pairs and ask them to take turns to tell their partner about the best place they've ever visited. Encourage them to ask each other follow-up questions.
- Ask some pairs to report back to the class about what they found out.

Language for Life (SB page 22)

1 1.18

- Focus the students' attention on the illustration. Explain that the people in the picture are Josh, Matt, and Erica. They're going to listen to them talking and they have to decide what nationality each of them is.
- Play the recording for them to listen and note down their answers. Encourage them to read the conversation as they listen.

> **ANSWERS:**
>
> Josh is American.
> Matt is American.
> Erica is British.

Cultural notes

Manchester

A city in northwest England. Manchester is credited as the world's first industrialized city. It's home to many modern bands, such as the Smiths, Stone Roses, Happy Mondays, and Oasis, and is also famous for its two soccer teams, Manchester City and Manchester United.

Los Angeles

"The City of Angels" is on the west coast of the United States. Founded in 1781, Los Angeles was part of Spain. It became part of Mexico in 1821 and was then ceded to the United States in 1848. In the last 150 years, Los Angeles has become the movie capital of the world.

2

Focus attention on the maps and ask the students to match each of the people with one of the maps. Tell them to put an X to show exactly where each person comes from.

> **ANSWERS:**
>
> Map 1: Erica Map 2: Matt Map 3: Josh

3 1.19

- Ask the students to complete the useful phrases. Remind them that they can look back at the conversation in Exercise 1 if they need help.
- Play the recording for the students to listen and check their answers. Then play it again for them to repeat the useful phrases.

> **ANSWERS:**
>
> **a** Where are you from?
> **b** I'm originally from England.
> **c** Where exactly?
> **d** A small town just outside Manchester.
> **e** Manchester's in the north.
> **f** I live in New York, but actually I'm from Los Angeles.
> **g** Which part of the city are you from?
> **h** Not far from the airport.
> **i** They live in the south.

4 Pairwork

Ask the students to write their conversations, using as many of the useful phrases as they can. Go around, monitoring and giving help where necessary. When they've finished, tell them to practice their conversations out loud. Ask a few confident pairs to perform their conversations for the class.

Life Skills: Prioritizing (SB page 22)

What to do ...?

1

Explain that when visiting a new city, it's customary to go sightseeing (see the most famous sites). This section focuses on prioritizing the best places to visit in the students' cities.

- Focus the students' attention on the text, and make sure that they understand the meaning of *tweet* (a post on the social media platform Twitter).
- Tell them that they are going to respond to Bob Denny's request. Focus their attention on the table, and put them into pairs to complete the table with ideas about their own cities/towns. Encourage them to come up with as many places as they can.

2

Still in their pairs, ask students to look at their ideas from Exercise 1 and to choose their top three places. When they're done, they should do the same for places to eat and places to stay.

Vocabulary Extra (SB page 23)

Places

1

- Focus the students' attention on the list of words and point out that they're all to do with places. Check that the students can pronounce the words correctly.

- Ask the students to look at the places in the picture and match each one with one of the words. Point out that the first one has been done for them.

ANSWERS:

art gallery 6	mosque 1
parking lot 10	museum 2
castle 3	shopping mall 8
church 7	square 9
library 5	theater 4

2 Pairwork

Go through the example question and answer with the class and then ask the students to take turns asking and answering similar questions using the places in Exercise 1.

Adjectives

1

Focus the students' attention on the adjectives in the box and tell them that all the adjectives describe cities. Ask the students to work individually and decide which words are positive and which are negative. Check answers with the class. Ask for choral and individual repetition to check that they're pronouncing the words correctly.

POSSIBLE ANSWERS:

Positive: beautiful, (big), exciting, fabulous, interesting, (modern), romantic, spectacular
Negative: (big), boring, crowded, dirty, dull, expensive, (modern), noisy, polluted
(Some people may regard big and modern as negative adjectives in this context.)

2 Pairwork

Ask the students to choose five adjectives to describe their own cities and to compare their choices with their partner.

Furniture

1

Focus the students' attention on the pictures and point out that they all show different kinds of furniture. Check that they can pronounce the words correctly.

- Ask the students to look at the pieces of furniture in the pictures and match each one with one of the words.

ANSWERS:

toilet 4	shower 1
bathtub 7	rug 8
desk 5	lamp 2
couch 6	sink 3

Focus on *like*

1

Ask the students to look at the table. Go through the different uses of *like* with the class and then ask them to match them to the example sentences.

ANSWERS:

a 4	**d** 2
b 3	**e** 1
c 6	**f** 5

2

Ask the students to write a sentence of their own for each use of *like* in the table. Go around, monitoring and giving help. In a class feedback session, put some of their suggestions on the board.

Further Practice Material

Need more classroom practice activities?
Photocopiable resource materials in the Teacher's Presentation Kit / Extra Resources

Need more tests?
Test Generator
Teacher's Presentation Kit / Extra Resources / Tests

Need more on important teaching concepts?
Key concepts in American Inside Out Evolution pages xxi-xxxvii

Need student self-study practice?
Workbook pages 8-11

Need more information and ideas?
American Inside Out Evolution website www.macmillan.com.br/americaninsideoutevolution

Need to check what your students can do by the end of this unit?
Self-evaluation checklists on pages xxxix-xliii

3 Love *Overview*

Section	Aims	What the students are doing
Listening SB page 24	Listening for specific information	Listening to two people talking about their relationship and answering questions. Completing sentences with *He*, *She*, or *They*.
Vocabulary & Speaking SB page 24	Relationship expressions; fluency practice	Completing sentences with relationship expressions. Discussing statements about relationships.
Vocabulary SB page 25	Relationship expressions	Matching verb phrases with pictures. Putting the stages of a relationship in a logical order.
Grammar SB page 25	Simple past	Writing affirmative and negative simple past forms of verbs. Writing sentences with simple past verbs.
Pronunciation SB page 25	Irregular simple past forms	Categorizing simple past forms according to their pronunciation.
Listening SB page 26	Listening for detail	Reading about a TV game show and answering questions. Listening to contestants and identifying the answers they give. Talking about the game show questions with a partner.
Grammar SB page 27	Past progressive	Identifying the uses of the simple past and past progressive. Writing sentences using simple past and past progressive to describe a picture.
Reading SB page 27	Reading for detail	Completing a story with past progressive or simple past verbs. Predicting the ending to the story.
Reading SB page 28	Reading for detail	Completing noun phrases. Completing a blog post with noun phrases. Discussing relationships in pairs.
Vocabulary & Speaking SB page 29	Time adverbials; telling a story	Finding time adverbials in stories and listing them in order. Retelling a story using time adverbials.
Grammar SB page 29	Adverbs of manner	Completing a table with adverbs and adjectives. Answering questions about forming adverbs from adjectives. Rewriting sentences in the correct order and then making them true for them.
Language for Life SB page 30	Things in common	Listening to a conversation to determine whether the speakers know each other. Answering true/false questions. Completing useful phrases for talking about things in common. Writing and responding to comments with the useful phrases.
Life Skills SB page 30	Decision-making: A Perfect Date	Listening and completing dating profiles. Discussing and choosing the perfect date for someone. Discussing their own perfect dates.
Vocabulary Extra SB page 31	Adjectives ending in *ed* or *ing*; *get*	Matching pictures with adjectives. Underlining the correct adjectives in sentences. Identifying the various uses of *get*. Writing example sentences using *get*.
Writing WB page 15		Using time expressions. Telling a story.

3 Love *Teacher's notes*

Warm-up

- Prepare a number of labels, each with the name of one member of a famous couple that the students are likely to know, e.g. *Romeo and Juliet, Bonnie and Clyde, Samson and Delilah, Minnie and Mickey Mouse*. You can use ones from the students' own culture(s) to ensure that they are well-known. You can even get the students to prepare the labels themselves.
- Pin the labels to the backs of the students' clothing so they cannot see them. They then have to walk around the classroom asking questions to find out who they are—the only questions they can't ask are *Who am I?* or *What is my name?* They then have to find their other half. Pairs then report back to the class on what they know about their famous couple. You could ask them to do all the pairwork exercises in this unit as a couple.

Listening (SB page 24)

1 1.20

- Focus the students' attention on the pictures. Ask the students what they notice about the pictures (they show the same couple now and when they were younger). Ask them to say how old they think Walt and Betty are now and how old they were in the earlier pictures.
- Go through the questions so that the students know what information to listen out for. Play the recording and ask them to answer the questions.

ANSWERS:

a Fifty years ago.
b Last summer.

1.20

(B = Betty; W = Walt)

B: We first met fifty years ago.
W: I joined the Navy and I went to Annapolis, Maryland, for my training. On the first day I went to the canteen, and this little lady was serving lunch.
B: Yes, I was. I liked him so I gave him extra fries.
W: Anyway, we started talking. Then, one night, there was a party.
B: I said to Walt, "I'll be your girl tonight," and that was it.
W: Yes, we dated for three wonderful months.
B: We did.
W: Then we both moved to different places. At first, we wrote to each other. We wrote twice a week.
B: Yes, but then we stopped. I don't know why. But we lost touch with each other. Then we got married to other people. I had two children, and Walt had a daughter.
W: That's right. I was married for forty-eight years, and then my wife died.
B: And I got divorced after thirty years of marriage.
W: So we were both single again.
B: And one day, my grandson took me to Annapolis for the day. I visited all the old places and I thought about Walt. I wanted to find him.
W: She didn't even know whether I was alive.
B: No, I didn't. So I wrote a letter to the editor of the local newspaper.
W: I have a cousin in Annapolis. She doesn't usually buy the newspaper, but on that day she did. She bought the paper and she saw the letter. And she realized that Betty was looking for me.
B: He called me. I nearly had a heart attack. I said, "Is that my Walt?" I was so happy.
W: We met soon after that. We realized we were still in love and we moved in together a few months later.
B: We got married last summer. I didn't want to lose him again!

2

- Go through the example with the class, then ask the students to read the remaining sentences and complete them with *He*, *She*, or *They*. Allow them to compare their answers in pairs before playing the recording again for them to check their answers.

- Ask the students for their reactions to this story. Can they imagine being in love and getting married in their seventies?

> **ANSWERS:**
>
> | | |
> |---|---|
> | **a** They | **f** She |
> | **b** They | **g** She |
> | **c** He | **h** He |
> | **d** She | **i** They |
> | **e** She | **j** They |

Cultural notes

Annapolis

Annapolis is a city on the eastern coast of the USA, situated at the mouth of the Severn River, which flows into the Chesapeake Bay. It is the capital of the state of Maryland. The United States Naval Academy is in Annapolis.

Vocabulary & Speaking (SB page 24)

1

Ask the students to read the sentences and complete them with the words in the box. Allow them to compare their sentences in pairs before checking answers with the class. Check answers by asking individual students to read their sentences aloud.

> **ANSWERS:**
>
> | | |
> |---|---|
> | **a** get | **d** live |
> | **b** have | **e** lose |
> | **c** love | |

2 Groupwork

Ask the students to discuss each of the statements in Exercise 1 and to decide whether they agree or disagree with them. Ask one member of each group to take notes on their discussion. The groups can then report back to the class on what they decided.

Vocabulary (SB page 25)

1

Focus the students' attention on the pictures. Give them a minute or two to take in what they see. Then ask them to match the verb phrases to the pictures.

> **ANSWERS:**
>
> flirt with somebody – b)
> have a crush on somebody – a)
> have a fight – d)
> move in together – c)

2

- This is an exercise about the different stages of a relationship. As such, you may need to adapt it to take into account the cultural sensitivities of your students. Point out that they have the option of adding or taking away any of the stages listed if they think it's necessary. You may find one of the alternative activities below more appropriate.
- Go through the stages of a relationship with the class and make sure everybody understands them. Ask them which of these stages comes first in a relationship. When they've identified that it's most likely d) You have a crush on somebody, ask them to work individually to work out the logical order of each of the other stages. There are no fixed answers to this and make it clear that they can add or take away any stages if they wish.
- Put the students into pairs and ask them to compare their ideas.

Grammar (SB page 25)

Simple past

1

- Go through the information in the margin on affirmative and negative simple past forms. Point out that *go* is an irregular verb and the simple past form is *went*. Ask several students to read out the sentences, questions, and answers in the margin.
- Go through the list of verbs in the box. Ask the students to write the affirmative and negative simple past forms as in the example.

> **ANSWERS:**
>
> be: was/were, wasn't/weren't
> can: could; couldn't
> get: got; didn't get
> go: went; didn't go
> have: had; didn't have
> flirt: flirted; didn't flirt
> kiss: kissed; didn't kiss
> like: liked; didn't like
> meet: met; didn't meet
> move: moved; didn't move
> study: studied; didn't study
> want: wanted; didn't want

Language note

Grammar: teaching irregular verbs

- There are approximately 180 irregular verbs. Some of these are rare, but most are very common and students need to learn them.
- Some people learn a list by heart. Others think you'll just gradually acquire them over time. However, one useful method is for students to note down new irregular verbs when they meet them in sentences rather than as individual words, for example, *go – I went to the movies last night with Jamie.*

2

- Do the first one with the class as an example and then ask the students to work individually to write the remaining sentences. Remind them that they should be true. Go around, monitoring and checking that the statements are being formed correctly.
- Go through the example question with the class. Then ask a student to form a question with the second statement. (With weaker classes, go through all the statements and get the students to change them into questions before moving into the pairwork stage.)
- Put the students into pairs and ask them to take turns asking and answering questions about the statements. Go around checking that all the questions are being formed correctly. Ask several pairs to report back to the class on what they learned about their partners.

ANSWERS:

Statements

a My mother and father met / didn't meet at college.
b My grandparents got married / didn't get married in a church.
c I had / didn't have a big breakfast this morning.
d I went / didn't go skiing last winter.
e I studied / didn't study German at school.
f I was / wasn't very busy yesterday.

Questions

a Did your mother and father meet at college?
b Did your grandparents get married in a church?
c Did you have a big breakfast this morning?
d Did you go skiing last winter?
e Did you study German at school?
f Were you very busy yesterday?

Language notes

Grammar: *did* auxiliary

- In the simple past, the auxiliary *did/didn't* functions in exactly the same way as *do/does/doesn't* in the simple present. For example, *yes/no*-questions and short answers: *Did you go to Chicago yesterday? Yes, I did.* And in open questions and negative sentences: *Who did you meet?* I didn't meet anyone.
- Note that there's only one form did for first, second, and third persons.
- Note also that you use the infinitive form of the verb after the auxiliary *did/didn't* rather than the past form. For example, *I didn't leave*, NOT ~~*I didn't left*~~. and *Did he go?* NOT ~~*Did he went?*~~

3 Grammar Extra 3 Part 1

Ask the students to turn to Grammar Extra 3 Part 1 on page 134 of the Student's Book. Here they'll find an explanation of the grammar they've been studying and further exercises to practice it.

ANSWERS:

1

a worked, went, called, helped
b took, made, woke, baked
c tried, played, studied, copied
d stopped, planned, hopped, walked

Verbs that don't belong in each set:
a go - went because it's irregular.
b bake - baked because it's regular.
c play - played because the y doesn't change to an i.
d walk - walked because it doesn't double the final consonant.

2

a taught **b** sat **c** said **d** knew **e** spoke
f made **g** began **h** rang **i** fell **j** learned
k caught **l** flew **m** sank **n** threw
o swam **p** read **q** understood **r** brought
s ran **t** slept **u** found **v** wore
w bought **x** came **y** met **z** thought

3

a My father didn't teach me how to drive.
b I didn't go to a private school.
c My parents didn't give me a gift for my birthday.
d I didn't have meat for dinner last night.
e I didn't study English at school.
f I didn't play basketball when I was young.

Pronunciation (SB page 25)

1 1.21

- Focus the students' attention on the table and explain that verbs which don't form their simple past by taking *-ed* are known as irregular. Point out that in each set, the infinitive is in the left-hand column and the simple past form in the right-hand column. Ask them to complete the table. Check answers with the class before moving on to the next part of the exercise.
- Point out that the irregular verbs have been grouped according to the pronunciation of their simple past forms. Read out the sounds in the instructions (/æ/, /e/, and /ɔ/) and make sure the students can identify them and say them correctly. You could write them on the board and ask the students to suggest words that contain each sound.
- Ask the students to label the past forms in each group with the sounds. Play the recording for them to check their answers, then play it again for them to listen and repeat all the words.

ANSWERS:

a meant
b meet
c began
d drank
e buy
f caught

Group 1 past forms: /e/
Group 2 past forms: /æ/
Group 3 past forms: /ɔ/

2 1.22

- Ask individual students to read out the verbs in the box. After each one, ask the other students to say what they think the simple past form is. When they produce the correct answer, ask them which group in the table they should add it to.
- Play the recording for them to check their answers. Then play it again for them to listen and repeat the words.

ANSWERS:

fight (fought): 3
read (read): 1
sing (sang): 2
sleep (slept): 1
swim (swam): 2
teach (taught): 3

Listening (SB page 26)

Warm-up

Ask the students to give you the names of some popular game shows that they watch on TV. Ask them to explain what the contestants have to do and what they can win. Find out which game show they like best.

1

- Focus the students' attention on the pictures and tell them that they show different TV shows. The biggest picture shows the host of a TV game show called *Get Personal*.
- Go through the questions with the class so that they know what information they're looking for, then ask them to read the description of the show and answer the questions.
- Check answers with the class and answer any questions about vocabulary.

ANSWERS:

a Rosie and Dave
b $10,000
c They have to give the same answers to the same questions.

2 1.23

Go through the questions and answers with the class. Then ask the students to listen to the recording and choose the answers that Rosie gives. Play the recording twice if necessary.

ANSWERS:

1 a
2 c
3 b
4 She a; He a
5 b

1.23

(I = Introducer; BB = Bobby Brown; R = Rosie; D = Dave)

I: It's time for our popular competition *Get Personal*, with your host, Bobby Brown.

BB: Good evening and welcome to this week's *Get Personal*. Let's meet our first couple, Rosie and Dave. As you know, Rosie and Dave are in separate studios—Rosie can't hear Dave, and Dave has no idea what Rosie is saying. But they can both hear me. OK, are you ready to play *Get Personal*?

R&D: Yes, Bobby.

BB: OK, we'll start with you, Rosie. We want you to remember exactly what was going on when you first met Dave. OK?

R: OK, Bobby.

BB: Now, Rosie, how did you first meet Dave?

R: Well, I was working as a nurse, and Dave was my patient. He came into the hospital for an operation.

BB: OK, Rosie. I want you to think about the moment when you first met. What time of day was it?

R:	Um, I was working nights that week. So early evening.
BB:	Uh-huh. And how was the weather?
R:	I think it was raining. Yes, it was raining when I arrived at work.
BB:	What were you both wearing when you saw each other for the first time?
R:	Now, that's easy. I was wearing my nurse's uniform, a white coat, and he was wearing pajamas. Blue pajamas. Or were they green? No, blue.
BB:	Finally, who spoke first and what did he or she say?
R:	Dave spoke first. In fact he shouted at me. He said, "Nurse, I'm going to throw up!"
BB:	Well, that's very romantic! Thank you, Rosie.

3 1.24

Go through the instructions with the class. Make sure they understand that they just have to circle the check or the X in the column for Dave's answers according to whether or not he gives the same answer as Rosie. Play the recording twice if necessary. Check answers with the class and ask how many points out of five Rosie and Dave scored.

ANSWERS:

1✓ 2✓ 3✗ 4✓ 5✗

1.24

(BB = Bobby Brown; D = Dave)

BB:	Now, Dave, it's your turn. Where and how did you first meet?
D:	Well, I went into the hospital for an operation, and Rosie was working there as a nurse.
BB:	What time of day was it?
D:	Oh, I don't know. Lunchtime? No, hold on, it was later than that. Early evening.
BB:	How was the weather?
D:	It was summer, so I guess the sun was shining.
BB:	What were you both wearing when you saw each other for the first time?
D:	Rosie was wearing her nurse's uniform, a white coat, and she was also wearing nice perfume. I was wearing my favorite blue pajamas.
BB:	Finally, Dave, who spoke first and what did he or she say?
D:	Rosie spoke first. She said, "How are you feeling?" And I think I said, "I feel terrible."

4 Pairwork

Ask the students to discuss the questions in pairs and then report back to the class.

Grammar (SB page 27)

Past progressive

1

- Go through the information in the margin, pointing out that the past progressive is formed with *was/ were* plus the *-ing* form of the main verb. Ask several students to read out the full sentences in the margin (*I was working, You were working*, etc.).
- Read out the extracts from the interview with Rosie and ask the students to answer the questions about them. Go around, monitoring and giving help as they do this.

ANSWERS:

a	Simple past	**c**	Past progressive
b	Past progressive	**d**	Simple past

Extra activity

Ask the students to write the simple past forms of these verbs and answer the questions. For example:

be – was/were

be can get go have kiss want

1. Which verbs have irregular past forms?
2. How do you form the simple past of regular verbs?
3. How do you spell the past forms of these regular verbs: *move, study, like*?
4. How do you make negatives for *be* and *can* in the simple past?
5. How do you make questions for *be* and *can* in the simple past?
6. How do you make negatives and questions for all other verbs?

Language note

Grammar: past progressive + *when* + simple past

The past progressive is used to talk about the circumstances surrounding an event in the past. It's often used with *when* in sentences where the event (in the simple past) interrupts the circumstances (in the past progressive): *It was raining* ***when*** *I arrived at work.* In these sentences, when is always followed by the event (in the simple past).

It's possible to change the order of the clauses, putting when at the beginning of the sentence, without changing the meaning. Where this happens, the two clauses are separated by a comma: *When I arrived at work, it was raining.*

2 Pairwork

- The pairwork exercise for this unit is on pages 121 and 126 of the Student's Book. Put the students into pairs and tell them who will be Student A, and who will be Student B.
- While they're doing the exercise, go around, monitoring and giving help. Take note of any errors which may need particular attention later, and also any examples of good language use.

3 1.25

- Focus the students' attention on the pictures. Explain to the class that they're going to listen to some sounds.
- Go through the example with the class. Point out the use of the past progressive for the action that was taking place when something else happened (simple past). Ask the students to work individually.
- Play the recording. Pause after each situation in the recording for the students to write sentences for them. When checking answers, make sure the students are using the past progressive and simple past correctly.

POSSIBLE ANSWERS

1 Jake was taking a shower when his cell phone rang.
2 Fiona and her friend were talking at the disco when a man asked Fiona for a dance.
3 Jake and Fiona were having dinner when Jake asked Fiona to marry him.
4 Jake and Fiona were sleeping when the baby started to cry.
5 Jake and Fiona were having an argument when somebody arrived.

4 Grammar Extra 3 Part 2

Ask the students to turn to Grammar Extra 3 Part 2 on page 134 of the Student's Book. Here they'll find an explanation of the grammar they've been studying and further exercises to practice it.

ANSWERS:

1
a coming **b** eating **c** hitting **d** leaving
e playing **f** putting **g** staying **h** studying
i swimming **j** waking **k** winning **l** working

2
a Were you having breakfast? Yes, I was. No, I wasn't.
b Were you driving to work? Yes, I was. No, I wasn't.
c Was your mother working? Yes, she was. No, she wasn't.
d Were you walking around town? Yes, I was. No, I wasn't.
e Were your parents watching TV? Yes, they were. No, they weren't.

3
a moved
b were studying
c started
d was raining
e turned on
f was talking

Reading (SB page 27)

1 1.26

- Focus the students' attention on the picture and ask them what they think is happening in it.
- Ask the students to read the story and complete it with past progressive and simple past verbs. When they've finished, check their answers and then ask them to work in pairs to decide what the ending of the story is. Get various suggestions from around the class and write them on the board.
- Play the recording for the students to listen and check their answers. Did any of them predict the original ending to the story?

ANSWERS:

1 met
2 tweeted
3 was moving
4 weren't following
5 agreed
6 were waiting
7 replied
8 was writing
9 met
10 asked

1.26

How I met my husband is a funny story. Three years ago, he tweeted that he was moving and he had lots of horror DVDs he wanted to give away. At the time, we weren't following each other on Twitter, but a friend showed me his tweet.

I am a huge horror movie fan, so I agreed to come and pick up the DVDs. They were waiting on the front porch when I got to his house, but he wasn't at home.

I tweeted to say "thank you". He replied and asked me out for a coffee. He's a writer, so he said he was writing a book and he wanted to interview me for it. I met him, and he asked me all sorts of questions about my business.

At the end of the meeting he then asked me if I would like to go out for dinner with him any other day. I had to laugh! I really thought he wanted to interview me and that was it. After we were seeing each other for a few months, I asked him when he was planning to write the book ...

That's when he told me there was no book! He just wanted to make sure I wasn't crazy before asking me out. And he has his DVDs back because...we got married last June!

Reading (SB page 28)

1

- Focus the students' attention on the pictures. Ask them to read the words in the box and use them to complete the noun phrases.
- Check answers with the class and tell them that they're going to read a blog post in which these things play an important part. Ask them to say what they think the post might be about.

ANSWERS:

a paint	**d** club
b party	**e** bag
c scissors	**f** mineral water

2 1.27

- Give the students plenty of time to read the blog post. Answer any questions they have about vocabulary. Tell the students to complete the blog post with the items from Exercise 1.

ANSWERS:

1 dinner party	**4** plastic
2 bottle	**5** can
3 pair	**6** night club

3 Pairwork

- First lead a brief whole class discussion by asking the students what they thought of Bill and Lisa's decisions. Ask them if they've ever been in a boring relationship or know someone who was and why the relationship was boring. List a few reasons on the board.
- Then refer the students to the question in Exercise 3 and ask them to discuss their views in pairs. Go around, monitoring and offering help.
- As a whole class, ask several pairs to share their opinions with the rest of the class, and have a vote on the best or most original ideas for making a relationship fun.

Vocabulary & Speaking (SB page 29)

1

- Focus the students' attention on the box and explain that these words are known as time adverbials; they tell us when or in what order things happened. Ask the students to look back at the blog post on page 28 and underline the time adverbials.
- Draw the students' attention to the list and point out that the first time adverbial has already been inserted. Ask them to write the others in the order in which they appear in the blog post.

ANSWERS:

1 Last year	**7** Next
2 That evening	**8** After
3 At first	**9** A week later
4 Then	**10** One day
5 That night	**11** At the end of August
6 The next morning	

2

- Ask the students to retell the story in the blog post to their partner, using the list of time adverbials to prompt them and without looking back at page 28. Go around, monitoring and giving help. Take note of any students who do this particularly well and ask them to retell their stories to the class.

Grammar (SB page 29)

Adverbs of manner

1

- Go through the information in the margin, explaining that adverbs of manner tell us how something is or was done. Point out the spelling changes in *carefully* and *angrily*.
- **Pairwork.** Ask the students to work together to complete the table with adverbs or adjectives from the blog post on page 28. Check answers with the class. Then elicit answers from the class to the questions below the tables.

ANSWERS:

a happily	**e** beautiful
b surprising	**f** unhappily
c angry	**g** quietly
d quickly	

a Add *ly*.
b Delete *y* and add *ily*.
c well, early, late

2

- Explain that it's important to put adverbs in the correct place in a sentence. Read out the example to the class and point out that the adverb is in the final position in the sentences. Explain that subject + verb + object + adverb is the usual order, though other positions are possible.
- Ask the students to work individually to rewrite the remaining sentences. As they do this, go around, monitoring and giving help where necessary. Check answers with the class before moving on to the next part of the exercise.
- Give the students a minute or two to decide which sentences are true for them and to change the ones that aren't to make them true. Then put them into pairs to compare their sentences.

ANSWERS:

a I eat my lunch very quickly.
b I drive my car very slowly.
c I plan my days very carefully.
d I spend my money very intelligently.
e I play tennis very badly.
f I clean my house very regularly.
g I speak English very well.

Language for Life (SB page 30)

1 1.28

- Focus the students' attention on the picture and ask them to describe the situation. Tell them that they're going to listen to a conversation between Tim and Anna, and all they have to do is decide whether they know each other or not.
- Play the recording. When you ask the students if they know each other, you could also ask what helped them decide (Tim's first words are "Excuse me", which is a way of starting a conversation with a stranger).

ANSWER:

They don't know each other.

1.28

(T = Tim; A = Anna)
T: Excuse me. Do you know what time we arrive in Atlanta?
A: Yes, I think we get there at about 2:30.
T: Thanks. I see you're reading *Pride and Prejudice*. Are you enjoying it?
A: Yes, I am.
T: I didn't like the movie.
A: Oh, I did. I thought it was great. I really like Keira Knightley.
T: Oh, so do I. I think she's really good in *Pirates of the Caribbean*.
A: Me, too. I love that movie. Johnny Depp's fantastic.
T: I know. I'm going to see his new movie tomorrow night.
A: Really? So am I. Where are you going to see it?
T: At the AMC Phipps Plaza.
A: Me, too!
T: Oh, that's great. I don't know what time it starts.
A: No, neither do I. But my husband has the tickets, so he knows.
T: Oh. That's good.

Cultural notes

Pride and Prejudice

This English novel by Jane Austen, published in England in 1813, tells the story of Mrs. Bennet and her desperate attempts to get her five daughters to marry wealthy men, as there were no sons to inherit Mr. Bennet's property and support the family should he die. Despite Mrs. Bennet's interference in her daughters' love lives, which leads to all sorts of misunderstandings, two of her daughters eventually get married to wealthy men.

Keira Knightley (born 1985)

Keira Knightley was born in London. She plays the role of Elizabeth Swan in the *Pirates of the Caribbean* movies. She also starred in the British films *Bend it Like Beckham* (2002), *Love Actually* (2003), and *Atonement* (2007).

Johnny Depp (born 1963)

Johnny Depp's movie debut was in *Nightmare On Elm Street* (1984). He then acted in the popular TV show *21 Jump Street*, before starring in the movie *Edward Scissorhands* (1990), directed by Tim Burton. His most popular role to date is probably playing Jack Sparrow in the *Pirates of the Caribbean* film franchise.

- Read the sentences with the class. Tell them to decide whether they are true or false. You could do this by reading each one in turn and asking the students to stand up if they think it's true or remain seated if they think it's false. Encourage them to try to persuade people who have made a different decision of their own point of view.
- Play the recording for the students to check their answers.

ANSWERS:

a True	**d** True
b True	**e** False
c True	

3 1.29

- Allow the students to work in pairs to complete the table. Play the recording for them to check their answers. Then play it again for them to listen and repeat the useful phrases.

ANSWERS:

1 Oh, I did.	**4** So am I.
2 So do I.	**5** Neither do I.
3 Me, too.	

4

Ask the students to work individually to write their comments. Explain that these can be on any subject they like. Elicit a few examples from the class before they begin to start them off, or put a few of your own on the board.

Extra activity

- Put the students into pairs to take turns reading out their sentences and agreeing or disagreeing with their partner's comments.
- Find as many things in common with one another as possible in three minutes. Talk about the following, or your own ideas: movies, books, music, food, places to go, sports, where you live, where you go on vacation, what you did yesterday / last year / for your last vacation, what you're going to do later / on the weekend / for your next vacation, etc.

Life Skills (SB page 30)

Decision-making: A Perfect Date

Cultural notes

Explain that some people use dating agencies to find partners. The agency generally asks you to provide personal information so they can find a suitable match for you. You then go on a date with this person, that is to say you meet them, usually in a public place like a bar or restaurant, and get to know each other.

1

- Refer the students to the dating profile boxes for Petra and Stevie. Make sure they understand the meaning of the headings.
- Play the recording once and have the students check their answers in pairs. Play the recording again if necessary.
- Write the answers on the board.

1.30

ANSWERS:

Petra
Age: 23
Job: Designer
Character: shy
Likes: French movies
Dislikes: expensive restaurants

Stevie
Age: 24
Job: Sales Manager
Character: loud and confident
Likes: sports
Dislikes: (going to) fancy places and (wearing) formal clothes

Donny
Age: 32
Job: company owner
Character: boring
Likes: new places
Dislikes: loud music

a My name is Petra and I'm twenty-three years old. I work as a designer in a web marketing company. I'm a bit shy, and don't go out much. I like French movies. I don't like expensive restaurants.
b I'm Stevie. I'm twenty-four. I work as a sales manager for a sportswear company. I'm very loud and confident! I love watching sports. I don't like going to fancy places and wearing formal clothes.
c Hi, my name's Donny. I'm thirty-two. I own a car rental company. I guess I'm a little bit boring, I'm afraid, as I take my work very seriously. I like going to new places. I don't like loud music.

2

- Refer the students to the question in Exercise 2 and look at the first item (a French restaurant) together. Ask the students which of the people would enjoy going to a French restaurant on a date and why.
- **Groupwork.** put the students in groups of 3 or 4 and have them decide the best place for a date for each of the couples. To complete the task ask the groups to share their answers with the whole class.

3 Pairwork

- You might like to provide an example for the task by telling the students about your perfect date, and why. You can use the speech bubble to start your answer. Then ask students to work in pairs and describe their perfect date to each other. At the end of the task, ask a few students to share their ideas with the rest of the class and hold a class vote on what they think is the best date.

Vocabulary Extra (SB page 31)

Adjectives ending in *ed* or *ing*

1

Focus the students' attention on the list of words and point out that they are all adjectives to describe how people *feel*, or to describe a situation (or people). Then focus the students' attention on the pictures and ask them to match them with the correct adjectives.

ANSWERS:

annoyed/annoying 5
bored/boring 1
confused/confusing 10
depressed/depressing 3
embarrassed/embarrassing 4
excited/exciting 8
frightened/frightening 6
interested/interesting 2
surprised/surprising 7
tired/tiring 9

2

- Go through the example with the class, explaining why the answer is *bored* and not *boring* (you need an adjective that describes how the students feel rather than the situation). Then ask the students to choose the correct adjectives in the remaining sentences. Point out that the sentences in this exercise describe the pictures in Exercise 1.
- Check answers with the class and then ask them to discuss in pairs whether any of the sentences are true for them.

ANSWERS:

1 bored	**6** frightened
2 interesting	**7** surprised
3 depressing	**8** exciting
4 embarrassed	**9** tired
5 annoying	**10** confusing

Focus on *get*

1

- Ask the students to look at the table. Tell them that *get* is an extremely common word in English, but it can mean a variety of things, depending on the words that it's combined with.
- Focus the students' attention on the first use of *get* in the table and the examples for it. Then ask the students to read the other example sentences and match them with the correct uses of *get*. Go around, monitoring and giving help.

ANSWERS:

a 2	**d** 3
b 5	**e** 4
c 1	

2

- Allow the students to work in pairs if they wish. Remind them that they can use a dictionary to help them. As they work, go around checking that their examples are accurate and are matched to the correct use of *get*. Check answers by taking a section at a time and asking several pairs to read out their own example sentences.

Writing

Workbook page 15
Using time expressions
Telling a story

Further Practice Material

Need more classroom practice activities?
Photocopiable resource materials in the Teacher's Presentation Kit / Extra Resources

Need more tests?
Test Generator
Teacher's Presentation Kit / Extra Resources / Tests

Need more on important teaching concepts?
Key concepts in *American Inside Out Evolution* pages xxi-xxxvii

Need student self-study practice?
Workbook pages 12-15

Need more information and ideas?
American Inside Out Evolution website www.macmillan.com.br/americaninsideoutevolution

Need to check what your students can do by the end of this unit?
Self-evaluation checklists on pages xxxix-xliii

Review A *Teacher's notes*

These exercises act as a check of the grammar and vocabulary that the students have learned in the first three units. Use them to find any problems that students are having, or anything that they haven't understood and which will need further work.

Grammar (SB page 32)

Remind the students of the grammar explanations they read and the exercises they did in the Grammar Extra on pages 130–135

1

This exercise reviews language from Unit 1. Check answers before putting the students into pairs to ask and answer the questions.

ANSWERS:

a Have – Present perfect
b Do – Simple present
c did – Simple past
d are – Future (*be*) *going to*
e are – Present progressive
f Have – Present perfect
g do – Simple present

2

This exercise reviews *such* (*a*), *so*, *too* and *very* from Unit 2.

ANSWERS:

1 such a
2 too
3 very
4 so
5 such a
6 too
7 so
8 very

Cultural notes

Rome

Italy's capital city, with a population of 2.8 million. Tourist attractions include buildings from Ancient Rome: the Forum, the Colosseum, and the Pantheon, and buildings from the Renaissance and Baroque period, such as St. Peter's Basilica.

The city is also home to paintings and sculptures from that era by artists such as Michelangelo, Leonardo da Vinci, and Caravaggio, and fountains by Bernini. Within Rome is the Vatican City: it's the home of the Pope, and the smallest nation in the world.

3

This exercise reviews the simple past and past progressive from Unit 3.

ANSWERS:

a was working; met
b was raining; got
c were having; called
d were talking; came
e was cooking; cut
f were watching; woke

4

This exercise reviews adjectives and adverbs. Check answers with the class before the students tick the sentences that are true for them and then compare their answers in pairs.

ANSWERS:

a regularly
b well
c quietly
d early
e carefully

5

This exercise reviews structures used in Units 1, 2, and 3.

ANSWERS:

1 a ~~What means your name?~~
2 a ~~Did they been to Miami?~~
3 b ~~How was Florida like?~~
4 b ~~We eat way too many chocolate.~~
5 b ~~You eat very slowly your food.~~
6 a ~~They speak Spanish very good.~~

Vocabulary (SB page 33)

1

This exercise reviews family words from Unit 1.

ANSWERS:

1 stepfather
2 half-brother
3 half-sister
4 daughter
5 stepmother
6 brother-in-law
7 niece
8 nephew
9 uncle

2

This exercise reviews the names of places in a city.

ANSWERS:

a art gallery
b bridge
c canal
d parking lot
e castle
f fountain
g library
h museum
i park
j shopping mall

3

This exercise reviews useful adjectives for describing places.

ANSWERS:

a crowded
b polluted
c dull
d romantic
e expensive
f beautiful
g spectacular

4

This exercise reviews direction words. You might like to ask a student to draw a compass on the board and label it with the direction words before the students complete the exercise.

ANSWERS:

Darwin is in the north.
Cairns is in the north-east.
Brisbane is in the east.
Sydney is in the south-east.
Melbourne is in the south.
Perth is in the south-west.
Alice Springs is in central Australia.

Cultural notes

Alice Springs

A mining town in the Northern Territory of Australia, Alice Springs has a population of 27,000. It became important as the telegraph station on the overland route from Adelaide to Darwin.

Brisbane

Brisbane (/ˈbɹɪzbən/) is the capital city of the Australian state of Queensland and has a population of 2.3 million.

Cairns

A small city in northern Queensland with a population of over 160,000, Cairns (/kɛɹnz/) is a popular destination because it's close to many tourist attractions including The Great Barrier Reef, The Daintree National Park, and Cape Tribulation.

Darwin

Darwin (/ˈdɑɹwɨn/) is the capital and most heavily populated city in the Northern Territory, with over 140,000 people. However, it's the least populated of Australia's capital cities. Its two main industries are mining and tourism.

Melbourne

Melbourne (ˈmelbərn) has the second biggest population in Australia, with over 4.5 million people. It is the state capital of Victoria and is often refered to as Australia's sporting and cultural capital.

Perth

The capital of the state of Western Australia, with over 2 million residents, Perth (/ˈpɝθ/) is the fourth most populated city in Australia and is currently growing faster than any other Australian city.

Sydney

With a population of over 5 million, Sydney is the most heavily populated city in Australia. Sydney is the state capital of New South Wales and is the site of the first European colony, established in 1788. Famous landmarks in the city include Sydney Harbor Bridge and Sydney Opera House

Pronunciation (SB page 33)

1

Remind the students that the circles show the syllables of a word and the large circles indicate the stressed syllables. Here they are being asked to classify words according to how many syllables they have and where the main stress falls. Encourage them to say each word aloud to get a feeling for what sounds right.

2 1.31

Point out the main stresses in the example words which are underlined. Ask the students to do the same for the other words in the table. Then play the recording for them to check their answers. Play it a second time for them to listen and repeat.

ANSWERS:

1 and 2
A: annoyed, Chinese, dessert, surprised
B: central, cousin, Cuba
C: beautiful, chocolate, finally, granddaughter, uniform
D: cathedral, Egyptian, extremely, together

Reading & Listening (SB page 34)

1 1.32

Focus the students' attention on the heading and ask them to guess what the news story is about. Ask the students to read the questions first and point out that they need to answer each question for both pairs of friends.

ANSWERS:

a Josh and Thomas met at elementary school. Sally and Phoebe met when Sally covered Phoebe's story for a local newspaper.
b Josh and Thomas see each other a couple of times a month. Sally and Phoebe see each other every weekend.

Language note

Pronunciation: *Phoebe*

Phoebe is a female first name. It is pronounced /ˈfibi/.

2

Go through the sentences with the students before they read the texts again and see if they can identify the false statements. Then ask them to read the texts again, check their answers, and correct the false statements.

ANSWERS:

a False (They met at elementary school.)
b False (Thomas makes jokes.)
c True
d True
e False (They always speak on the phone.)
f False (They hang out in the local park.)

3 1.33

Focus the students' attention on the picture. Play the recording and ask the students to identify Matt's nationality. Then focus attention on the information in the box. Play the recording again and ask the students to underline the correct information.

ANSWERS:

Matt is Australian.
1 At college.
2 Five years ago
3 She didn't like him.
4 Scuba diving.

1.33

(C = Carol; J = Jennifer)
C: OK, so who's that in this picture, Jennifer?
J: Oh, that's my friend, Matt.
C: Friend? Really?
J: OK, boyfriend!
C: Hmm. Where did you meet him?
J: At college in California – about five years ago.
C: Oh, OK.
J: Yeah. I didn't actually like him at first. And I already had a boyfriend. But one day, a group of us spent the day together at the beach. We went swimming and talked and I discovered that Matt was a very interesting person and he really liked traveling.
C: You like traveling too, don't you?
J: Yes, I love it. Anyway, we talked all evening, and after that we became really good friends. But after college he went back home to Australia—he's Australian—and I stayed here.
C: Oh, no!
J: Then Matt and I started emailing and calling each other a lot because we wanted to go scuba diving in Egypt with friends.
C: Ah. In the Red Sea?
J: That's right. Anyway, I saw Matt in Egypt with all our friends. It was a lot of fun. Then, last summer, I went to Australia to visit him. I asked him to come back to the USA with me, and he did.
C: Really? That's wonderful.
J: Yes, we're good together. In fact, we're planning a trip to the Bahamas right now ... Hey, life is good.

4

Go through the questions with the students before playing the recording again. Elicit answers from the class.

ANSWERS:

a They went swimming and talked.
b He went back to Australia.
c They wanted to go scuba diving in the Red Sea.
d Yes, she has.
e Last summer.
f The Bahamas.

Writing & Speaking (SB page 35)

1

Ask the students to work into pairs to match the questions and answers listed on the note.

ANSWERS:

a 3
b 2
c 5
d 1
e 4

2

Ask the students to read the text and match the different parts to the questions in Exercise 1.

ANSWERS:

a My best friend ...
b We met on the first day ...
c Adriana knew everybody ...
d We are very different ...
e We do everything together ...

3

Give the students a minute or two to think of ideas, then ask them to make notes in answer to the questions in Exercise 1 about their own best friend. Discourage them from writing full sentences at this stage so that they don't simply read out their answers in Exercise 4.

4

Put the students into pairs to tell each other about their best friends. Go around, monitoring and giving help with vocabulary.

5

Remind the students that they can use the text in Exercise 2 as a model and that they should use long answers to the questions in Exercise 1 to structure their writing.

Further Practice Material

Need more classroom practice activities?
Photocopiable resource materials in the Teacher's Presentation Kit / Extra Resources

Need more tests?
Test Generator
Teacher's Presentation Kit / Extra Resources / Tests

Need more on important teaching concepts?
Key concepts in *American Inside Out Evolution* pages xxi-xxxvii

Need more information and ideas?
American Inside Out Evolution website www.macmillan.com.br/americaninsideoutevolution

4 Shopping *Overview*

Section	Aims	What the students are doing
Speaking SB page 36	Fluency practice	Discussing giving and receiving gifts.
Reading SB page 36	Reading for specific information	Reading and answering questions on a text about gifts. Discussing the worst Valentine's Day gifts.
Vocabulary SB page 37	Collocations	Matching words to make common phrases. Talking about common items to give as gifts.
Pronunciation SB page 37	Plural forms	Listening and repeating plural forms. Adding plural nouns to a table according to their pronunciation.
Grammar SB page 37	Adverbs of frequency	Studying the use and position of adverbs of frequency. Adding adverbs of frequency to sentences and discussing if they are true for them.
Speaking: anecdote SB page 38	Fluency practice	Listening and talking about the last time they bought someone a gift.
Grammar & Vocabulary SB page 38	Verb patterns (1)	Studying sentences with verbs with two objects. Completing a table. Completing questions with indirect objects and answering them in pairs.
Speaking SB page 39	Fluency practice	Completing statements and discussing them.
Grammar SB page 39	Verb patterns (2)	Completing two interviews with *ing*-forms and the *to*-infinitive. Completing sentences and comparing with a partner.
Reading & Vocabulary SB page 40	Reading for detail	Completing texts describing clothes. Discussing their opinions on clothes. Completing a table with descriptions. Clothes and accessories. Listening and repeating items of clothing. Completing sentences that are true for them.
Reading SB page 41	Reading for gist	Reading a text and answering a question. Matching words to their meaning. Discussing the trend towards ethical clothing.
Grammar SB page 41	Simple present and present progressive	Matching simple present and present progressive forms with uses. Writing simple present and present progressive sentences in the negative and checking the ones that are true for them.
Language for Life SB page 42	Useful phrases in a clothes store	Matching lines from conversations with speakers. Completing a conversation with useful phrases. Writing and practicing new conversations about shopping.
Life Skills SB page 42	Planning: A shopping trip	Listening to a conversation and writing a shopping list. Planning a route in a shopping mall.
Vocabulary Extra SB page 43	Review of words from the unit: clothes and accessories; verbs used with clothes	Matching pictures with descriptions. Matching verb phrases with meanings. Underlining appropriate verb phrases in sentences.

4 Shopping *Teacher's notes*

Warm-up

- Bring to class several objects wrapped up in paper to make interesting-looking parcels. If possible, disguise the shapes a little. Ask the students to pass them around, feel them, shake them, smell them, and talk about what they think is inside. Ask which one they would most like to receive as a gift. Finally, allow them to open the parcels to reveal the contents.

Speaking (SB page 36)

1

- **Groupwork.** Go through the questions with the class, making sure that they understand them all. Then put the students in groups to discuss their answers. As they do this, go around, monitoring and giving help with vocabulary.
- Ask a representative from each group to report back to the class on their discussions.

Reading (SB page 36)

Cultural notes

Valentine's Day

Valentine's Day is celebrated on February 14. It is generally seen as the day for people in love to celebrate and it is customary for partners to exchange cards or gifts on the day.

1

- Refer the students to the introduction and elicit a few bad gifts they have received in the past.
- Go over the four questions in Exercise 1 and deal with any new vocabulary.
- Set the task and remind students they are only scanning for specific information so they should be skimming the tweets quickly.
- Ask the students to share their answers in pairs before checking as a whole class.

ANSWERS:

a 3
b a box of chocolates
c Phil Plumber
d silver jewelry

2

- Ask the students who is more likely to be bad at buying gifts, men or women, and why.
- Then ask students to discuss the question in pairs. Go around, monitoring and giving help, and encourage some pairs to share their views in a whole class discussion once they have finished.

Extra activity

Extend the whole class discussion by asking the students if it's important to celebrate Valentine's Day and whether they would prefer to get an expensive present or one that is made by the other person.

Vocabulary (SB page 37)

1

- Go through the example with the class and explain that all the words in column A can be matched with one of the lists of items in column B. Allow the students to work in pairs if they wish as they match the items. When checking answers, say the collocations aloud or get the students to say them so that they hear all the combinations of words.

ANSWERS:

a 4	**d** 3	**g** 8
b 7	**e** 2	**h** 6
c 1	**f** 5	

Language notes

Pronunciation: sentence stress

- English is a stress-timed rather than a syllable-timed language. This means that the time it takes to say a sentence depends on the number of stressed syllables, not the number of syllables itself. This explains why students often think that native speakers of English speak very quickly, or swallow some of their words. The syllables that aren't stressed are shortened, and the *schwa* sound /ə/ is very common. For example, in the phrase *A bunch of flowers* the unstressed words *a* and *of* are pronounced /ə/ and /əf/

2

- **Pairwork.** Go through the questions with the class and make sure they understand them all. Then put them into pairs to discuss their answers.
- If you have a multicultural class, make sure that you get feedback from a representative of each nationality for the second question. Be prepared to talk about your own country and your own experiences of gift giving.

Pronunciation (SB page 37)

1 1.34

This exercise practices pronunciation of the endings of plural nouns. Focus the students' attention on the table which gives them three categories of plural nouns, those ending with the /s/ sound, those with /z/, and those with /ɪz/. Play the recording and ask them to listen and repeat the plural forms.

Language notes

Pronunciation: voiced versus unvoiced

- In this exercise, where possible, the plurals which end in an unvoiced sound are pronounced /s/; the plurals which end in a voiced sound are pronounced /z/, and where neither of these are possible the plural is pronounced /ɪz/.
- One way to make your students more aware of the difference between voiced and unvoiced sounds is to get them to touch their throats as they are practicing. They should be able to feel the vibration as they make voiced sounds.
- You can give extra practice by giving them the words that they've already met and asking them to classify them into voiced and unvoiced. For example:
  Voiced: *the, their, them, that, there, this, these, they*
  Unvoiced: *thing, third, thirty, think, thank, thirteen, three, Thursday*

2 1.35

- Focus the students' attention on the headings in the table and point out that there are rules which govern the pronunciation of plural endings. Explain that it's the sound that a word ends in that is important here, not the letter it ends with. So *cake* ends with the /k/ sound although the final letter is an e. Read out the sounds in each of the columns.
- Ask the students to say the words in the box aloud. Then allow them to work in pairs if they wish as they match them to the correct columns. Encourage them to say the words and their plural forms aloud as they work so they can match the final sounds to the columns more easily. Play the recording for the students to check their answers. Then play it a second time for them to listen and repeat all the words.

ANSWERS:

A: /s/ grapes, pots, socks
B: /z/ bars, keys, ties
C: /ɪz/ bridges, bunches, pieces

Grammar (SB page 37)

Adverbs of frequency

1

- Focus the students' attention on the information in the margin. Read the adverbs of frequency aloud or ask a student to do it and point out the scale from 100% to 0%. Then go through the information about where the adverb goes in a sentence, pointing out the exception with the verb *be*.
- Ask the students to look back at the tweets on page 36. Point out that eight adverbs of frequency are highlighted. Ask a number of students to read out the sentences that contain adverbs of frequency. Then ask the class to answer the true/false questions. If necessary, write some of the sentences on the board and label the adverbs, the main part of the verbs, the auxiliary verbs and instances of the verb *be*.

ANSWERS:

a True
b True

Language notes

Grammar: adverbs of frequency

- While the rule states that the adverb comes between the subject and the main verb (and after the verb *be*), it's possible to use some adverbs at the beginning of the sentence, to emphasize the frequency.
  From the selection in the Student's Book, adverbs which can start a sentence are: *usually*, *normally*, *sometimes*, and *occasionally*.
  Sometimes I call her five times a day. / I sometimes call her five times a day.
  Normally they cost $25. / They normally cost $25.
- It's probably just as well not to mention this to your students at this stage, unless someone brings up the subject, as the rule in the Student's Book covers all adverbs of frequency.

2

- Go through the instructions with the class and make sure the students understand that they must not ask their partner for information. They should write their sentences based on what they think they know about the person next to them. Give them a few minutes to do this and discourage any talking or comparing of notes.
- **Pairwork.** The students work in pairs to check their sentences and see how many were true. Ask the pairs to report back to the class on how accurate their sentences were and how similar/different they are to each other.

Speaking: anecdote (SB page 38)

For more information about how to set up, monitor, and repeat Anecdotes, see page xviii-xx in the Introduction.

1 1.36

- Ask the students to look at the pictures. Ask the students if they know what the object is and what it's used for (a foot spa, used to massage and relax the feet). Then tell them that the man is named Eddie and they're going to hear him talking about the last time he bought someone a gift.
- Go through the sentences and choices with the class. Explain any unknown vocabulary and ask the students to listen and underline the answers Eddie gives.
- Check answers with the class and ask them what they think about Eddie's story. Do they sympathize with him or with his sister?

ANSWERS:

a sister
b birthday
c On the internet.
d No, I didn't.
e A foot spa.
f $50
g Yes, I did.
h No, she didn't.
i Yes, it was.

1.36

The last gift I bought was for my sister. It was her birthday. In fact, it was her thirtieth birthday. Thirty isn't very old, but she was pretty upset. She liked being in her twenties, and she thought thirty was really old. Anyway, I didn't know what to get her, so I went on the internet to find something. I didn't have any ideas, but I wanted something special. Eventually, I found a really good gift. I thought it was unusual, and just perfect for her—it was a foot spa. My sister's a teacher and she stands up all day, so a foot spa is great for relaxing in the evening. It was expensive—about $50—but she's my sister, and thirty is a special birthday.

I bought a nice card and wrote a funny message in it—I put, "Now that you're thirty, you're too old to die young!" Ha-ha. On her birthday, I gave her the gift, but unfortunately she didn't like it—at all. She said that a foot spa is a gift for a grandmother, not for a young woman. I was really surprised—I'd love a foot spa. And then, when she read the card, she cried! What a disaster.

2

- Give the students a minute or two to decide what they're going to talk about. Then ask them to look at the questions in Exercise 1 again and decide how they would answer them. Allow them to make notes of what they're going to say and how they're going to say it, but discourage them from writing a paragraph that they can simply read out. Go around, monitoring and giving help.
- **Pairwork.** Put the students into pairs and ask them to take turns to tell their partner about the last time they bought someone a gift. Encourage them to ask each other follow-up questions to get further information.
- Ask some pairs to report back to the class about what they found out.

Grammar & Vocabulary (SB page 38)

Verb patterns 1

1

- Remind the students they've just talked about when they last *bought someone a gift*. Point out that bought someone a gift is an example of a verb with two objects. Focus the students' attention on the information in the margin and point out that there are other verbs which can take two objects. Explain that in the sentence *I bought somebody something*, *somebody* is called the indirect object and *something* the direct object.

- Focus the students' attention on the two example sentences and either read them aloud or ask a student to read them. Elicit answers to the questions from the class.

ANSWERS:

a Yes
b Blue
c Red

Language notes

Grammar: verbs with two objects

- The sentence *I bought a gift* is an example of verb (*bought*) + object (a *gift*). If you want to say who you bought it for, you need another object. *I bought my mother a gift* is an example of verb (*bought*) + indirect object (*my mother*) + direct object (*a gift*). The indirect object (usually the recipient) can be put after the direct object with *to* or *for* (*I bought a gift* ***for*** *my mother*).
- Other verbs which can be followed by two objects include: *cost, give, leave, make, offer, play, promise, send, teach, tell, write*.

2

- Remind the students that the two sentences about Eddie in Exercise 1 were two ways of saying the same thing. Ask them to look at the table. Point out that *I never lend my car to anybody* and *I never lend anybody my car* also mean the same thing. The difference is in the position of the indirect object and the addition of *to* when the indirect object follows the direct object.
- Ask the students to complete the table and check answers with the class. Point out the use of *for* instead of *to* in the last sentence.
- Ask the students to check the sentences that are true for them and to compare their results with a partner.

ANSWERS:

a I never lend anybody my car.
b My friends send me lots of texts.
c I sometimes buy my mom flowers.

3

- Read the example to the class. Ask the students to complete the remaining questions and go around, monitoring and giving help as they do this. Check answers with the class before putting the students into pairs to take turns asking and answering the questions. As they do this, go around, making sure they are forming the questions correctly and that the indirect objects are in the right position.

ANSWERS:

a you bought your family gifts?
b you made somebody coffee?
c your bank sent you a letter?
d you gave somebody a ride?
e you lent your best friend some money?
f a friend told you a joke?

4 Grammar Extra 4, Part 1

Ask the students to turn to Grammar Extra 4, Part 1 on page 136 of the Student's Book. Here they'll find an explanation of the grammar they've been studying and further exercises to practice it.

ANSWERS:

1
a Anna gave Grandpa some socks.
b John gave Tony a cell phone.
c Dick gave Molly some chocolate.
d Sue gave Carlos a cook book.
e Becky gave Eric a DVD.
f Jimmy gave Sally some earrings.

2
a to **b** to **c** for **d** to **e** to **f** to
g for **h** to **i** for **j** to

3
a Could you send me the money?
b (Not possible to change.)
c My dad bought me this for my birthday.
d I've told everybody that joke!
e (Not possible to change.)
f We showed him pictures of our vacation.
g Ian is getting us some ice cream.
h (Not possible to change.)
i I don't want to make him breakfast!
j Can you lend Sue your bike?

Speaking (SB page 39)

1

- Go through the statements with the class and make sure they understand them all.
- Ask the students to work individually to decide whether each statement refers to men or women, and to complete them accordingly.

2

- **Pairwork.** Ask the students to compare and discuss their answers to Exercise 1 with their partner. Do they agree on which ones describe men and which women?
- Ask the students to widen their discussion to include which of the statements are true for them and to report back to the class.

Grammar (SB page 39)

Verb patterns 2

1 1.37

- Go through the information in the margin, pointing out that some verbs are followed by an *ing*-form and others by a *to*-infinitive. Read out the example sentences or ask a student to do it. Then focus their attention on the statements they completed in Exercise 1 of the Speaking section on this page. Ask them to underline all instances of verb + *ing*-form and circle all those of verb + *to*-infinitive.
- Focus the students' attention on the pictures of Conor and Jim. Tell them that these two men were interviewed about their attitudes to shopping. Ask the students to say, just by looking at the men, whether they think they would enjoy shopping or not.
- Tell the students that they have to complete the interviews with the *ing*-form or the *to*-infinitive of the verbs in brackets. Go through the example with the class, pointing out that it has to be *going* because *mind* is one of the verbs that takes an *ing*-form.
- Give them a few minutes to complete the rest of the text. Go around, monitoring and giving help. If students aren't sure which form they need, remind them that they can look back at lists of verbs in the margin.
- Play the recording for the students to check their answers. Then ask them to say whether they know of any men with similar attitudes.
- **Pairwork.** Ask the students to take turns asking and answering the questions from the interviews. Encourage them to report back to the class any interesting answers.

ANSWERS:

1 going
2 to go
3 going
4 to go
5 going
6 reading
7 to buy
8 looking
9 to buy
10 going
11 to buy
12 going
13 to go
14 to buy
15 buying
16 to buy
17 having
18 to find

1.37

ANSWERS:

(I = Interviewer, C = Conor, J = Jim)

I: OK. Question one. Do you mind going to the shopping mall?
C: Not really. But after about an hour, I want to go home.
J: Actually, I can't stand going to the mall. My girlfriend knows this, so she usually chooses to go without me.
I: OK. Um, let's see. Question two. What kind of stores do you enjoy going into?
C: Bookstores. I spend a lot of time reading book reviews so I always have a list of books I'd like to buy.
J: I enjoy looking at electronic equipment but I can't afford to buy it. It's usually way too expensive.
I: OK. Question three. Are there any kinds of stores you hate going into?
C: I hate grocery stores. I usually forget to buy the things I went there for, so I avoid going into them. Fortunately, I can do most of my food shopping online.
J: I refuse to go into shoe stores with my girlfriend. She tries on ten pairs and then decides to buy the first pair.
I: OK. Last question. Question four. Do you enjoy buying clothes for yourself?
C: Not really. I only go into a clothing store when I need to buy a new shirt or something. For me, shopping is a necessity, not a pleasure.
J: I love having new clothes, but I never manage to find time to go shopping.

Language notes

Grammar: verbs + *ing*-form and *to*-infinitive

- Some verbs can be followed by an *ing*-form or by a *to*-infinitive without changing the meaning: *He started running* = *He started to run*. Other verbs that follow this pattern include: *begin, continue, prefer*.
- Other verbs can be followed by an *ing*-form or by a *to*-infinitive, but the meaning changes in each case. Compare *He stopped reading* (He stopped the action of reading) with *He stopped to read* (He stopped what he was doing in order to read). Other verbs where there is a change of meaning include: *forget, remember, try*.

2

- Ask the students to work individually to complete the sentences. As they do this, go around offering help where needed.
- Put the students into pairs to compare their sentences.

Reading & Vocabulary (SB page 40)

1 1.38

- Write the word "clothes" on the board and brainstorm clothes items the students know. Try to elicit the words listed in the word box by using pictures, descriptions or real objects.
- Refer the students to the gapped texts and point out that the first one has been done for them. Ask the students to complete Exercise 1 individually and then compare with a partner before checking their answers with the whole class.
- Play the recording for them to check their answers. Encourage them to keep a record of any new vocabulary in their notebooks. You could suggest that they have a special page for clothing words.

ANSWERS:

1 top	**4** boots	**7** jacket
2 skirt	**5** shirt	**8** pants
3 earrings	**6** scarf	**9** shoes

2

Pairwork. Put students into pairs to discuss what they think of the clothes in the pictures. Go around, helping with vocabulary, then some pairs to share their opinions with the class.

3

- Focus the students' attention on the table. Explain that they're going to complete it with words from the descriptions in Exercise 1. Explain *design*, *material*, and *accessories* and elicit a few examples of words which can go in these columns before asking the students to complete the task.

ANSWERS:

Design/Color: black, striped green, brown, white, red, blue
Material: cotton, linen, silk, leather, plastic, woolen, denim
Clothes and accessories: top, boots, earrings, coat, scarf, shirt, skirt, shoes, jeans

Language notes

Grammar: adjective word order

- When describing someone's clothes, it's often necessary to use two or more adjectives. When there are two or more adjectives, the order is:
  - size (*big, small*)
  - design (*plain, checked*)
  - color (*black, red, cream*)
  - material (*cotton, leather, denim*)
- So, for example, you could say: *A small plain red cotton T-shirt.*

Vocabulary: accessories

- A small thing such as a piece of jewelry (*a necklace, earrings, a bracelet, a watch*, etc.) or an additional item of clothing (*a belt, a bag, a scarf*, etc.) that you wear with clothes to give them more style.

4 1.39

- Ask the students to look at the pictures. Then play the recording and ask them to listen and repeat the items of clothing.
- Tell the students to add the words to the table in Exercise 3.

ANSWERS:

Design: pinstriped, patterned, checked
Material: silk, woolen
Clothes and accessories: tie, jacket, hat, shirt

1.39

a a red woolen hat
b patterned silk ties
c a pinstriped jacket
d a checked shirt

5

Go through the example with the class. Point out the position of *blue* in *I'm wearing a blue cotton top* and remind the students that you usually put color words before material or design words. Ask the students to work individually to complete the sentences so that they are true for them. Go around, monitoring and giving help, then ask them to compare their sentences in pairs.

Extra activities

- Teach the word *bargain* and ask the students to describe the best bargain they ever bought.
- Ask the students to describe the oldest piece of clothing that they possess and that they still wear. Where did they get it? How much did it cost? What is so special about it that they've kept it for so long?

Reading (SB page 41)

1

- Ask the students if they know any clothing companies and elicit a few names.
- Refer the students to the pictures and ask them if they recognize anyone (Bono in the

second picture). Ask students to predict what the connection might be between Bono and the clothing company they are going to read about.

- Look at the question and remind the students that they are reading for gist so they should only try to get the general meaning of the article in order to answer the question.

ANSWER:

Edun is an "ethical trade" company which tries to provide jobs in poor sub-Saharan African countries and invests all profits back into the business

Cultural notes

Bono

Bono is the stage name of Paul David Hewson, lead singer of the Irish rock group U2.

2

- Focus the students' attention on the words listed and point out that the first answer has been done for them. Encourage the students to determine the meaning of the words by looking at the context.
- Ask the students to complete the exercise individually before checking in pairs. Then check answers as a whole class.

ANSWERS:

a 5
b 3
c 1
d 6
e 4
f 2

3

- Make sure the students are clear on the meaning of "ethical clothing" before starting the discussion.
- Go over the questions with the class and deal with any unknown words.
- Put the students into pairs to discuss the questions. Then have pairs join to form small groups and compare their ideas.

Grammar (SB page 41)

Present tenses

1

- Focus the students' attention on the information in the margin and go through the form of the simple present and present progressive with the class. Read out the example sentences.
- Read the sentences in Exercise 1 to the class and ask them to match the underlined verb forms with their uses.

ANSWERS:

1 b **2** a **3** c

Language notes

Grammar: simple present versus present progressive

- The difference between the simple present and the present progressive can be confusing for students even at an advanced level. However, here the difference is clear. You use the simple present to talk about what you do regularly, and you use the present progressive to talk about what you are doing at, or around, the moment of speaking. Expressions like *right now* and *now* are commonly used in present progressive sentences. Adverbs of frequency (*sometimes*, *always*, *never*, etc.) are commonly used in simple present sentences.
- Further uses and differences will be met at higher levels. For the moment, pre-intermediate students need a lot of practice to consolidate their understanding of this fundamental difference.

2

- Go through the example with the class and then ask them to write the remaining sentences in the negative. Check these answers with the class before asking the students to match them with the uses in Exercise 1.
- Ask the students to work individually to check the sentences that are true for them. Point out that they can check the affirmative sentences in the book or the negative ones that they've produced. They then compare with a partner.

ANSWERS:

a I'm not sitting near the door. = Use b
b My parents don't go to church. = Use a
c I'm not saving money for my next vacation. = Use c
d My mother doesn't work in a bookstore. = Use a
e I'm not studying for an exam. = Use b or c
f It isn't raining. = Use b
g I'm not learning to play the piano. = Use c
h The cost of living isn't going up fast. = Use c

3 Pairwork

- The pairwork exercise for this unit is on pages 121 and 126 of the Student's Book. Put the students into pairs and tell them who will be Student A, and who will be Student B.

- Take note of any errors which may need particular attention later, and also any examples of good language use which you can praise.

> **ANSWERS:**
>
> **Student A**
> **a** He/She is trying to eat less sugar.
> **b** He/She is writing a book.
> **c** He/She is applying for a job.
> **d** He/She is learning to dance.
> **e** Personal answer.
>
> **Student B**
> **a** He/She is trying to do more exercise.
> **b** He/She is learning to drive.
> **c** He/She is planning a trip abroad.
> **d** He/She is reading a good book.
> **e** Personal answer.

4 Grammar Extra 4, Part 2

Ask the students to turn to Grammar Extra 4, Part 2 on page 136 of the Student's Book. Here they'll find an explanation of the grammar they've been studying and further exercises to practice it.

> **ANSWERS:**
>
> **1**
> **a** is **b** cries **c** does **d** goes **e** has **f** hears **g** pays **h** pushes **i** says **j** studies **k** takes **l** touches
>
> **2**
> **a** becoming **b** choosing **c** cutting **d** flying **e** living **f** meeting **g** shining **h** shutting **i** sitting **j** starting **k** staying **l** wearing
>
> **3**
> **a** Do you wear perfume? / Are you wearing perfume?
> **b** Do you use an electronic dictionary? / Are you using an electronic dictionary?
> **c** Do you plan your vacations? / Are you planning your vacations?
> **d** Do your parents work? / Are your parents working?
> **e** Does your teacher wear glasses? / Is your teacher wearing glasses?
> **f** What do you do? / What are you doing?
>
> **4**
> **a** Where do you come from?
> **b** How many languages do you speak?
> **c** What are you wearing today?
> **d** Why are you learning English?
> **e** What time do you usually go to bed?
> **f** What color pen are you using to do this exercise?

Language for Life (SB page 42)

1 1.40

- Focus the students' attention on the picture and ask them what they can see. Explain that the young man is Russell and that he wants to buy a gift for his girlfriend. The woman in the picture is a sales clerk. Go through the phrases and ask the students to decide who says them, Russell or the sales clerk.
- Before checking answers by playing the recording, read the phrases out one by one and ask the students to stand up if they think it's Russell and remain seated if they think it's the sales clerk. Tell the students to try to convince classmates who have made a different choice to change their minds.
- Play the recording for the students to check their answers. Then play it again for them to repeat the useful phrases.

ANSWERS:

a	R	**f**	R
b	R	**g**	SC
c	SC	**h**	SC
d	R	**i**	SC
e	SC	**j**	R

2 1.41

- Ask the students to read the conversation and decide where the useful phrases should go. Allow them to work in pairs if they wish.
- Play the recording for the students to check their answers.
- Put the students into pairs and ask them to practice the conversation, taking turns to be Russell and the sales clerk.

> **ANSWERS:**
>
> **1** Can I help you?
> **2** I'm just looking, thanks.
> **3** What sort of thing are you looking for?
> **4** What colors do you have?
> **5** What size is she?
> **6** I'll take it.
> **7** How would you like to pay?
> **8** By credit card.
> **9** Here's your receipt.
> **10** Can she exchange it if it doesn't fit?

1.41

(**SC = Sales clerk; R = Russell**)
SC: Can I help you?
R: I'm just looking, thanks. Well, actually, I'm looking for something for my girlfriend.
SC: What sort of thing are you looking for?
R: I don't really know. A sweater?
SC: OK, and what color would you like?
R: What colors do you have?
SC: We have any color you want, sir. Purple is very fashionable right now.
R: Purple's fine.
SC: OK. What size is she?
R: Ah, well, she isn't very big, but she's not particularly small.
SC: So she's medium.
R: Yes, medium.
SC: Well, we have this nice purple sweater here ...
R: Good. I'll take it.
SC: Are you sure you don't want to see any more ...
R: No, that's great. I'll take it. Thank you. How much is it?
SC: That's $70, sir. How would you like to pay?
R: Seventy?! By credit card, please.
SC: Fine. If you could just sign ...
R: Here you go. Goodbye.
SC: Just a minute, sir. Here's your receipt.
R: Oh, yes, er ... Can she exchange it if it doesn't fit?
SC: Yes, but she needs to keep the receipt.

3

- **Pairwork**. Go through the instructions and explain anything that is unclear. Give the students a few minutes to write their conversations. Go around, monitoring and giving help. Encourage them to use as many of the useful phrases as possible and make sure they include at least six of the words in the box.
- Ask the pairs to practice their conversations and then perform them for the class.

Extra activity

Ask the students to discuss their shopping preferences. Do they like grocery stores where you can just take things off the shelves, put them in a basket or cart, and have no contact with the sales staff until you get to the checkout? Do they prefer stores with clerks who help you, or do they prefer to be left alone to make their own choices? Have they ever felt uncomfortable in a store where a sales clerk was too persistent, or showed too much interest in the items they were buying? Or do they like the interaction with the staff?

Life Skills (SB page 42)

Planning: A Shopping Trip

1 1.42

- Write "shopping" on the board and brainstorm all the names of stores the students know and what you can buy there. Elicit possible new words from the listening (*wrapping paper*, *ribbon*). Point out that things we buy are called "items".
- Ask the students what they usually do if they have many items to buy. Elicit "make/write a shopping list" and refer them to the list in Exercise 1.
- Explain that they are going to listen to a conversation and they have to complete Paul's shopping list.
- Play the recording once and ask students to compare their answers in pairs. Then play the recording again if necessary.
- Write the answers on the board or have one of the more confident students write the answers.

ANSWERS:

Item(s)	Store
shampoo	drugstore
ribbon and wrapping paper	stationery store
bunch of flowers	flower shop
muffins and coffee	coffee shop
new phone	phone store

1.42

(**M = Man; W = Woman**)
W: Paul, can you go to the mall for me?
M: Well...yes...but I only have, like 20 minutes as I have to go pick Emily up.
W: I'm sure it won't take too long.
M: Okay, what do you need?
W: I need some shampoo—I think there's a drugstore on level 3.
M: Right. Shampoo.
W: Emily has a party tomorrow so I need some ribbon and wrapping paper. I think there's a stationery store either on level 1 or level 2.
M: Any color?
W: It's for Emily, right? It's going to be pink! I also need a bunch of flowers as a gift to Larry and Susie. There's a flower shop somewhere there ...
M: Okay. A bunch of flowers. Is that it?
W: Could you pick up some muffins and a coffee at the coffee shop? Oh, and can you see if my new phone is ready to pick at the phone store?
M: You know I only have 20 minutes, right?
W: I'm sure you can do it. Thanks, hon!

2

- Ask the students what they do if they have to go to different stores in a big mall with different levels. Elicit that they are likely to "plan their route", which means they will map out which store they will start with and where they will go after that.
- Focus the students' attention on Exercise 2 and explain they will have to plan Paul's route using the words in the box. Go over the words and deal with any new vocabulary.
- Remind the students to plan the route using the shopping mall guide. They have to include all the items and stores in the shopping list they completed in Exercise 1.
- Ask the students to complete the route individually and to write this down using the linkers in the word box. Then put students into pairs to describe their route to their partner and compare answers.
- Ask a few students to share their route with the whole class and vote for the best route.

Extra activity

Play 'Where am I?' Demonstrate the game by saying "I'm in a place where you can book your holiday". The students must understand where you are in the mall (*Fallow Travel*). Students can play this game in pairs or groups.

Vocabulary Extra (SB page 43)

Clothes and accessories

1

Focus the students' attention on the list of words and point out that they're all words used to describe clothing and accessories. Then focus the students' attention on the pictures and ask them to match them with the correct descriptions. When they've finished, ask them to complete the descriptions.

ANSWERS:

7 a checked scarf
9 brown leather gloves
11 a plain white cotton T-shirt
2 a blue denim jacket
8 a pinstriped suit
10 a silver necklace
12 a patterned woolen sweater
5 a floral top
6 gold earrings
1 striped socks
4 plastic sunglasses
3 a light blue silk dress

2 Pairwork

Demonstrate first with a confident student by getting them to ask and answer the example questions with you. Then ask the students to work in pairs asking and answering questions about the pictures.

Focus on verbs used with clothes

1

Ask the students to work individually to match the verb phrases with their meanings. Then allow them to compare answers in pairs before checking with the class.

ANSWERS:

a 4	**d** 3
b 1	**e** 5
c 6	**f** 2

2

Ask the students to underline the most appropriate verb phrases. Check answers with the class before asking the students to tick the sentences that are true for them and compare with a partner.

ANSWERS:

a get dressed	**d** trying on
b wear	**e** look good on
c put on	**f** get changed

Further Practice Material

Need more classroom practice activities?
Photocopiable resource materials in the Teacher's Presentation Kit / Extra Resources

Need more tests?
Test Generator
Teacher's Presentation Kit / Extra Resources / Tests

Need more on important teaching concepts?
Key concepts in *American Inside Out Evolution* pages xxi-xliii

Need student self-study practice?
Workbook pages 16–19

Need more information and ideas?
American Inside Out Evolution website www.macmillan.com.br/americaninsideoutevolution

Need to check what your students can do by the end of this unit?
Self-evaluation checklists on pages xxxix-xliii

5 In Shape *Overview*

Section	Aims	What the students are doing
Reading SB page 44	Reading for detail	Reading an interview and answering questions. Completing statements with numbers. Discussing extreme sports in pairs.
Vocabulary SB page 45	*How* + adjective/adverb	Completing a table about how long it takes them to do things and guessing their partner's answers. Completing questions with *How* + adjective/adverb then asking and answering them in pairs.
Speaking: anecdote SB page 45	Fluency practice	Listening and talking about experiences of doing sports at school.
Listening SB page 46	Listening for specific information	Matching famous sportspeople with their birthdates. Listening to a discussion and identifying which sports star is chosen for an advertising campaign. Completing comparative sentences.
Grammar & Vocabulary SB page 46	Comparatives	Making comparisons in a general knowledge test. Making comparative statements with words in boxes.
Pronunciation SB page 47	The *schwa* sound	Completing expressions with *as ... as*. Practicing the *schwa* sound. Talking about expressions in their own language.
Grammar SB page 47	Superlatives	Writing superlative forms for different groups of adjectives. Completing questions with superlative adjectives and discussing them in pairs.
Vocabulary SB page 47	Numbers	Listening and repeating fractions and decimals. Writing numbers in words. Matching numbers with facts.
Reading SB page 48	Reading for detail	Reading about ways to relax. Discussing ways to relax and the things that stop them from relaxing.
Vocabulary SB page 48	Phrasal verbs	Completing sentences with phrasal verbs. Discussing the sentences with a partner.
Grammar SB page 49	Phrasal verbs	Answering questions about the form and use of phrasal verbs. Putting words in the correct order to make answers to questions.
Listening & Speaking SB page 49	Listening for gist; fluency practice	Listening to a radio show about laughter clubs and marking statements true or false. Trying to make a partner laugh. Discussing questions about laughter.
Language for Life SB page 50	Useful conversational phrases for giving instructions	Listening to three conversations to identify sports. Matching people with sets of instructions. Completing a conversation with useful phrases then listening and practicing it with a partner.
Life Skills SB page 50	Time management: An exercise routine	Matching phrases with pictures. Listening to a podcast and identifying which exercises it includes. Creating a workout routine and comparing it with a partner.
Vocabulary Extra SB page 51	Review of words from the unit: sports; verbs used with sports	Matching equipment with sports to complete a table. Adding more sports words to a table. Underlining the correct verbs in sentences. Completing verb phrases with *do*, *go*, or *play* and adding more sports.
Writing WB page 23		Organizing a text. Linking sentences with *although*. Describing a sports event.

5 In Shape *Teacher's notes*

Warm-up

Write the word *sports* on the board and ask the students to suggest as many words and expressions as they can to do with sports. They should be able to name a number of sports, but try to widen the lexical field by prompting them to think of other aspects of sports, such as health. Write all their suggestions in a spidergram, grouping them according to topic (all the sports together; words to do with health together; etc.).

Reading (SB page 44)

1

- Focus the students' attention on the picture and ask them if they know what kind of athlete the woman is. Elicit/Explain that she is a "triathlete", write this word on the board. Then ask if anyone knows or can guess the meaning (triathletes take part in triathlons, which generally involve swimming, cycling, and running in immediate succession over various distances.)
- Refer students to the two questions and have them predict the answers. Then ask the students to scan the text quickly and check with the whole class if their predictions were right. Are they surprised by the answers?

ANSWERS:

- She tries to run, swim, and ride every morning, but each day she focuses on one area more than the others.
- Yes, she'll join the World Triathlon Series.

2

- Explain that the students will read the text again, but this time they are looking for specific information.
- Give students a minute to look at the statements and deal with any new vocabulary as needed.
- Ask the students to complete the task individually, then check answers with a partner. Encourage some students to report back to the class with their answers.

ANSWERS:

a three
b 10
c 40
d 75 (an hour and fifteen minutes)
e 10

3

- Show some pictures of extreme sports and ask the class if anyone has ever tried any of these or other extreme sports. Encourage students to share experiences with the class.
- **Pairwork.** Refer the students to the question and have them discuss this in pairs. Go around, monitoring and giving help. Then, as a whole class, ask a few students to tell the rest of the class what they discussed with their partner.

Extra activity

Extend the speaking activity by starting a discussion on why extreme sports have become so popular and whether they should be more strictly regulated.

Vocabulary (SB page 45)

1

- Focus the students' attention on the picture in the margin. Ask them if this is a fair representation of their own morning routine or whether theirs is more leisurely.
- Ask the students to look at the table. Go through the activities listed and make sure everyone understands them. Put the students into pairs, but ask them to work individually to write down the time it takes them to do the activities. Ask them also to guess how long it takes their partner to do the activities and to write their guesses down as well. Ask them not to exchange opinions at this stage.
- **Pairwork.** When the students have finished completing the table, they can take turns asking each other about how long it takes them to do the activities to find out how accurately they guessed. You might like to complete the table for yourself and ask the students at the end to guess as a class how long it takes you to do these things.

Extra activity

Ask the students to brainstorm more questions with *How long ...?* Then get the students to ask about other people in their family, e.g. *How long does it take your brother/sister to ...?*

2

- Remind the students that the questions in Exercise 1 were all *How long does it take you to ...?* Point out that this is a question about time using *How* plus the adjective *long*. Go through the words in the box and explain that these adjectives and adverbs can all be used with *How* to make questions.
- Ask the students to complete the questions individually. Check answers before the students take turns asking and answering the questions in pairs.

ANSWERS:

a often	**d** much
b long	**e** far
c many	**f** fast

Extra activity

- Extend the activity by getting the students to brainstorm another question for each *How* + adjective/adverb combination.

Speaking: anecdote (SB page 45)

For more information about how to set up, monitor, and repeat Anecdotes, see pages xviii–xx in the Introduction.

1 1.43

- Ask the students to look at the girl in the picture and explain that she's going to talk about her experiences of sports at school.
- Go through the sentences and the answers with the class. Explain any unknown vocabulary and ask the students to listen and check the answers Tina gives that are correct and put an X next to any that are wrong.
- Check answers with the class and ask them whether they had similar experiences to Tina of sports at school.

ANSWERS:

a ✗ **b** ✓ **c** ✓ **d** ✗ **e** ✗

1.43

When I was in high school, we did sports every Wednesday afternoon. Two hours, from 1:30 to 3:30. Wednesdays were my worst day of the week. I hated doing sports at school. In summer we did swimming and tennis, and in winter we did lacrosse. I really, really hated lacrosse. It was always cold when we played lacrosse, but we wore shorts! Horrible, gray shorts. My legs were very thin and they were so cold that they turned blue. I was always happy when it was raining or snowing—then we stayed inside and did dancing. I loved that.

At my school we had a sports field, tennis courts, and a swimming pool. I love swimming, but the swimming pool wasn't heated so it was freezing.

I didn't like my gym teacher, and she didn't like me. Her name was Ms. Rockham. We called her Rocky. She looked like a boxer, and she had a very loud voice. She loved lacrosse. In fact, I think she played for the national lacrosse team.

Of course, I didn't play for the school lacrosse team, but I loved dancing so much that I joined a dance club after school. My best sports moment was when my dance club won a competition for disco dancing. Rocky didn't think that dancing was a real sport, but I disagree. Dancing kept me in shape, and I didn't have to wear gray shorts.

2

- Allow the students time to decide what experience they're going to talk about. Remind them that it could be a good or a bad experience. Then ask them to look at the questions in Exercise 1 again and decide how they would answer them about their experiences of sports at school. Allow them to make notes of what they're going to say and how they're going to say it, but discourage them from writing a paragraph that they can simply read out. Go around, monitoring and giving help.
- **Pairwork**. Put the students into pairs and ask them to take turns to tell their partner about their experiences. Encourage them to ask follow-up questions to get further information. Then ask some pairs to report back to the class about what they found out.

Listening (SB page 46)

1 1.44

- Draw the students' attention to the pictures and ask them if they know anything about these sports stars. They may be able to say that Ronaldo and Neymar are soccer players, Maria Sharapova is a tennis player, Simone Biles is a gymnast, Rory McIlroy is a golfer, and Stephen Curry plays basketball. Then ask them to say who they think is the oldest and who the youngest. Don't confirm answers at this stage, but try to get the class to reach a consensus decision.

- Ask the students to try to match the sports stars with the list of birthdates. Allow them to discuss this in pairs or small groups and to try to come to a consensus.
- Play the recording for the students to check their answers. Ask them if they were surprised by any of the information.

ANSWERS:

04/19/1987 e)	03/14/1997 c)
02/05/1985 a)	03/14/1988 d)
05/04/1989 b)	02/05/1992 f)

1.44

The soccer player Ronaldo is the oldest. He was born in 1985. Amazingly, he has the same birthday as Neymar, though Neymar was born in 1992. Maria Sharapova is the next oldest - the tennis star was born in 1987. Two other stars with the same birthday, March 14, are the NBA star Stephen Curry, born in 1988, and the gymnast Simone Biles, born in 1997. And finally the golfer Rory McIlroy was born in 1989.

Cultural notes

Ronaldo (born 1985)

Christiano Ronaldo is a Portuguese soccer player. He played for Portugal and Manchester United before being signed Spain's **Real Madrid** soccer team in 2009.

In January 2017, Ronaldo won FIFA's best player of the year for the fourth time.

Rory McIlroy (born 1989)

Rory McIlroy is a Northern Irish professional golfer. He is a member of both the European and PGA Tours. He was world number one in the Official World Golf Ranking for 95 weeks.

Simone Biles (born 1997)

Simone Arianne Biles is an American artistic gymnast. Biles is the 2016 Olympic individual all-around, vault and floor gold medalist. She was also part of the gold medal-winning team at the 2016 Summer Olympics in Rio de Janeiro.

Stephen Curry (born 1988)

Stephen Curry is an American professional basketball player for the Golden State Warriors in the National Basketball Association. Many players and experts consider him to be the greatest shooter in NBA history.

Maria Sharapova (born 1987)

Maria Sharapova is a Russian professional tennis player. She has competed on the WTA (Women's Tennis Association) tour since 2001 and she has been ranked world No. 1 in singles by the WTA five times.

Neymar (born 1992)

Neymar da Silva Santos Júnior, commonly known as Neymar or Neymar Jr., is a Brazilian professional soccer player. In August 2017, Neymar moved from Barcelona to Paris Saint Germain in a transaction worth €222 million, making him the world's most expensive player.

2 1.45

- Explain the roles of a marketing director and an advertising executive. A marketing director is the person in a company who is responsible for making sure that its product sells well. Advertising is just one way of doing this and the marketing director will use an advertising executive from an advertising agency to help put together a campaign to get the product widely known. Ask the students how many advertising campaigns they can name which use famous sports stars to advertise a product.
- Tell the students that they're going to listen to a conversation between a marketing director and an advertising executive. They're discussing the marketing of a new energy drink called "Isotonic" and they want to use a famous athlete in the advertising campaign. Ask the students to listen and say who they would choose.
- Check the answer and then go through the gapped sentences with the class. Play the recording again and ask the students to listen and complete the sentences with the names of the athletes in Exercise 1. Point out that they'll need to use some names more than once.

ANSWERS:

a Sharapova; McIlroy
b tennis; golf
c Siomne Biles; Sharapova
d Soccer; basketball
e Neymar; Ronaldo

1.45

(W = Woman; M = Man)
M: OK, what are we looking for exactly?
W: We're looking for the new face of "Isotonic," the new energy drink.
M: Yes, I know ... but what kind of face are we looking for?
W: Ah, well, we need a sports star. Someone good-looking and healthy.
M: Good. Do we have any ideas?
W: Yes, we're thinking of Maria Sharapova or Rory McIlroy.
M: Hmm, Sharapova, tennis is more popular than golf. McIlroy ...
M: Hmm. I think we need someone younger. How about Simone Biles? She is not as old as Sharapova.
W: I don't know... How about Stephen Curry?
M: Who's he?
W: He's an NBA star - he's young, successful ...
M: But NBA is too American. We want this man to be the face of "Isotonic" globally. Soccer is much more popular than basketball. Who else? Neymar, Ronaldo ...?
M: Neymar is much younger than Ronaldo so he could be more successful in the future.
W: Hmm.
M: OK, who's your favorite sports star?
W: Oh, Ronaldo. I think he's the best looking, most interesting, most talented sportsman in the world.
M: Well, let's use him then. Perfect. I want you to get in touch with him immediately.

3

- **Pairwork.** Ask the students to list the most famous atheletes in their country. If you have students from more than one country, make sure that the pairs are made up of students from the same country. If this isn't possible, allow them to make two lists.
- Ask the students to complete the exercise using the names they've listed and choosing one of them for a new sports car advertisement. As they do this, go around, monitoring and giving help. Make sure each pair has enough information to feed back to the rest of the class.

Extra activity

Ask the students to find a picture of the athlete they've chosen and to make their advertisements. They'll need to think of slogans and any other wording that will appear on them. Display the finished ads in the classroom for everyone to see. Encourage discussion of them using comparative adjectives.

Grammar & Vocabulary (SB page 46)

Comparatives

1 1.46

- Remind the students that they used comparative structures to talk about the sportspeople in the last section. Go through the information in the margin to reinforce the structures.
- Focus the students' attention on the sentences and read out the example to the class. Ask the students to complete the remaining comparisons. Encourage them to work individually, but to compare their results with a partner when they've finished.
- Play the recording for the students to listen and check their answers.

ANSWERS:

a is not as wet as
b isn't as big as
c is much smaller
d is a little bit busier
e is a little bit taller

Language notes

Grammar: *a little bit / much*

- Quantifiers *a little bit* and *much* come between the verb *be* and the comparative adjective: *He's much older than his sister. She's a little bit taller than her sister.* They help by giving more information about the differences between two things or people.

Grammar: comparative structures

- The comparative form can be divided into five categories:
  1) short adjectives take *-r/-er* (*old - older*).
  2) adjectives that end in consonant-vowel-consonant double the final consonant + *-er* (*th-i-n - thinner*).
  3) adjectives that end in *-y* drop the *-y* and take *-ier* (*happy - happier*).
  4) longer adjectives remain unchanged, but are preceded by *more* (*interesting - more interesting*).
  5) Some adjectives are irregular and don't follow any of the rules above (*good - better; bad - worse*).

2

- Give the students time to choose the words they want to use and form their comparative statements. Remind them that they can use their own ideas if they wish and encourage them to work individually. Go around, monitoring and giving help where necessary.

- Ask the students to show their statements to a partner and discuss whether they agree or disagree with each other's comparisons. Ask a selection of pairs to report back on their statements to the class.

3 Grammar Extra 5, Part 1

Ask the students to turn to Grammar Extra 5, Part 1 on page 138 of the Student's Book. Here they'll find an explanation of the grammar they've been studying and further exercises to practice it.

ANSWERS:

1
a kind - kinder than, nice - nicer than, strong - stronger than,
b sad - sadder than, thin - thinner than, wet - wetter than
c happy - happier than, lazy - lazier than, lucky - luckier than
d bad - worse than, good - better than
e famous - more famous than, interesting - more interesting than, successful - more successful than

2
a France is a little bit bigger than Spain.
b India is much hotter than Canada.
c The Nile River is a little bit longer than the Amazon.
d Tokyo is much more expensive than Bangkok.
e Rome is a little bit farther north than Barcelona.
f Manila is much more crowded than Helsinki.

a Spain isn't as big as France.
b Canada isn't as hot as India.
c The Amazon isn't as long as the Nile River.
d Bangkok isn't as expensive as Tokyo.
e Barcelona isn't as far north as Rome.
f Helsinki isn't as crowded as Manila.

Pronunciation (SB page 47)

1

- Go through the example with the class and explain that there are several English expressions which use the structure *as ... as*. Ask them to look at the expressions and try to decide on appropriate words to complete them. Emphasize that you don't expect them to know them all. Allow them to work in pairs if they wish and encourage them to be creative.

2 1.47

- Play the recording for the students to check their answers. Then play it again for them to listen to and ask them to notice how the schwa sounds are pronounced. Ask them to repeat after the speaker and try to copy these sounds exactly.
- Check that the students understand the meanings of these phrases, i.e.

a) *It's as light as a feather.* = very light
b) *He's as free as a bird.* = very free
c) *They're as good as gold.* = very well-behaved (usually refers to children)
d) *She's as pretty as a picture.* = very pretty
e) *It's as solid as a rock.* = very strong, not likely to break (of a person = very reliable or calm)
f) *It's as old as the hills.* = very old

- Ask the students if they particularly like or dislike any of the expressions. Then find out if they can think of people or things they could use the expressions to describe. Write any good suggestions on the board. Ask if they have similar expressions in their own language(s).

ANSWERS:

a feather
b bird
c gold
d picture
e rock
f hills

Extra activity

Point out that expressions with *as ... as ...* are known as similes and that the English language is full of them. Although these similes are used more in daily conversation these days than proverbs are, students should be careful not to overuse them. However, they may be interested in knowing a few more. Here is a matching exercise to try; ask the students when they've matched them how appropriate they think the similes are.

1 as strong as	a) a pancake
2 as brave as	b) ice
3 as green as	c) a cucumber
4 as cold as	d) an ox
5 as hot as	e) a lion
6 as flat as	f) hell
7 as cool as	g) grass

ANSWERS:

1 d 2 e 3 g 4 b 5 f 6 a 7 c

Grammar (SB page 47)

Superlatives

1

- Remind the students that up till now they've compared two things. Tell them that now they're going to look at how to compare three or more things. Focus their attention on the information in the margin and go through the superlative forms with the class. If students ask how long an adjective has to be to be considered "long," a good rule of thumb is three syllables or more, although there are exceptions and some adjectives which can be either "long" or "short" (e.g. *clever*). Focus their attention on the spelling change with *funny* – *funniest*.

- Go through the example in the exercise with the class. Elicit the superlative forms of *exciting* and *great* and then ask the students which superlative adjective in the group is formed in a different way from the other three (*the most exciting*). Ask them to complete the exercise, in each group underlining the one that is formed differently.

ANSWERS:

a the oldest / the richest / <u>the most exciting</u> / the greatest
b <u>the most valuable</u> / the biggest / the hottest / the thinnest
c the funniest / <u>the most interesting</u> / the sexiest / the happiest
d the worst / the furthest / the best / <u>the most talented</u>

Language notes

Grammar: superlatives

The superlative form can be divided into five categories:

1 short adjectives take *-est* (*old – the oldest*).
2 adjectives that end in consonant-vowel-consonant double the final consonant + *-est* (*th-i-n – the thinnest*).
3 adjectives that end in *-y* drop the *-y* and take *-iest* (*happy – the happiest*).
4 longer adjectives remain unchanged, but are preceded by *the most* (*interesting – the most interesting*).
5 Some adjectives are irregular and don't follow any of the rules above (*good – the best; bad – the worst*).

2

- Tell the students that they can use the adjectives in Exercise 1 or their own ideas to complete the questions. However, the questions must make sense. As they complete them, go around, monitoring and giving help.
- Ask the students to work in pairs and ask their partner their questions.

Vocabulary (SB page 47)

1 1.48

- Ask the students what they notice about the numbers in the box. Teach the words *fraction* and *decimal*.
- Play the recording and ask the students to listen and repeat the numbers. When they've done this chorally, ask for individual repetition of the numbers.
- Ask the students to find pairs of numbers with the same value. Read out the example to the class. When they've matched up the decimals and fractions, check answers by asking various students to read the pairs aloud. Then put them into pairs to practice saying the numbers.

ANSWERS:

3/4 is the same as 0.75.
0.25 is the same as 1/4.
0.33 is almost the same as 1/3.
1 1/2 is the same as 1.5.
1/8 is the same as 0.125.

2 1.49

- Play the recording and ask the students to listen and repeat the numbers in column A. When they've done this chorally, ask several students to repeat the numbers individually. Point out the way the first one can be written out in full. Ask the students to write out the others. Go around, monitoring and giving help.
- Focus the students' attention on column B and ask them to match these facts with the numbers. Allow them to discuss this in pairs or small groups.

ANSWERS:

a two hundred and sixty-three kilometers an hour
b forty-two point one nine five kilometers
c seventy million, six hundred thousand dollars
d thirty-one-nil

a 3
b 4
c 1
d 2

> **Cultural notes**
>
> **Cristiano Ronaldo**
>
> (See notes about Cristiano Ronaldo on page 52.)
>
> **Australia versus Samoa**
>
> The biggest international soccer score ever was by Australia against Samoa. On April 11, 2001, in a FIFA World Cup qualifying round, Australia beat American Samoa 31 goals to 0.
>
> **Samuel Groth (born 1987)**
>
> Samuel Groth is a former professional tennis player. In 2012, he recorded the fastest serve ever at 263 km/h, but went on to lose the game to Uladzimir Ignatik in straight sets, 4-6, 3-6.

3 Pairwork

- The pairwork exercise for this unit is on pages 121 and 126 of the Student's Book. Put the students in pairs and tell them who will be Student A, and who will be Student B.
- While they're doing the exercise, go around, monitoring and giving help. Take note of any errors which may need particular attention later, and also any examples of good language use which you can praise.

> **ANSWERS:**
>
> **Student A**
> **a** 30 km/h
> **b** $80,137,000
> **c** 7,120
> **d** 20%
> **e** 40,075.16 km
>
> **Student B**
> **a** 105 km/h
> **b** $93,820,000
> **c** 2,175
> **d** 2%
> **e** 4,203 km

Reading (SB page 48)

1

- Focus the students' attention on the picture and ask them what the woman is doing (taking a selfie on a hammock). Ask them if sitting on a hammock is a good way to relax. Elicit a few opinions from the students.
- Next, refer them to the question at the start of the text. Point out there is no right or wrong answer. Explain that "chill" in the hashtag is an informal way to say "relax."
- Give students time to read the posts individually then lead a whole class discussion on who they would like to be and why.

2 Pairwork

- Refer the students to the two questions and ask them to discuss their answers in pairs. Go around, monitoring and giving help as they do this.
- Ask several pairs to report back to the whole class and write students' ideas on how to relax/chill on the board and do a survey on which are the most common. Have you listed any ways which they have never tried and would like to try?
- Then elicit from a few students the reasons that stop them from relaxing. Invite the others to think of ways to remove the obstacles.

Vocabulary (SB page 48)

1

- Remind the students that the phrasal verbs in the box were in the text in the previous section. Ask them to find and underline them.
- Allow them to work in pairs to complete the sentences. Go around, monitoring and giving help.

> **ANSWERS:**
>
> **a** take off
> **b** turn off
> **c** put on
> **d** give up
> **e** turn on
> **f** throw away
> **g** hang up

2

- Ask the students to discuss in pairs whether any of the sentences are true for them.
- Ask several pairs to report back to the class on their discussion.

Grammar (SB page 49)

Phrasal verbs

1

- Focus the students' attention on the information in the margin. Ask the students to identify the particles in the phrasal verbs in the margin (*down, off, after*). Read aloud the example sentences in the margin or ask several students to read them. For more information on phrasal verbs, see the Language notes below.
- Put the students into pairs to look at the sentences and answer the questions. Go around, monitoring and giving help.

> **ANSWERS:**
>
> **a** sat down (sit down)
> **b** took off (take off)
> **c** ran after (run after)

2

Elicit the answer to the question from the class. Ask them to look at the example sentences in Exercise 1 and in the margin to help them decide.

ANSWERS:

a Between the verb and particle.
b After the verb and particle.

Language notes

Grammar: phrasal verbs

- There are many phrasal verbs in English. When your students encounter a phrasal verb in a text, encourage them to try to guess the meaning from the context. This will help if they then look it up in a dictionary, as there can sometimes be several meanings of the same phrasal verb. A good dictionary will tell you if the verb needs an object (transitive) or doesn't (intransitive). There are two types of transitive phrasal verbs: separable and non-separable.
- In separable phrasal verbs the object can separate the phrasal verb or come after it: *Throw the banana peel away. / Throw away the banana peel.* But if the object is a pronoun it must separate the phrasal verb: *Throw it away.*
- In non-separable phrasal verbs the object always comes after it: *Could you deal with the problem? / Could you deal with it?* If a phrasal verb has two particles (*get along with*), the object always comes after them: *My husband gets along with my parents. / He gets along with them.*

3

- Go through the example with the class, then ask the students to work individually to put the words in the correct order in the answers for the questions. Allow them to compare answers in pairs before checking with the class. If the students don't have dictionaries to consult, answer any questions about vocabulary.
- Check answers by having one student read out a question and another give the appropriate answer.

ANSWERS:

a Throw it away.
b Clear it up.
c Hang them up.
d Deal with it.
e Fill it in.
f Call it off.

4 Grammar Extra 5, Part 2

Ask the students to turn to Grammar Extra 5, Part 2 on page 138 of the Student's Book. Here they'll find an explanation of the grammar they've been studying and further exercises to practice it.

ANSWERS:

1

a Can you turn the light off, please?
b She threw away my letter.
c I'd like to try this dress on, please.
d Pick up all the papers before you leave!
e Write your name down, please.
f I gave his pen back.

2

a take after her
b get along well with them
c take care of it
d brought me up
e put them away
f make them up
g gave it up
h look it up

Listening & Speaking (SB page 49)

1 1.50

- Focus the students' attention on the picture and ask them what the people are doing (smiling/ laughing). Tell them that the people are at a laughter club and that they're going to listen to a radio show about these clubs.
- Read the statements with the class and ask them if they can predict whether they are true or false. Encourage them to try to persuade other students to change their minds if they disagree with them.
- Play the recording for the students to listen and check their answers.

ANSWERS:

a True
b False (They started in India.)
c True
d True
e False. (They don't need anything to make them laugh—they do exercises.)

1.50

(P = Presenter; A = Avril)

P: We all know the expression "laughter is the best medicine." But a recent study shows that adults don't laugh enough. The study shows that young children laugh up to four hundred times a day, while adults only laugh seventeen times a day. According to medical research, fifteen to twenty minutes of laughter a day really does keep the doctor away. Well, now you can join one of the laughter clubs to get your regular twenty minutes of laughter. It sounds funny, and it even looks a little funny, but this is a laughter club. Avril is the teacher here. Avril, how did the laughter clubs start?

A: They started in India eleven years ago. Dr. Kataria started a club in Mumbai, and now there are hundreds of laughter clubs all over the world. In India, people are very serious about the benefits of laughter.
P: And what are the benefits of laughter?
A: When you laugh, you release happy chemicals—endorphins. This can reduce the effects of stress and you feel more relaxed. Laughter boosts the immune system and relaxes the mind. Also, laughing is good for the heart and good for the lungs.
P: What happens in a laughter club? What exactly do you do?
A: We just laugh.
P: Do you listen to funny stories?
A: Oh, no. We don't need anything to make us laugh. We do exercises, and when you start laughing, you can't stop.
P: What kind of exercises?
A: Well, we start the class with a laughing exercise called Ho Ho Ha Ha Ha. After that, we do different kinds of laughing. There's "social laughter"... "silent laughter"... and the "loud, explosive laugh"... which exercises the lungs.

2

- Tell the students they can use any reasonable means to make their partner laugh, but not physical contact. Elicit a few suggestions first for things they might try, and put these on the board. You may have to start them off with a few ideas of your own, e.g. tell a joke, make a funny face, make a funny noise, etc.
- **Pairwork.** In pairs, the students take turns trying to make each other laugh. Give them a time limit. See which methods are most successful and encourage those students to try to make the whole class laugh.

3

Pairwork. Go through the questions with the class and then ask them to discuss them in pairs. Encourage them to report back to the class on anything interesting that came out of their discussion.

Language is Life (SB page 50)

1 1.52

- Focus the students' attention on the illustrations. Explain that the people in the pictures are Selma, Jimmy, and Rebecca and they're each learning a sport. They're going to listen to them talking and they have to decide what sport each of them is learning.
- Play the recording for them to listen and note down their answers.

ANSWERS:

a windsurf
b soccer
c tennis

1.51

a) (P = Paul; S = Selma)
P: OK, are you ready?
S: Yes.
P: Stand up on the board.
S: OK. Ohhhhh!
P: Ha, ha, ha!
S: Don't be mean.
P: Oh, sorry. OK. Try again. Good! Great. Hold on. Don't let go.
S: Ohhhh! It's too difficult. I can't do it.
P: Don't be silly. Of course you can do it. Be patient. Come on, try again.
S: I look stupid.
P: Don't worry. Everyone looks stupid the first time. Now, stand up on the board. That's it. Be careful. Good. Now, don't go too fast. Selma. Selma! Come back!
S: Wheeee!
b) (F = Father; J = Jimmy)
F: OK, Jimmy, kick the ball to me.
J: Daddy, Daddy, look at me.
F: Oh, that's very good, Jimmy. Now, this time, don't throw the ball –kick it.
J: Kick?
F: Yes, with your foot. Look, like this.
J: Like this?
F: No, no, don't pick it up—that's it. Now, kick it. No, don't touch the ball with your hand. Use your foot. Yes, that's it. Ouch!
J: Are you OK, Daddy?
F: Aagh!
c) (M = Mother; R = Rebecca)
M: OK, watch me. Throw the ball in the air. Watch the ball, and hit it. OK? Now you try. Throw the ball in the air and hit the—oh, OK, try again. This time, don't look at me - look at the ball. Throw the ball in the air. Watch the ball and, ... oh, no.
R: I hate this stupid game. I want to go horseback riding. You're horrible.
M: Don't be rude, Rebecca. Pick up your racket and try again.

2

Focus the students' attention on the instructions and ask them to match each of the people with one of the sets of instructions. Check answers with the class and point out the use of the imperative in both the affirmative and negative forms. If anyone asks about the use of *do* in affirmative imperatives, tell them that this is only used for very strong advice, as in *Do be careful!*

ANSWERS:

a 2
b 3
c 1

Language notes

Vocabulary: sports equipment

- Tennis and squash players use a racket; golfers use a club; baseball players use a bat, (wind) surfers use a board.

3

- Ask the students to complete the conversation by replacing the highlighted phrases with their equivalent from the box. In most cases, negative imperatives will be replaced with positive imperatives carrying the same meaning and vice versa. You may need to do the first one with the class as an example.
- Play the first conversation on the recording again for the students to listen and check their answers. Then ask them to practice the conversation with a partner.

ANSWERS:

1 Don't be mean.
2 Try again.
3 Be patient.
4 Don't worry.
5 Be careful!
6 Come back!

Life Skills (SB page 50)

Time management: An exercise routine

1 1.52

- Ask students if they have ever attended an exercise class and what exercises they did. If they do not know the name of the exercise, encourage them to mime the action and elicit or provide the name of the exercise.
- Refer the students to the pictures and elicit any exercises they know. Then focus their attention on the phrases and ask them to match each to a picture. Encourage them to deduce meaning by looking at the verbs and the actions in the pictures, e.g. push/pull.
- **Pairwork.** Put the students into pairs to complete the exercise then play the recording for the students to listen and check their answers.

ANSWERS:

a 3	d 5
b 6	e 4
c 2	f 1

2 1.53

- Explain that the students will now listen to a trainer give instructions for a workout. They will have to identify which of the exercises from Exercise 1 the workout includes. You may have to stop the recording after the first answer to demonstrate the task.
- After listening the first time, students compare their answers in pairs. Play the recording as needed then ask several students to share their answers with the rest of the class.

ANSWERS:

jogging in place	pull-ups
lunges	squats
push-ups	planks

1.53

Hi, I'm Tim, your personal trainer. And welcome to my six-minute workout. This is so easy to do, and can really get you into great shape! Begin with 30 seconds of jogging in place as a warm-up. Afterwards, take a 10-second break. Now, do two sets of lunges–each set should last for 20 seconds. Then take another 10-second break. Right. Now onto push-ups. Do as many as you can in 1 minutes and then take another 10-second break. Pull-ups can be tricky, so use a chair to help you. Again, as many as you can in 1 minutes and another break of the same length. You're doing really well! Now, 30 seconds of squats and straight into the plank–try to hold for a minute. And you're done ...and feeling good!

3

- You might have to demonstrate the next task by creating a timed workout yourself and reading it out to the students. Include 3-4 of the exercises featured in the pictures and ask students to identify them.
- Depending on the abilities of the students, ask them to create their workout individually or pair a weak student with a strong partner. Encourage students to write down and practice their workout before reading it out to their peers. Each time a student reads out their routine, the others must identify the exercises it includes.
- If the group is particularly sporty, you can even try the workout in class!

Vocabulary Extra (SB page 51)

Sports

1

- Focus the students' attention on the table and look at all the items in the first row. Read them aloud and ask the students to repeat them. Make sure they get the stress right on *athletics* (/æθˈletɪks/). Point out that the final column (*Equipment*) is incomplete and there are illustrations of the missing equipment. Ask them to find the picture of the running shoes.
- Give the students a few minutes to identify the sports that the other pieces of equipment are associated with and to add them to the table.
- Check answers with the class, making sure they can pronounce all the items correctly.

ANSWERS:

1 running shoes
2 a helmet
3 cleats
4 golf clubs
5 swimming trunks
6 goggles
7 a tennis racket
8 a net

2

- Brainstorm another sport that could be added to the table and elicit the appropriate words to put in the Person, Place, and Equipment columns of the table. Then allow the students to work in pairs to add their own sports and words. Go around, monitoring and giving help.
- Ask several pairs to read out their answers to the class.

Focus on verbs used with sports

1

- Explain that you use different verbs to talk about doing different sports. There are no hard and fast rules, but *play* tends to be used with ball games and games played in teams, such as ice hockey, or between two opponents, such as chess; *go* is used with sports that end in *-ing*, such as swimming, and *do* with other sports, such as track. Explain that *practice* refers to spending time working on a sport in order to improve one's performance.
- Ask the students to underline the appropriate verbs in the sentences. Check answers with the class before putting them into pairs to discuss how many are true for them.

ANSWERS:

a do
b been
c go
d did
e played
f practice

2

Ask the students to complete the table. Check answers with the class before asking them to add more sports to each list. Go around, monitoring and checking that they put the new sports in the correct columns.

ANSWERS:

a go
b do
c play

Extra activities

- Write the following stems on the board and ask the students to complete them to make true statements about their participation in sports and then compare with a partner.
  a) *I often* ... b) *I sometimes* ... c) *I don't* ...
  d) *I've never* ... e) *I'd like to* ...
- Discuss the various things you can do with a ball: throw, catch, pass, kick, hit, smash, etc.

Further Practice Material

Need more classroom practice activities?
Photocopiable resource materials in the Teacher's Presentation Kit / Extra Resources

Need more tests?
Test Generator
Teacher's Presentation Kit / Extra Resources / Tests

Need more on important teaching concepts?
Key concepts in *American Inside Out Evolution* pages xxi-xxxvii

Need student self-study practice?
Workbook pages 20-23

Need more information and ideas?
American Inside Out Evolution website www.macmillan.com.br/americaninsideoutevolution

Need to check what your students can do by the end of this unit?
Self-evaluation checklists on pages xxxix-xliii

6 Job Overview

Section	Aims	What the students are doing
Listening SB page 52	Listening for specific information	Listening to people and identifying the question they are asked. Checking the jobs each person mentions. Discussing what they wanted to be when they were young.
Speaking SB page 52	Fluency practice	Listing all the jobs they, their parents, and their grandparents have done. Discussing questions about jobs.
Reading SB page 53	Reading for detail	Discussing the best job in the world. Reading an article on the best job in the world and answering questions.
Grammar SB page 53	*can/can't*; *have to/don't have to*	Matching verbs and meanings. Matching the beginnings and endings of sentences. Discussing what is and isn't allowed at work or school.
Reading SB page 54	Reading for specific information	Discussing first job experiences. Answering questions on a text.
Vocabulary SB page 54	Collocations (jobs)	Adding words and phrases to sets of collocations about jobs. Writing sentences about themselves.
Grammar SB page 55	Present perfect	Identifying the uses of the present perfect. Completing a table and completing sentences with time expressions.
Pronunciation SB page 55	Past participles of irregular verbs	Completing a table with past participles and categorizing them according to vowel sound. Practicing saying them.
Speaking SB page 55	Fluency practice	Forming questions using the present perfect. Asking and answering questions about past experience.
Listening SB page 56	Listening for specific information	Listening to an interview with a businessman and answering questions. Deciding if statements are true or false.
Vocabulary SB page 56	Job-related words	Using job-related words from a text to complete sentences. Identifying the meaning and use of *should*. Discussing statements about working practices.
Writing SB page 57	A letter of application	Improving a job application letter. Writing their own letter of application for a dream job.
Speaking: anecdote SB page 57	Fluency practice	Listening and underlining the correct information. Talking about someone who has a good job.
Language for Life SB page 58	Presenting yourself	Listening and underlining the correct information. Completing presentations for three other people. Writing a short presentation of themselves.
Life Skills SB page 58	Negotiatiing: Who's doing it?	Listening to two people negotiating and identifying who's doing what. Writing a list of tasks they do at work or school. Negotiating with a partner to help them with their tasks.
Vocabulary Extra SB page 59	Office equipment; *job* and *work*	Matching pictures with words. Completing questions with *job* or *work*. Writing further questions and discussing them.

6 Job *Teacher's notes*

Warm-up

- Ask the students how easy they think it is to decide what someone's job is just by looking at them. Ask what things can give them a clue, e.g. someone's clothes, perhaps a uniform they wear, their voice, whether or not they have a suntan, the condition of their hands, etc.
- Encourage them to tell the class of any times when they've correctly or incorrectly guessed someone's job and what the consequences were, if any.

Listening (SB page 52)

1 1.54

- Focus the students' attention on the pictures. Ask the students if they think that the people in the pictures look as if they do these jobs and to give reasons why.
- Tell the students they're going to hear the four people each answering the same question. Ask them to listen and identify the question.

POSSIBLE ANSWERS:

What did you want to be when you were a child?
What job did you want to do when you were a child?
When you were a child, what did you want to be when you grew up?
When you were a child, what job did you want to do when you grew up?

1.54

a Mark, a CEO
I think I wanted to be a soldier—I liked the uniform, and lots of boys want to be soldiers when they're young, don't they? Later on, I thought about being an engineer, but I didn't do any work at school so I couldn't go to college. In the end, I started working with my father, and now I'm the CEO of my own company, so I'm really happy with the way things turned out.

b Karen, a surgeon
I've always wanted to be a surgeon, right from when I was a small child. It's my vocation. When I was at school, my best friend wanted to be a ballet dancer, but even then I knew what I wanted to do. There's never been a doctor in our family, but my father's a butcher, so I suppose it's similar!

c Frank, a teacher
When I was five, I wanted to be a farmer or a vet because I loved animals. Later, I wanted to be a pilot, but my eyes weren't good enough. When I was at college, I wanted to be a snowboarder, but I wasn't good enough to be a professional. After college, I had no idea what I wanted to do, so I became a teacher, and I love it.

d Mia, a model
My dream was to be an archaeologist. My family went on vacation to Mexico and I loved the pyramids and ruins so much that I became really interested in ancient history. But when I was sixteen, I had the chance to earn a lot of money as a model, so I stopped studying, and I've been working as a model for five years now. I want to start studying again when I'm thirty.

2

- Go through the job choices in each line and make sure the students understand and can pronounce them all.
- Play the recording again and ask the students to check the ones that each person mentions.
- Have a class discussion about what the students wanted to be when they were children. Depending on the age of the students, find out if they did, in fact, become what they wanted to be, or whether they now have different ambitions.

ANSWERS:

a Mark: a soldier, an engineer, a CEO
b Karen: a surgeon, a ballet dancer, a doctor, a butcher
c Frank: a farmer, a vet, a pilot, a snowboarder, a teacher
d Mia: an archaeologist, a model

Speaking (SB page 52)

1

Ask the students to call out the jobs and write them on the board. Give help with any vocabulary they need. (Depending on the age of the students, you could widen this to include siblings and friends.)

2

Groupwork. Go through the questions with the class and make sure everyone understands them. Then put the students into small groups and ask them to discuss the questions with reference to the jobs listed on the board. Ask one member of each group to act as a secretary and take notes on their discussion. The groups can then report back to the class on what they decided.

Reading (SB page 53)

1

- **Pairwork.** Ask a few students what jobs they do and whether these are good jobs. Then refer the students to the instructions in Exercise 1 and ask them to discuss their dream jobs in pairs. Go around, monitoring and giving help with vocabulary.
- Ask a few students to share their answers with the rest of the class and take a vote on which is the most popular dream job.

2

- Focus attention on the title of the article and ask the students to predict the answer. Write their guesses on the board. Then refer the students to the reading questions and tell them to complete the task individually.
- Once the students have finished, ask them to compare their answers in pairs before checking with the whole class. Ask them if their predictions were right.

ANSWERS:

a You have to stay in 12 luxury vacation homes and share your experiences on social media.
b You can use social media and can make these luxury homes look desirable.
c Make a one-minute video explaining exactly why you're the best candidate.

Extra activity

- Ask the students whether they would like to have this job. Would they get bored? Why? Why not?

Grammar (SB page 53)

1

- This exercise focuses on *can* and *can't* for permission and *have to* and *don't have to* for necessity. Go through the information in the margin. Point out the difference between *can* and *can't* and read out the example sentences. If students ask, tell them that the form of *can* and *can't* is the same for talking about ability, but here the focus is on permission.
- Go through the information in the margin about *have to* and *don't have to*. Emphasize that *You don't have to do something* isn't the same as *You mustn't do it*. Read out the example sentences.
- Do the first sentence with the class and then ask the students to work individually to match the remaining sentences with their meanings. Go around, monitoring and giving help where necessary.

ANSWERS:

a 4
b 2
c 1
d 3

Language notes

Grammar: modal verbs

- There are nine single-word modal verbs in English: *can, could, may, might, must, shall, should, will,* and *would*. They don't take the third person *s*. (*He can ski* NOT ~~*He cans ski*~~.) They are followed by the infinitive without *to*. (*I must go* NOT ~~*I must to go*~~.) To make negatives add *not* or *n't*. (*I shouldn't* NOT ~~*I don't should*~~.) To make questions invert the subject with the verb. (*Could you help?* NOT ~~*Do you could help?*~~)
- Two-word modal verbs like *have to* and *need to* take the third person *s* and use the auxiliary *do* to form negatives and questions. (*Do you have to go?* NOT ~~*Have you to go?*~~ / *She needs to be here before four o'clock* NOT ~~*She need to be here before four o'clock*~~).
- You use modal verbs to express possibility, probability, obligation, permission, necessity, etc. In this unit, *can/can't* are used to express permission and *have to / has to / don't have to / doesn't have to* are used to express necessity.

2

- Ask the students to match the beginnings and endings of the sentences in the exercise.
- Check answers with the class before asking them to think about what they can do and have to do at work or school.

ANSWERS:

a 3
b 1
c 6
d 5
e 4
f 2

3 Grammar Extra 6, Part 1

Ask the students to turn to Grammar Extra 6 Part 1 on page 140 of the Student's Book. Here they'll find an explanation of the grammar they've been studying and further exercises to practice it.

ANSWERS:

1
a can
b don't have to
c can
d don't have to
e can
f have to
g can
h don't have to

Reading (SB page 54)

1

- **Pairwork.** Make sure the students understand all the jobs, then ask them to list all the good experiences they think you could have in these jobs. You may need to start them off with a few ideas.

2

- Ask the students if anyone has ever had a good experience with their first job and what happened. You could give an example of a good work experience of your own.
- Give the students time to read the tweets and decide which was the best first job, and why. Elicit a few answers and take a vote on the best job. Remind them that there is no right or wrong answer.

3

- Explain that the students are going to read the tweets again, but this time they are looking for specific information. Refer them to the questions and deal with any new vocabulary where necessary. Ask them to identify what the auxiliary is.
- Set this as a timed task and encourage the students to read quickly as they scan for answers. Allow the students to compare their answers in pairs before whole class feedback.

ANSWERS:

a Sam Olive
b Saskia Phillips
c Pete Kirtley
d Tim Thomas
e Dan Ley
f Saskia Phillips

Vocabulary (SB page 54)

1

- Tell the students that collocations are pairs or groups of words that commonly occur together. Read the first set of collocations aloud, substituting the middle part, i.e. *some time*, *two weeks*, *a day*, so that the students hear the complete collocation each time. Point out that *to have a day off* is a collocation from Saskia's tweet in the previous section. She says *I had one day off a week.*
- Ask the students to find collocations in the tweets to complete the other sets. Go around, monitoring and giving help as they do this. It may be helpful if they underline the collocations in the tweets as they find them.
- Check answers with the class and answers any questions about vocabulary.

ANSWERS:

a a day off
b get
c living
d part-time
e break
f permission

2

Demonstrate the activity and get the students started by writing some sentences about yourself on the board using the collocations from Exercise 1. Then give the students time to write some sentences of their own. Encourage them to work individually and allow them to compare with a partner when they've finished. Ask several students to read out their sentences to the class.

Grammar (SB page 55)

Present perfect

1

- Read the two sentences in the exercise to the class and ask them to answer the questions underneath.
- Ask the students to look at the information in the margin about the form of the present perfect. Focus their attention on the meaning and use of *ever* which is commonly used in present perfect questions, but point out that it isn't used in the

answers to them. Also point out that the main verb (*worked*) isn't repeated in short answers to present perfect questions.

ANSWERS:

a Sentence 1. Simple past.
b Sentence 2. Present perfect.

Language notes

Grammar: present perfect

- Many students have difficulty with the present perfect tense. The tense may look similar to a composite tense (auxiliary *have/ be* + past participle) they use in their own language. However, these students will find that the present perfect in English is used rather differently from the tense they know.
- The present perfect has many different usages. It can be used to ask questions about past experience (completed events in the past) using the adverb *ever* (*What's the best party you've ever been to?*). In this context, *ever* means at any time (in your life up to now). The present perfect is never used with precise past time references, and so any answer requiring precise time references must revert to the simple past.
- In contrast with the present perfect, the simple past is used to describe completed events in the past where a precise time (e.g. at *10:00 a.m.*, *yesterday*, *two days ago*) is specified.
- *been* is the past participle *of be*, but it's often used as a past participle of *go* (or *come*). Note that this use of *been* is only for completed visits, i.e. *gone* and *returned* (*She's been to New York many times ... but now she's in Chicago.*) If the visit does not involve a return trip, then *gone* should be used (*She's gone to New York ... and she's still there.*)

2

- Focus the students' attention on the headings in the table. Explain that you can categorize time expressions according to whether they refer to time which has already finished or to time "up to now." They've already seen that *ever* is used to refer to time "up to now."
- Read out each time expression in turn and ask the students to decide which column of the table it should go in.
- Explain that you use the simple past to talk about finished time and the present perfect to talk about time "up to now."

ANSWERS:

Finished time: a few minutes ago, in 2015, last week, recently, when I was a student, years ago
Time "up to now": in the last two weeks, never, over the years, recently, this week, today

Language notes

Grammar: *recently* and *today*

- *Recently* is in both columns because although it's very often used with the present perfect, it can also be used with the simple past, e.g. *I saw a great movie recently* (describing a past event).
- Although *today* belongs in the time "up to now" column, it can sometimes be used with the simple past if we're talking at the end of the day, or distancing ourselves from the earlier part of the day. This will depend on whether what happened is still affecting us now. Compare *I've had a bad day today* with *I bought a new dress today.*
- Note that it's often possible to use the "time up to now" adverbials with both tenses in the affirmative: e.g. *I've been to the movies recently. / I went to the movies recently.*

3

- Remind the students that you use the simple past for finished time and the present perfect for time "up to now." Do the first sentence with the class as an example, then ask them to complete the remaining sentences.
- Go around, monitoring and giving help as they work. Make sure they are using appropriate tenses and time expressions. Take note of any particularly good sentences and ask the students to write them on the board.

ANSWERS:

a bought / 've bought
b didn't go / haven't been
c met / 've met
d spent / 've spent
e didn't see / haven't seen
f did / 've done
g read / 've read
h lost / 've lost

4 Pairwork

- The pairwork exercise for this unit is on pages 122 and 127 of the Student's Book. Put the students into pairs and tell them who will be Student A, and who will be Student B.

- While they're doing the exercise, go around, monitoring and giving help. Take note of any errors which may need particular attention later, and also any examples of good language use which you can praise.

> **QUESTIONS:**
>
> **Student A**
> **a** Have you ever broken your leg?
> **b** Have you ever sung karaoke?
> **c** Have you ever ridden a motorcycle?
> **d** Have you ever been fishing?
> **e** Have you ever eaten escargot?
> **f** Have you ever bought a painting?
>
> **Student B**
> **a** Have you ever been to Canada?
> **b** Have you ever given a speech?
> **c** Have you ever broken the speed limit?
> **d** Have you ever cut somebody's hair?
> **e** Have you ever cried at the movies?
> **f** Have you ever forgotten your mother's birthday?

5 Grammar Extra 6, Part 2

Ask the students to turn to Grammar Extra 6, Part 2 on page 140 of the Student's Book. Here they'll find an explanation of the grammar they've been studying and further exercises to practice it.

> **ANSWERS:**
>
> **1**
> 1 been 2 done 3 taken 4 drunk 5 broken 6 seen 7 eaten 8 written 9 forgotten 10 ridden 11 become 12 stood 13 given 14 gone 15 been
>
> **2**
> **a** I haven't been on TV.
> **b** I haven't sung karaoke.
> **c** I haven't driven a sports car.
> **d** I haven't met a famous person.
> **e** I haven't climbed a mountain.
> **f** I haven't called up a TV show.
>
> **3**
> **a** Have you been on TV?
> **b** Have you sung karaoke?
> **c** Have you driven a sports car?
> **d** Have you met a famous person?
> **e** Have you climbed a mountain?
> **f** Have you called up a TV show?
>
> **4**
> **a** 've never been
> **b** didn't do
> **c** haven't called
> **d** 've never eaten
> **e** went
> **f** had

Pronunciation (SB page 55)

1 1.55

- Explain that the present perfect tense is formed with the auxiliary verb *have* and the past participle of the main verb. With regular verbs, this is formed by adding *-ed* to the infinitive. Tell the students to look back at the example sentences in Exercise 1 of the previous section and point out the simple past form of the irregular verb *do* (*did*) and the past participle (*done*).
- Ask the students to look at the table. Read the first four infinitive forms aloud, following each one with its past participle so that the students hear them together. Then read the past participle forms only and ask the students to identify the one with the different vowel sound (*seen*).
- Tell the students to write the past participle forms of the remaining verbs in the right-hand column. Suggest that they say them aloud as they do this. Then ask them to underline the one in each line that has a different vowel sound.
- Play the recording for the students to check their answers. Then play it again for them to listen and repeat. When they've done this chorally, ask for individual repetition of the past participle forms.

> **ANSWERS:**
>
> **a** said, read, fed, <u>seen</u>
> **b** known, <u>bought</u>, flown, grown
> **c** rung, sung, <u>brought</u>, hung
> **d** <u>drunk</u>, taught, thought, fought

Speaking (SB page 55)

1

- Read the example aloud and remind students of the use of *ever* in present perfect questions about people's experiences up till now.
- **Pairwork.** Put the students into pairs to make the remaining questions from the prompts. Go around, monitoring and giving help as they do this.

> **ANSWERS:**
>
> **a** What's the best/worst party you've ever been to?
> **b** What's the best/worst vacation you've ever been on?
> **c** What's the best/worst meal you've ever eaten?
> **d** What's the best/worst joke you've ever heard?
> **e** What's the best/worst car you've ever been in?
> **f** What's the best/worst T-shirt you've ever worn?
> **g** What's the best/worst bed you've ever slept in?

2

- Give the students a moment or two to choose their questions. Emphasize that they should choose either the *best* or the *worst* in each case. Demonstrate the example dialogue with a confident student. Point out the switch to the simple past in the answer (to talk about a specific finished event in the past) and in the follow-up question.
- Put the students into pairs and ask them to take turns asking and answering their questions. As they work, go around making sure they are using the tenses correctly. Encourage them to use follow-up questions to elicit more information, and to report back to the class on what they found out about each other.

Listening (SB page 56)

1

- **Pairwork.** Focus Focus the students' attention on the picture of Mr. McClusky and ask the students to discuss the questions in pairs.

2 1.56

Play the recording for them to check their answers. Then ask them if they were surprised by anything they heard.

ANSWERS:

a A department store.
b In 1948.
c He's 85 (nearly 86).

1.56

(P = Radio presenter; I = Interviewer; Mr. M = Mr. McClusky)

P: And this week, in our regular report, we visit a department store with a difference ...

I: Mr. McClusky, can you tell us what is so special about your department store?

Mr. M: Well, McClusky's is a large department store and you can find everything you want for the home here. Oh, and it stays open late on Thursdays and Saturdays.

I: Yes, that's right, but isn't there something special about the staff–you know–has anybody retired recently?

Mr. M: Ah, oh, I see. No. Nobody has retired recently, and we never force anybody to retire here.

I: How old is your oldest employee?

Mr. M: Well, that's Art. Art is our cleaner, and he's 87.

I: 87!And he cleans the store every day?

Mr. M: Well, not alone, no. He works with two other cleaners. They're not so old ... Marshal's 70 and Ivy's 75–no, 76. That's right, she's just had her birthday.

I: And they don't want to retire?

Mr. M: No, I think they enjoy the work, and it keeps them young. Also, we pay a decent salary, and they get four weeks of paid vacation a year.

I: So how many workers do you have who are over retirement age?

Mr. M: Well, we employ a staff of 105 and half of those are over 65. The young ones work in the office–we've got computers now, you know.

I: Really? Has the store changed much over the years?

Mr. M: No, not really. I started working here in 1948 and I've only had two secretaries in all that time. Barbara, my first secretary, resigned when she was 72.

I: Oh, why did she leave McClusky's so young?

Mr. M: Well, she was getting married to somebody who lived in another town.

I: Wow! That's amazing ... Do you think you will ever retire, Mr. McClusky?

Mr. M: Oh, yes. I'm almost 86! My son's going to take over the business next year. He's only 64.

3

- Go through the statements with the class so the students know what information they are listening out for.
- Play the recording again and ask the students to mark the statements true or false. Tell them to correct the false statements to make them true.

ANSWERS:

a True
b False (The oldest employee at McClusky's is 87.)
c True
d False (Employees get four weeks of paid vacation.)
e False (About half the staff are over the retirement age.)
f True
g False (Mr. McClusky's son is going to run the business from next year.)

Vocabulary (SB page 56)

1

- Tell the students to look back at the statements in Exercise 3 in the previous section. Ask them to use the underlined words to complete the sentences. Allow them to compare their answers in pairs before checking answers with the class.

> **ANSWERS:**
>
> **a** paid vacation
> **b** decent salary
> **c** retirement age
> **d** to retire
> **e** run
> **f** resign

2

- Point out the use of *should* in each of the sentences in Exercise 1. Ask several students to read the sentences containing *should* aloud.
- Ask them to decide which ending best describes the meaning of *should* in these statements.

> **ANSWER:**
>
> a good idea

3

Groupwork. Put the students in small groups to discuss whether or not they agree with the statements in Exercise 1. Ask a representative from each group to report back to the class on their group's decisions.

Writing (SB page 57)

1

- Focus the students' attention on the letter and explain that the highlighted parts are those where Michele has used either the wrong word or expression, or one that isn't suitable for a formal letter. Explain the concept of *formal* and *informal language* and establish that a letter of application for a job requires formal language. Point out the example: formal letters to someone you don't know should begin *Dear Sir or Madam*. *Dear Mr. McClusky* would be acceptable in a less formal letter, but *Dear McClusky* is wrong.
- Read out the expressions in the box and ask the students to use them to improve the letter by replacing the highlighted parts. Go around, monitoring and giving help.

> **ANSWERS:**
>
> **1** Sir or Madam:
> **2** would like to apply for
> **3** attached
> **4** reached retirement age
> **5** a new challenge
> **6** look forward to hearing

2

- This exercise could be set for homework. Explain the concept of a dream job (the one that you would most like to have). Give the students a minute or two to decide what their dream job would be. You could start by telling them about your own dream job.
- Point out the different sections of Michele's email in Exercise 1. She begins by saying that she saw the advertisement and makes it clear which job she's applying for. In the second paragraph, she talks about her experience (why she would be a suitable candidate for the job) and refers to her résumé. In the third paragraph, she explains why she wants the job. In the fourth paragraph, she says when she's available for a job interview.
- Ask the students to write their own letter of application for their dream job. Tell them that they can use Michele's email as a model, but remind them to keep the language formal and appropriate, and to change the details to match the job they have in mind.

Speaking: anecdote (SB page 57)

For more information about how to set up, monitor and repeat Anecdotes, see page xviii-xx in the Introduction.

1 1.57

- Ask the students to look at the picture. Explain that Kim, a friend of the woman in the picture, is going to talk about her friend's job. Go through the questions and the answer choices with the class. Explain any unknown vocabulary and ask the students to listen and underline the answers Kim gives.
- Check answers with the class and ask them whether they would like a job like Hannah's.

> **ANSWERS:**
>
> **a** Hannah
> **b** personal trainer
> **c** She's self-employed.
> **d** 7:00 a.m.
> **e** $35 an hour
> **f** She helps people get in shape.
> **g** Yes, because she doesn't have to work in an office.

1.57

My friend Hannah has the best job in the world—she's a personal trainer. She has about ten clients, and she writes an exercise program for each person. She doesn't work for anybody—she's self-employed.

She starts work very early every day because some of her clients like to exercise before they go to work. I think she starts her first client at seven o'clock in the morning.

I think it's a great job, because Hannah loves sports and so she gets money for doing what she loves. She earns a reasonably good salary. I think she charges $35 an hour, so her salary depends on the number of hours she works. She loves her job because she helps people get in shape and stay healthy.

I'd love to do her job, because she doesn't have to work in an office all day and she doesn't have to go to the gym in her free time either. She's her own boss so she can go on vacation when she wants, and she always looks fantastic in a swimsuit.

2

- Give the students a minute or two to decide who they're going to talk about. Then ask them to look at the questions in Exercise 1 again and decide how they'd answer them about the person and the job they're going to talk about. Allow them to make notes on what they're going to say and how they're going to say it, but discourage them from writing a paragraph that they can simply read out. Go around, monitoring and giving help.
- **Pairwork.** Put the students into pairs and ask them to take turns to tell their partner about the person they know who has a good job. Encourage them to ask each other follow-up questions.
- Ask some pairs to report back to the class about what they found out.

Language for Life (SB page 58)

1 1.58

- Focus the students' attention on the picture and ask them to describe the situation. Tell them that all these people are in a group for volunteers. This is their first meeting and they're going to introduce themselves. Give them a minute or two to read through the information.
- Play the recording and ask the students to underline the correct information for each person. Then check answers with the class.

ANSWERS:

Layla: audio equipment; sales and promotion
Mike: unemployed; publishing
Jack: in Detroit; a lot of foreign travel
Elise: the photography department; taking pictures

1.58

(C = Chair; L = Layla; J = Jack; E = Elise; M = Mike)

C: Good afternoon, everybody. Welcome to our *Volunteer Program*. I'm John, the program coordinator. Can you tell the group who you are, and what you do?
L: Hello. My name's Layla. I work for a big company and we produce high-quality audio equipment. I'm responsible for sales and promotion.
M: Good morning. My name's Mike. I just graduated from college. Right now I'm unemployed. I'm looking for a job in publishing.
J: Hi. I'm Jack and I work as a bodyguard. I'm self-employed and I'm based in Detroit, but my job involves a lot of foreign travel. I have to take important clients safely from one place to another.
E: My name's Elise. I'm a photographer and I work for a music magazine. We're based in Detroit. I run the photography department and I'm in charge of taking pictures of rock stars and bands, so I travel a lot.
C: Thank you for being here. I'm sure everybody can help ...

2 1.59

- Focus the students' attention on the next set of pictures. Tell the students that these people are also joining the volunteer program group, but they're late. Ask the students to look through the notes and complete their presentations with words from Exercise 1.
- Allow them to compare their answers in pairs before you play the recording for them to check.

ANSWERS:

1 as
2 for
3 charge
4 for
5 involves
6 looking
7 in
8 run
9 sell
10 based

3

- Ask the students to work individually to write their presentations. Remind them that they can use the ones in Exercises 1 and 2 as a model and that they can invent information if they wish, based on their ideal job.
- As they work, go around, monitoring and giving help. Make sure they use at least three of the useful phrases from Exercise 1.
- Ask the students to make their presentations to the class.

Life Skills (SB page 58)

Negotiating: Who's doing it?

- Refer the students to the picture and ask them to describe the picture (a man and a woman shaking hands). Point out that the theme of this section is "negotiating." Ask students what this involves (*talking, compromising, reaching an agreement*), and if they remember the last time they had to negotiate something.

1 1.60

- Focus the students' attention on the instructions and go over each of the tasks listed in the box, explaining any new vocabulary. Tell the students they are going to listen to a conversation at work and to note down who agrees to do the task.
- Play the recording once and have students check their answers in pairs. You may need to play the recording more than once.
- Go through the answers with the students and ask them what they heard to help them understand.

ANSWERS:

Get stationery items	B
Write the report	N
Print out the report	B
Make the coffee	N
Do the filing	B
Set up the conference room	N

1.60

(B = Beatrice; N = Nathan)

B: Okay, I need to finish early today. Can you help me to do some of these tasks?
N: Really? I have to do lots of work already. Look—I have to finish writing this report.
B: Sorry, I can't help you with that—I don't know anything about sales.
N: But once I've finished, can you help print it out? The boss wants it on her desk before she leaves.
B: Okay, I can do that. But can you help with this filing?
N: Sorry, I'm useless at filing. But why don't you do the filing, and I'll help setting up the conference room for the morning meeting.
B: Oh, great. Everyone needs a pen, notepad, and pack of Post-its.
N: But if I do that—can you make me a coffee?
B: Oh, no! My coffee is terrible! But I will get you some stationary supplies? Okay?
N: You have a deal—I need paperclips and folders.

2

- With the whole class, brainstorm as many tasks as they know that they have to do at work or school. Write these up on the board. Ask the students which of these they particularly dislike doing and why.
- Ask the students to choose five of the tasks listed (or they can think of some of their own) and to write these in the table.

3

- Before starting the task, elicit from the students some language they can use to negotiate, e.g. making a request ("Can you ..."), making an offer ("I'll ..."), agreeing ("Okay, I can do that."), disagreeing ("Sorry, ...") and write these on the board.
- **Pairwork.** Refer the students to the instructions and ask them to work with a partner in making similar dialogues to the example. Go around, helping with new vocabulary.
- At the end of the task, ask some of the more confident pairs to perform their negotiation for the rest of the class.

Vocabulary Extra (SB page 59)

Office equipment

1

- Focus the students' attention on the list of words and point out that they're all words to do with office equipment. Check that the students can pronounce the words correctly.
- Ask the students to match the pictures with the words. Let them use dictionaries if they wish.

ANSWERS:

15 a briefcase
5 a calculator
11 a desk lamp
13 a filing cabinet
14 a folder
9 a hole punch

10 a keyboard
8 a mouse
6 a note pad
2 paper clips
12 a photocopier
3 Post-its
1 a printer
7 a screen
4 a stapler
16 a trash can

2

Pairwork. Demonstrate the example dialogue to the class with a confident student. Then put them into pairs to continue asking and answering questions about office equipment.

Focus on *work* and *job*

1

- Tell the students that *work* and *job* are used slightly differently in English. *Work* is usually used as a verb and *job* is a noun.
- Ask them to complete the sentences in pairs.

ANSWERS:

a job
b work
c job

2

- Elicit a few example questions around the class. Then ask the students to write at least six more questions using the words in the box. Go around, checking that they are using *work* and *job* correctly.
- Put them into pairs to take turns asking and answering six questions each.

ANSWERS:

had can be replaced with: applied for, looked for, lost, resigned from
abroad can be replaced with: from home, in marketing, outdoors
dangerous can be replaced with: badly paid, boring, stressful, well-paid

Further Practice Material

Need more classroom practice activities?
Photocopiable resource materials in the Teacher's Presentation Kit / Extra Resources

Need more tests?
Test Generator
Teacher's Presentation Kit / Extra Resources / Tests

Need more on important teaching concepts?
Key concepts in *American Inside Out Evolution* pages xxi-xxxvii

Need student self-study practice?
Workbook pages 24–27

Need more information and ideas?
American Inside Out Evolution website www.macmillan.com.br/americaninsideoutevolution

Need to check what your students can do by the end of this unit?
Self-evaluation checklists on pages xxxix-xliii

Review B *Teacher's notes*

These exercises act as a check of the grammar and vocabulary that the students have learned in Units 4–6. Use them to find any problems that students are having, or anything that they haven't understood and which will need further work.

Grammar (SB page 60)

Remind the students of the grammar explanations they read and the exercises they did in the Grammar Extra on pages 136–141

1

This exercise reviews adverbs of frequency from Unit 4. Check answers with the class before the students rewrite the sentences to make them true for them.

ANSWERS:

a We always get up at 7:00 a.m.
b You never get to class on time!
c We occasionally eat meat.
d They are often at home on Sunday evenings.
e Cecilia hardly ever goes out in the evening.

2

This exercise reviews comparative and superlative forms from Unit 5.

ANSWERS:

a healthiest
b sensitive
c expensive
d best-looking
e cheapest
f noisier

3

This exercise reviews the simple present and present progressive from Unit 4.

ANSWERS:

1 love
2 like
3 have
4 doesn't understand
5 has
6 wear
7 'm trying
8 'm not buying
9 'm saving
10 look

4

This exercise reviews *can, can't, have to,* and *don't have to* from Unit 6.

ANSWERS:

1 have to
2 have to
3 can
4 can't
5 have to

5

This exercise reviews simple past and present perfect verb forms from Unit 6.

ANSWERS:

1 Have you worked
2 've done
3 Have you had
4 've been
5 worked
6 went
7 finished

Vocabulary (SB page 61)

1

This exercise reviews collocations in Unit 4.

ANSWERS:

a chocolates, tissues
b keys, flowers
c beans, paint
d perfume, water

2

Go through the example first and explain that *necklace* doesn't belong because it's the only one that is jewelry; the others are all materials. Ask the students to give explanations of their choices for the other items in the exercise.

ANSWERS:

a necklace
b boots
c woolen
d checked

3

This exercise reviews questions with *How ...?* from Unit 5. Check answers with the class before the students work in pairs to ask and answer the questions.

ANSWERS:

a 6
b 5
c 4
d 1
e 3
f 2

4

This exercise reviews job-related collocations.

ANSWERS:

a part-time
b a pay-raise
c decision
d time
e lost

Pronunciation (SB page 61)

1

Remind the students that the circles show the syllables of a word and the large circles indicate the stressed syllables. Here the students are being asked to classify words according to how many syllables they have and where the main stress falls.

2 1.61

Point out the main stresses in the example words which are underlined. Ask the students to do the same for the other words in the table. Then play the recording for them to check their answers. Play it a second time for them to listen and repeat.

ANSWERS:

1 and 2
A: doctor, flowers, leather, racket, sandals
B: advice, afford, au pair, avoid, receive
C: horrible, company, interested, quality, talented, valuable

Reading & Listening (SB page 62)

1

Ask the students to read the questions first so that they know what information they're looking for when they read the posts.

ANSWERS:

a They're step-brother and step-sister.
b She's proud to have him as her step-brother. / She feels like he's her brother, not her step-brother.

2

Go through the statement first to see if the students can answer any of them. Then ask them to read the posts again and find the answers to any remaining questions. When you've checked their answers, ask them to correct the false information.

ANSWERS:

a False (Clara is older than Johnny. / Johnny is younger than Clara.)
b False (Johnny is still studying for a PhD. Clara runs her own company.)
c False. (Only Clara likes to exercise in the morning. Johnny doesn't like any exercise.)
d False (Johnny likes wearing jeans and T-shirts, but Clara likes to wear nice dresses.)
e False (He thinks she's kind and generous.)
f True

3 1.62

Tell the students they're going to hear Tom and Patsy (shown in the picture) talking about their relationship. Go through the questions so that they know what information they're listening for. Play the recording again and ask the students to answer the questions.

ANSWERS:

a They're husband and wife.
b She loves him.

4

Go through the choices with the students before playing the recording again. Ask them to underline the correct information.

ANSWERS:

a younger
b Tom
c always
d never
e likes
f very funny

1.62

(T = Tom; P = Patsy)
T: Patsy and I are very different ...
P: Yes, very different. In fact, we're complete opposites. Tom's water and I'm air. He's a Scorpio and I'm an Aquarius.
T: Mm, I don't really believe in all that ...
P: And Tom's much older than me. I think that also makes a difference.
T: I don't see what difference ...
P: The clothes he wears make him look older, too.
T: That's true. On the other hand, Patsy dresses like a teenager.
P: No, I don't. But I do enjoy finding fashionable clothes at good prices. I always buy him really good clothes, but he never wears them.
T: We've been married for twenty-two years ...
P: Is it that long?
T: ... and sometimes we can't understand why we've stayed together ...
P: Yes. He likes watching sports on TV, whereas I like getting out there and playing them. I can't stand watching sports on TV.
T: She loves shopping, but I prefer sitting in my backyard with a newspaper.
P: So, why are we together? Simple—I love him. He's a good husband and a good father to our children. And he's one of the funniest people I've ever met.
T: I think I'm the luckiest person I know.

Writing & Speaking (SB page 63)

1

Go through the questions with the class, then ask the students to read the text and check the ones that are answered.

ANSWERS:

Questions a, b, c, d, e, f, g, and h are answered.

2

Ask the students to read the text and underline the words from the box as they find them. When they've finished, ask them to complete the rules with these words and phrases.

ANSWERS:

a both
b whereas, but
c however, on the other hand

3

Encourage the students to read the sentences aloud to get a feel for what sounds right.

ANSWERS:

a However
b whereas
c On the other hand,
d but

4

Check answers with the class before putting the students into pairs to discuss whether or not the sentences are true for them.

ANSWERS:

a We both love dancing (*both* comes before the main verb)
b We have both been to the USA (*both* comes after the auxiliary)

5

Give the students a minute or two to decide who they're going to talk about. Remind them that they can choose questions from Exercise 1 to answer. Give them time to prepare what they're going to say and allow them to make notes if they wish, but discourage them from writing a script.

6

Remind the students that they can use the text in Exercise 1 as a model. Go around, monitoring and giving help, and encourage them to use expressions to describe contrast and similarity.

Further Practice Material

Need more classroom practice activities?
Photocopiable resource materials in the Teacher's Presentation Kit / Extra Resources

Need more tests?
Test Generator
Teacher's Presentation Kit / Extra Resources / Tests

Need more on important teaching concepts?
Key concepts in *American Inside Out Evolution* pages xxi-xxxvii

Need more information and ideas?
American Inside Out Evolution website www.macmillan.com.br/americaninsideoutevolution

7 Eco Overview

Section	Aims	What the students are doing
Reading & Vocabulary SB page 64	Reading for detail Climate change	Reading about a protest march and identifying true and false statements. Matching phrases with similar meaning. Talking about climate change.
Listening & Vocabulary SB page 65	Listening for gist Opinions	Matching four protesters with their opinions. Completing sentences which state opinions and discussing them.
Grammar SB page 65	Subject questions	Studying the structure and use of subject questions. Writing subject and object questions.
Pronunciation SB page 66	Words ending in *-tion*	Completing a table with words ending in *-tion*. Listening and repeating the words.
Grammar SB page 66	Dynamic and stative meanings	Studying verbs with dynamic and stative meanings. Writing sentences using the present progressive. Completing sentences describing actions and states, and making them true for classmates.
Speaking SB page 67	Fluency practice	Discussing what's good or bad for the environment. Conducting a survey on environmental issues.
Writing SB page 67	Writing a report	Completing a survey report on green issues. Writing a survey report.
Reading & Listening SB page 68	Reading for detail Listening for specific information	Discussing voluntary work. Matching projects from a volunteer website with duties. Listening and identifying which project a volunteer is going to join. Discussing which projects they would like to do.
Grammar SB page 68	Future: *(be) going to*	Correcting mistakes in sentences. Studying the future *(be) going to*. Writing and asking questions about the future.
Listening SB page 69	Listening for detail	Listening and identifying the speakers' feelings. Listening and underlining the correct information. Discussing when their parents worry about them.
Grammar SB page 69	Future: present progressive	Studying the present progressive to talk about the future. Deciding when you can use *(be) going to* or the present progressive.
Language for Life SB page 70	Useful phrases on the telephone	Underlining appropriate expressions in a phone conversation. Listening and repeating useful phrases. Practicing a phone conversation.
Life Skills SB page 70	Social responsibility: How green are you?	Listening to a podcast and categorizing tips on green living. Discussing and listing things they can do to be more environmentally friendly. Comparing actions.
Vocabulary Extra SB page 71	Review of words from the unit: environmental problems and solutions; *have / have got*	Matching pictures with phrases. Categorizing expressions and adding their own ideas. Completing sentences with *do*, *don't*, *have*, and *haven't*. Writing questions with *have / has got*. Comparing the use of *have / has* and *have / has got*.
Writing WB page 31		Linking sentences with *because*, *as*, *since*. Making written suggestions.

7 Eco *Teacher's notes*

Warm-up

- Write the word *protest* on the board. Explain what it means (verb and noun).
- Brainstorm issues that people protest about. Write all suggestions on the board and then ask the students which ones they feel strongly about. Ask if anyone feels strongly enough about any of the issues to join a protest. Ask in what ways people can protest about these issues (e.g. by writing letters to politicians, signing petitions, taking part in a demonstration, etc.)

Reading & Vocabulary (SB page 64)

1

Focus the students' attention on the picture, which shows people demonstrating about climate change. Then ask the questions in the exercise. Ask what kind of things may happen when the protest is violent.

2

- Ask the students to read the article. Give them a time limit to do this.
- Go through the statements one by one and ask the students to say whether they're true or false and to correct the false statements.

ANSWERS:

a True
b True
c False (The protesters wanted world leaders to do something immediately about environmental issues.)
d False (The protest demanded action from world leaders)
e True
f True

Language notes

Vocabulary: *demonstration*

An occasion when a large group of people gather to protest about something.

3

- Focus attention on the highlighted phrases. Ask the students to work in pairs to match them to similar phrases in the statements in Exercise 2.

ANSWERS:

broke away = separated
marchers = protesters
demanding urgent action on = wanted world leaders to do something immediately about
slogans = political messages
took part in = participated in
made their way = went to see
swarming with people = extremely crowded
buzzing with activity = very busy

4

Pairwork. Ask for some suggestions from the class and put them on the board before putting the students into pairs to discuss the questions. Go around, monitoring and helping with vocabulary. Note any interesting vocabulary and expressions on the board. Encourage the pairs to report back to the class on their discussions.

Listening & Vocabulary (SB page 65)

1 2.01

- Tell the students that they're going to listen to four protesters at the climate change march described in the article on page 64. Ask them to look at the pictures and encourage them to speculate on what kind of people they are and what their interests might be.
- Before you play the recording, go through the opinions with the class and make sure everyone understands them.
- Play the recording and ask the students to match the people with their opinions.

ANSWERS:

1 Jake
2 Debbie
3 Carlos
4 Jo

2.01

Jo, 26:	I work for an organization called Eco Vacations, and we're demonstrating against mass tourism. I'm not against tourism but I believe in responsible tourism. We're against big hotels and big tour groups. With Eco Vacations you can really experience the local culture. We organize accommodations with local families. Would you like some information about our vacations?
Jake, 14	I'm having a good time with my friends. It's my first demonstration. I don't feel strongly about politics, but I'm worried about global warming. I don't really care about people–they can take care of themselves. I'm in favor of protecting wild animals–I want to help polar bears and penguins. If the ice caps melt, where will they live?
Debbie, 37	I'm here because we're destroying the planet. I'm protesting against multinational companies. They're polluting our rivers and oceans and they're causing global warming. I'm in favor of small family-run companies. I'm against food imports. I support local farmers and I buy food from farmers' markets, not large grocery stores.
Carlos, 27	I'm riding my bicycle today because I'm against big cars in the city. I'm not anti-cars–in fact, I have a car–but I just think more people should use public transportation. Leave your car at home–ride a bicycle!

2

- Give the students a minute or two to complete the sentences.
- When checking answers, make sure that the students understand all the sentences. Then put them into pairs to discuss whether or not they agree with them. Go around, monitoring and giving help. See if there's any consensus regarding the sentences.

ANSWERS:

a anti
b really care
c believe
d in favor
e against
f support
g don't feel

Grammar (SB page 65)

Subject questions

1

- Focus the students' attention on the information in the margin. Point out that the statement John hates cars can generate two different questions: one focusing on the subject of the sentence and the other on the object.
- Go through the information and questions with the class.

ANSWERS:

a Who
b Jo
c No, you don't.

Language note

Grammar: subject questions

If a question word (e.g. *who*) is the subject of the question, you don't use *do*, *does*, or *did*. Compare:
Who went to the party? (*Who* is the subject)
Who did you go with? (*Who* is the object; *you* is the subject)
Who saw him? (*Who* is the subject)
Who did he see? (*Who* is the object; *he* is the subject)

2

- Look at the two example questions with the class and make sure that the students understand the principles. Then ask them to work individually to complete the exercise.
- Check answers with the class before putting the students into pairs to take turns asking and answering the questions.

ANSWERS:

a What did Mahatma Gandhi believe in?
b Who said, "I have a dream" in a famous speech?
c What does "slogan" mean?
d Which organization has a boat called "Rainbow Warrior"?
e What did thirty-six million people protest against in 2003?
f Who fought against apartheid for over fifty years?

a Non-violent protest
b Martin Luther King
c Political message
d Greenpeace
e The Iraq war
f Nelson Mandela

Cultural notes

Mahatma Gandhi (1869–1948)

Political and spiritual leader in India who helped his country, through peaceful resistance, to achieve independence in 1947 from the British Empire. Gandhi was committed to non-violence, and so his assassination at the hands of an extremist Hindu (Gandhi's own faith) gunman was all the more ironic.

Martin Luther King, Jr. (1929–1968)

One of the leaders of the US civil rights movement, Luther King was a Baptist minister who, inspired by Gandhi's success in India, advocated civil disobedience to gain rights for the black citizens of the United States. Luther King was also assassinated by a gunman's bullet in 1968.

Greenpeace

An international environmental organization founded in Canada in 1971. It's well known for its campaigns against whaling. Its boat, Rainbow Warrior, often makes the news around the world for efforts on behalf of marine ecology.

Nelson Mandela (born 1918–2013)

Nelson Mandela was President of South Africa from 1994 to 1999. Before that he was in jail for 27 years for his involvement with the armed wing of the African National Congress. In earlier life, Mandela had been inspired by Gandhi's non-violent protest, but was eventually brutalized by the apartheid system in South Africa and took up arms against it. He died in 2013, at the age of 95.

Pronunciation (SB page 66)

1

- Ask the students to look at the table. Remind them that the circles show the syllables of a word and the large circles indicate the stressed syllables. Read the word demonstration aloud and ask the students to repeat it. Make sure that they're pronouncing it correctly.
- Ask the students to put the words in the box in the correct columns of the table according to how they are pronounced. Encourage them to say the words aloud so they get a feeling for what sounds right.

ANSWERS:

A: destruction, pollution, solution
B: demonstration, education, explanation, revolution
C: globalization, modernization, organization

2 2.02

Play the recording for the students to check their answers to Exercise 1. Then play it a second time for them to listen and repeat the words. When they've done this chorally, ask individual students to repeat the words after you, and check that they're putting the stress on the correct syllables.

Grammar (SB page 66)

Dynamic and stative meanings

1

- If necessary, explain the difference between a verb with dynamic meaning (one describing an action when something happens) and one with stative meaning (one describing a state, not something that happens).
- Focus attention on the information in the margin and go through the example sentences. Point out that there are some verbs which can have both meanings.
- Focus attention on the two example sentences in the exercise and ask the students to answer the questions in pairs.

ANSWERS:

a Actions
b Present progressive

Language notes

Grammar: dynamic and stative verbs

- Stative verbs describe states or conditions which continue over a period of time. *Like, love, hate, want, need, hear,* and see are examples of stative verbs. These verbs aren't normally used in the progressive form. *I want to be an engineer one day*, NOT ~~*I'm wanting to be an engineer one day*~~.
- Dynamic verbs describe things which happen within a limited time. *Come, bring, buy, get,* and *learn* are examples of dynamic verbs. *I'm learning English at the moment*, NOT ~~*I learn English at the moment*~~.
- Some verbs, like *have, look,* and *think* can have both stative and dynamic meanings.

Compare:

1 *I have an old car* (state) with *I'm having a great time!* (something happening within a limited time).
2 *He looks tired* (condition) with *That woman is looking at me in a strange way.* (something happening within a limited time).
3 *Do you think Brazil will win the World Cup?* (state) with *I'm thinking of going downtown today.* (something happening within a limited time).

* Recently there's been a trend to make the verbs *like* and *love* take a dynamic form but retain a stative meaning. Thus, *I'm really liking that song!* is a modern colloquial way of saying *I really like that song!* Burger chain McDonald's® have introduced the slogan "I'm lovin' it!" with the intention of appealing to the 15–24 age group market.

2

- Ask the students to work individually to complete the sentences. When checking answers, make sure that the students have spelled *making* correctly. Then ask whether the sentences describe actions or states or both.

ANSWERS:

a A telephone is ringing.
b A teacher in another class is talking.
c The traffic is making a lot of noise.
d A clock is ticking.
e Birds are singing.
f Rain is falling.
g A student is laughing.
h People are talking.

- Tell the class that they must stay absolutely silent for the next 15 seconds and check any of the things that they hear during that time. Then they should write sentences using the present progressive. to describe anything else that they notice is happening. Agree on a signal for the beginning and end of the 15 seconds. Make sure the students are completely silent before you begin.
- See if everyone agrees on which things were happening and ask several students to read out their additional sentences.

3

- Read the example sentences to the class. Ask the students to look at the verbs in these sentences and answer the questions.

ANSWERS:

a States
b Simple present
c No

4

- Remind the students that some verbs can have both dynamic and stative meanings. Go through the two examples with the class and get the students to identify that sentence a) describes an action, and sentence b) a state. Point out the use of the present progressive in a) and the simple present in b).
- Ask the students to work individually to complete the remaining sentences. Go around, monitoring and helping anyone who's having difficulty.
- Check answers with the class before asking the students to replace the names in the sentences with those of members of the class. Emphasize that they should try to make true sentences and encourage them to ask each other questions as in the examples.
- Get several students to read their sentences aloud and ask the subjects of those sentences to confirm whether or not they're true.

ANSWERS:

a is thinking
b thinks
c has
d is having
e looks
f is looking
g likes
h knows

5 Grammar Extra 7, Part 1

Ask the students to turn to Grammar Extra 7, Part 1 on page 142 of the Student's Book. Here they'll find an explanation of the grammar they've been studying and further exercises to practice it.

ANSWERS:

1
a is taking
b 's thinking
c 's listening
d has
e loves
f thinks
g looks
h knows
i 's planning
j seems

Speaking (SB page 67)

1

- **Groupwork.** Put the students in groups and ask them to look at the list of activities and decide which ones are good for the environment and which are bad. Go around, monitoring and giving help with any difficult vocabulary.
- When the students have finished, ask them to make a list of any other activities they can think of which are good or bad for the environment.
- In a feedback session, find out if there is consensus of opinion and encourage the groups to share their other suggestions with the class.

> **ANSWERS:**
>
> Good for the environment: a, c, g, i, k
> Bad for the environment: b, d, e, f, h, j, l

2

- Go through the instructions with the class and then ask them to work in the same groups. Tell them to follow the instructions to prepare their surveys. Go around, monitoring and giving help.
- When the students are ready, tell them to go around the class asking their questions and noting down the answers. When they write down the results of their survey in their groups, make sure each member takes a copy as they'll need this in the next section.

Writing (SB page 67)

You might like to discuss the various meanings of the word *green* as an introduction to this section. It can mean new and naïve (as in *He only recently joined the company and he's still very green*), as well as *concerned with protecting the environment*, the meaning used in this section.

1

- Go through the information in the box, pointing out the different expressions for referring to larger or smaller numbers of people.
- Focus attention on the Greenville survey and the title *How green are you?* If you haven't already done so, explain the meaning of *green* to the class. Ask the students to read the report and complete it with either *very green* or *not very green*.

> **ANSWER:**
>
> not very green

2

- Remind the students of the survey that they did in the previous section. Ask them to take the results of that survey and use it to rewrite the Greenville survey, making any changes that are necessary.
- Go around, monitoring and giving help. Ask several students (from different groups) to read out their reports and find out how green the class is.

Language note

Vocabulary: cycling / biking / bike riding

Cycling, biking, and *bike riding* all mean the same thing. In American English, *cycling* is often reserved for cycle racing, rather than for biking to work or for leisure.

Reading & Listening (SB page 68)

1

- Introduce the idea of projects involving volunteers that try to help people in other countries. Ask the students if it's common for people in their countries to do unpaid voluntary work, either at home or overseas.
- Ask the students to read the list of duties that people volunteer to do.
- Put the students into pairs to discuss which of the duties they feel they could and couldn't do and have a class feedback session on the most popular and least popular duties.
- Then ask the students to read the information from the website and match the duties to the projects. Point out that some of the duties aren't mentioned.

> **ANSWERS:**
>
> Project 1: e, g
> Project 2: a, b, d
> Project 3: c, h
> Not mentioned: f

Language note

Vocabulary: *Orphanage*

An orphanage (/ˈɔːf(ə)nɪdʒ/) is an institution where children with no parents live.

Cultural notes

Organic farming

Organic farming describes a method of farming that doesn't use artificial chemicals. It claims to be better for the environment as it doesn't use fossil fuels, and it's kinder to animals. Organic produce is growing in popularity in the USA. Many people believe organic food is healthier for you and some think it tastes better.

2 2.03

Tell the students that they're going to listen to Helen, a young woman who's going to volunteer to join one of the projects in Exercise 1, talking to a friend. Ask them to decide which project Helen is going to join.

> **ANSWER:**
>
> Project 2.

2.03

> **(H = Helen; F = Friend)**
> **H:** I've decided I'm going to change my life.
> **F:** Yeah, me too. I want a bigger house, a bigger salary, and a better boyfriend.
> **H:** No, I'm serious. I'm going to do something important.
> **F:** What do you mean?
> **H:** I want to help people less fortunate than me—I'm going to go abroad and work with children.
> **F:** Oh. Well, that's, uh ... Where are you going?
> **H:** Ethiopia.
> **F:** Ethiopia? What about the animals?
> **H:** No, I'm not going to work with animals—I want to help people.
> **F:** No, I mean the dangerous animals—crocodiles, lions, snakes, ...
> **H:** Oh, I see. I'm not just going there alone. I've joined an organization, and they're going to arrange everything for me. I'm going to work in an orphanage.
> **F:** Good for you. How much are they going to pay you?
> **H:** Nothing. I'm a volunteer. In fact, I'm going to pay them $25 a week.
> **F:** You're going to pay them. I see. When are you going?
> **H:** Soon—next month.
> **F:** Wow. How exciting! I'd love to visit South America.
> **H:** Africa. Ethiopia's in Africa.
> **F:** Oh, is it? There are a lot of dangerous animals in Africa.
> **H:** I told you, I'm not ...

3

Ask the students to listen to Helen again and to check the things she says she's going to do. After checking answers with the class put the students into pairs to talk about which projects they'd like to be involved with.

> **ANSWERS:**
>
> ✓: a, c, e

Grammar (SB page 68)

Future: *(be) going to*

1

Focus the students' attention on the information in the margin. Explain that *be going to* is one of the ways you can use to talk about the future, and that it's usually used to talk about decisions people have made about the future. Go through the examples and then ask the students to look at the incorrect sentences in the exercise and tell them to correct them.

> **ANSWERS:**
>
> **a** I'm going to change my life.
> **b** I'm not going to work with animals.
> **c** How much are they going to pay you?

Language notes

Grammar: (*be*) *going to*

- There's no future tense in English, but there are various ways of talking about the future including *(be) going to*, the present progressive, and *will*.
- *(be) going to* is the most common way to talk about future plans and intentions. It's usually used when you've already decided about a future action—you know what you're going to do.
- When *(be) going to* is used with *go*, it's often shortened. For example: *I'm going to go shopping* becomes *I'm going shopping*.
- *going to* is often written in an abbreviated form as *gonna* in pop songs. Encourage students to use the full form when doing their own writing.

2

Do this exercise with the class, but give all the students a chance to decide how the sentence should be completed before you ask for the answers.

> **ANSWERS:**
>
> **1** past **2** future

3

- **Pairwork.** Ask the students to work individually to write their questions. Go around, monitoring and giving help as they do this.
- Check answers with the class before putting the students into pairs to take turns asking and answering the questions.

ANSWERS:

a Are you going to drive home after the class?
b Are you going to watch TV this evening?
c Are you going to learn another foreign language one day?
d Are you going to buy any new clothes this weekend?
e Are you going to do anything interesting next week?
f Are you going to travel abroad next year?

Listening (SB page 69)

1 2.04

- Remind the students that in the last section they heard Helen talking to a friend about her plans to join a volunteer project. Elicit that she's going to Ethiopia to work in an orphanage. Ask the students what Helen's friend's reaction to the news was (surprised, uncomprehending, concerned). Ask them to predict what Helen's father's reaction will be when he hears Helen's news.
- Check that the students understand all the options in the sentences. Then play the recording and ask them to underline the ones that they think are correct.

ANSWERS:

a confident
b worried

2.04

(H = Helen; D = Dad)
D: Who's picking you up at the airport?
H: I told you, Dad.
D: I know, but I'm worried. Ethiopia's a long way from here.
H: OK. Let's go through it again. I'm arriving in Addis Ababa at ten o'clock in the morning, and the volunteers' coordinator is meeting me. That's Bob White. He's taking me to my accommodations.
D: And you're staying with a host family?
H: Yes, I'm staying with an Ethiopian family.
D: Don't you want to stay in a hotel?
H: No, I want to have an authentic experience, so I'm staying with the Odoi family.
D: You have to write down their name and address for me.
H: Yes, don't worry. Then, I'm starting work on Monday.
D: And where exactly are you working?
H: In a small town near Addis Ababa.
D: How are you getting there?
H: By bus. Mrs. Odoi's going to make sure I get the right bus.
D: When are you coming back?
H: On September 15. Just in time for your birthday.

2

- Go through the options with the class, then play the recording again and ask them to choose and underline the correct information.
- Check answers with the class. Then ask the students to give examples of situations in which their parents worry about them.

ANSWERS:

a a.m.	**d** Monday
b accommodations	**e** small
c Ethiopian	**f** dad's

Grammar (SB page 69)

Future: present progressive

1

- Remind the students about the use of *be going to* to talk about future decisions. Explain that the present progressive can also be used to talk about the future. It's generally used to talk about future arrangements. Focus attention on the information in the margin and read the example sentences aloud to the class or ask students to read them out.
- Focus attention on the sentences in Listening Exercise 2 and ask them if the explanation is true or false.

ANSWER:

True.

Language notes

Grammar: present progressive

- Using the present progressive is the most common way to talk about future arrangements. It's usually used when you've already made plans (with someone else) to do something in the future. Compare:
  I'm going to learn Chinese one day. (intention/decision)
  I'm seeing an old friend on Friday. (arrangement)
- The present progressive is often used with a time expression to make the future meaning clearer. *I'm having dinner with a friend this evening.*

2

- Remind the class that *(be) going to* is used to talk about decisions made about the future and the present progressive is used for future arrangements. Explain that sometimes the two overlap and both forms are possible. Focus attention on the two examples. Explain that in the first sentence both options are possible because the sentence describes both a decision that has been made about the future and an arrangement that has been made. However, in the second sentence, a decision to start guitar lessons has been made but no actual arrangement has been made, so the present progressive isn't possible. Point out that time expressions like *one day* and *one of these days* aren't sufficiently concrete to establish an arrangement.

- Ask the students to work in pairs and look at the remaining sentences. They should decide whether both options are possible or not. Check answers with the class. You may need to explain in sentence f) that the present progressive isn't possible because it's impossible to predict precisely the outcome of a tennis match, so even though the time expression suggests an arrangement, no arrangement is possible.
- Students tell their partner if any of the sentences are true for them.

ANSWERS:

a ✓	e ✗
b ✗	f ✗
c ✓	g ✓
d ✓	h ✗

3 Pairwork

- The pairwork exercise for this unit is on pages 122 and 127 of the Student's Book. Put the students into pairs and tell them who will be Student A, and who will be Student B.
- Take note of any errors which may need particular attention later, and also any examples of good language use which you can praise.

4 Grammar Extra 7, Part 2

Ask the students to turn to Grammar Extra 7, Part 2 on page 142 of the Student's Book. Here they'll find an explanation of the grammar they've been studying and further exercises to practice it.

ANSWERS:

1
a I'm going to join the Green Party.
b I'm going to start yoga classes.
c I'm going to get a better job.
d I'm not going to eat so much fast food.
e I'm going to change my hairstyle.
f I'm not going to watch so much TV.
g I'm going to give up smoking.
h I'm going to spend less time on the computer.

2
1 I'm going to the dentist.
2 I'm meeting Mom in town.
3 I'm having lunch with Vicky.
4 I'm playing tennis.
5 I'm picking up the children from school.
6 I'm having dinner with Tim.

Language for Life (SB page 70)

1 2.05

- Focus the students' attention on the picture and ask the students what they can see. Explain that the young man is Mo Finkelstein and that he's speaking on the phone to the receptionist at a big chemical company. Ask them to read the conversation and underline the most appropriate expressions to complete it.
- Play the recording for the students to check their answers. Explain that these choices are correct because they're more polite and more formal than the other options. On the phone, particularly when you're talking to strangers, more formal polite language is usually used.

ANSWERS:

1 Could I speak to the CEO, please?
2 Who's speaking?
3 I'll try to put you through.
4 I'm afraid Mr. Carr is out right now.
5 Would you like to leave a message?
6 Hold on a moment, please.

2 2.06

Ask the students to listen and repeat the useful phrases. Ask several students to repeat the words individually and make sure that they're using the correct pronunciation and intonation.

3

- **Pairwork.** Ask the students to practice the conversation, taking turns to be Mo and the receptionist. They may find it helpful to sit back to back so that they cannot see each other as they do this.

Life Skills (SB page 70)

Social responsibility: How green are you?

Climate change and "going green" are issues debated by world leaders and scientists nowadays. Point out that the focus of this lesson is on how we as individuals can address the problem and make our homes "green".

1 2.07

- Ask the students what they do in their daily lives to help the environment. For example, do they recycle waste, car-pool (group of car owners agree to travel together to work, school, etc.), use eco friendly products?
- Explain that they will listen to an interview with an expert on what we can do to have "green" homes. Before playing the recording, ask the students to predict what the interviewee will say and write the students' predictions on the board.

- Refer the students to the question and point out that they are only writing the issue for now, i.e. what the problem is in each room.
- Play the recording once, ask students to check in pairs and play the recording a second time if necessary.
- Ask some pairs to report back to the class with their answers.

> **ANSWERS:**
>
> Living room: TV on standby
> Bedroom: window is open when the heating is on
> Bathroom: run the tap when brushing your teeth
> Kitchen: fruit and vegetables from the supermarket

2.07

(Pr = Presenter)

Pr: Today, we're talking green issues, we are here at my home, with our resident expert, Phil. Hi, Phil, how are you today?

Phil: I'm good. Today, I want to talk about your home. You may think you are very green – recycling your garbage, for example, but there is so much more you can do. I'm going to pick on you Katy, if that's OK.

Pr: Er, sure!

Phil: Let's go into your living room. Is your TV on standby?

Pr: Yes, the red light is on. I always turn it off when I'm not watching it.

Phil: But it's still on if it's on standby, and it's still using electricity. To save energy we have to turn it off completely.

Pr: Oh, okay.

Phil: Let's go into the bedroom. Is the window open?

Pr: Yes, it gets really stuffy in here...

Phil: And the heating is on?

Pr: Ah, I see...wasting more energy.

Phil: Exactly. And in the bathroom, do you run the tap when you are brushing your teeth?

Pr: Er, sometimes?

Phil: Up to 14 liters of water comes out every minute! We waste a lot of water.

Pr: You're making me feel really bad. Finally, we're in the kitchen.

Phil: I guess the fruit and vegetable are from the supermarket?

Pr: Yes. What's wrong with that?

Phil: Nothing. But if you buy from local markets you only buy local produce–just think of all the gas used to transport melons from another continent?

Pr: You got me again...

2

- **Pairwork.** Refer the students to the question and ask them to discuss possible actions with a partner. If students cannot think of any, ask them to look at the issues listed in Exercise 1 and think of alternative solutions. For example, kitchen: grow your own vegetables.
- Ask the pairs to share their ideas with the rest of the class and write these on the board.

3

- Refer the students to the question and focus their attention on the actions listed on the board.
- Set the students in small groups and ask each group to choose one action they think is the most practical.
- Then ask one spokesperson from each group to tell the rest of the class which action they are going to take to be more environmentally aware. Challenge stronger students by asking them to explain why their group chose this action over others.

Vocabulary Extra (SB page 71)

Environmental problems and solutions

1

Focus the students' attention on the pictures and ask them to match the pictures with the phrases.

> **ANSWERS:**
>
> 9 a carbon footprint
> 1 environmentally friendly products
> 7 global warming
> 6 mass-produced clothes
> 2 organic vegetables
> 5 a plastic container
> 4 public transportation
> 3 a recycling bin
> 8 renewable energy

2

Focus attention on the table and point out that global warming is a problem for the world, and organic vegetables represent a solution to the problem of introducing too many chemicals into the environment. Ask the students to categorize the other expressions from Exercise 1 as either problems or solutions. Encourage them to say what problems the various solutions apply to.

ANSWERS:

Problems: global warming , a carbon footprint, mass-produced clothes, a plastic container
Solutions: organic vegetables, environmentally friendly products, public transportation, a recycling bin, renewable energy

Focus on *have* and *have got*

The use of *have* or *have got* for talking about possession is largely a matter of personal taste, with *have got* being slightly more common in British English. The forms are manipulated in slightly different ways. *Have got* can only be used when talking about possession.

1

- Go through this exercise with the class, eliciting the correct words to fill the gaps. Explain that when *have/has* means to *own* or *possess*, you can also use *have/has got*.

ANSWERS:

a Do you have a car? Yes, I do. No, I don't.
b Have you got a car? Yes, I have. No, I haven't.
1 have/has
2 have/has got

2

Go through the example with the class and then ask the students write the remaining questions. Check answers before putting them into pairs to take turns asking and answering the questions.

ANSWERS:

a Have you got any brothers and sisters?
b Have you got more than one credit card?
c Have you got a pet?
d Have you got a headache?
e Has your mother got the same eyes as you?
f Has your father got any hobbies?

3

Look at the example with the class and elicit how sentence a) would be formed using *have got* instead of *have* (*Have you got a laptop?*). Ask the students to look at the remaining sentences and decide whether *have/has got* could be used in them. When checking answers, if students say that *have/has got* can be used, ask them to produce the sentence. When you've finished, get the students to write down the sentences with *have got*.

ANSWERS:

✓: a, c, d, e
a Have you got a laptop?
c My mother has got short, gray hair.
d I haven't got a smart TV.
e Have you got any children?

Writing

Workbook page 31

Linking sentences with *because*, *as*, *since*.

Making written suggestions.

Further Practice Material

Need more classroom practice activities?
Photocopiable resource materials in the Teacher's Presentation Kit / Extra Resources

Need more tests?
Test Generator
Teacher's Presentation Kit / Extra Resources / Tests

Need more on important teaching concepts?
Key concepts in *American Inside Out Evolution* pages xxi-xxxvii

Need student self-study practice?
Workbook pages 28–31

Need more information and ideas?
American Inside Out Evolution website www.macmillan.com.br/americaninsideoutevolution

Need to check what your students can do by the end of this unit?
Self-evaluation checklists on pages xxxix-xliii

8 Education *Overview*

Section	Aims	What the students are doing
Reading SB page 72	Reading for detail	Reading about a trainee circus performer and identifying true and false statements. Talking about their families' hopes for their future.
Vocabulary SB page 73	Education and training	Completing sentences with words from the Reading section. Discussing whether statements are true for their country.
Pronunciation SB page 73	Stress in school subjects	Saying names of school subjects with correct stress. Discussing their attitudes to school subjects.
Speaking: anecdote SB page 73	Fluency practice	Listening and underlining the correct information. Talking about favorite school subjects.
Reading SB page 74	Reading for gist and detail	Discussing how electronic devices have changed. Answering questions about the text. Talking about how life has changed over the generations.
Grammar SB page 75	*could* for permission and obligation	Completing a table with *can* and *have to*. Completing questions and answers. Discussing permission and obligation in their school or college.
Listening SB page 75	Listening for gist	Identifying topics discussed in a conversation. Writing sentences about then and now. Talking about permission and obligation in their own countries.
Reading & Listening SB page 76	Reading for detail Listening for main ideas	Offering and accepting advice for "meeting the parents." Labeling comments with advice. Listening and identifying the advice the person follows.
Vocabulary SB page 76	Words from a text	Completing sentences with words from a text. Discussing sentences with a partner.
Grammar SB page 77	*should* and *must* for advice	Matching phrases with meanings. Completing sentences with should and must.
Reading & Speaking SB page 77	Reading for detail Fluency practice	Completing advice on being the perfect romantic partner. Discussing the advice with a partner.
Language for Life SB page 78	Useful conversational phrases for giving opinions	Identifying topics from a conversation. Completing sentences from the conversation. Listening to and practicing useful phrases. Putting phrases for agreeing and disagreeing in order. Rewriting statements to show their own opinions.
Life Skills SB page 78	Giving advice: Education options	Listening to a conversation and listing decisions the speakers have to make. Writing down the advice they would give the speakers, then role-playing the advice.
Vocabulary Extra SB page 79	Review of words from the unit: education stages; words used with education	Matching pictures with stages of education. Comparing the stages with those in their countries. Describing their own education. Completing questions about education and discussing them.

8 Education *Teacher's notes*

Warm-up

Write the word *school* on the board and ask the students to think back to their first day at school. What can they remember about it? Start them off by telling them about your first day at school (or a memorable incident in your early school years).

Reading (SB page 72)

1

- Focus the students' attention on the picture and ask them what they can see (*a circus, circus performers / acrobats*). Ask the students if they would like to work in a circus. Why? / Why not?
- Tell the students they are going to read the blog quickly to find just one piece of information and refer them to the scan question. Set this as a timed reading competition (30 seconds). Check the answer with the class / Ask students for the answer.

ANSWER:

(At the end of the month Kim will become) a circus acrobat.

2

- Explain that the students are going to read more slowly this time and answer some true or false questions.
- Focus the students' attention on the statements and go over any new vocabulary as needed.
- Have the students complete the task individually then ask them to check their answers with a partner before whole class feedback.
- Go through the answers as a whole class and then ask the students to correct the false statements and write them on the board.

ANSWERS:

a False. She is training to be an acrobat.
b False. She studies in a classroom.
c False. Frannie has to pass an exam and sings in the morning.
d True.
e True.
f False. She will officially be a circus acrobat.

3

- Focus the students' attention on the fact that her parents did not want her to be an acrobat. Ask them if they would want their children to work in a circus.
- Refer the students to the question and example in the Student's Book. You might want to demonstrate the task by telling the students about your own personal experience.
- **Pairwork.** Ask the students to tell each other about what their parents wanted them to study and what they chose to do. Go around, monitoring and giving help as needed.
- Wrap up the task by asking a few students to share their experiences with the rest of the class, and whether they were right (not) to follow their parents' advice.
- Time permitting, extend the task by asking the class to discuss to what extent parents and family should get involved in their children's career decisions.

Vocabulary (SB page 73)

1

Tell the students that the words they need to complete the sentences are all in the text on page 72. They should use the line references to locate them

ANSWERS:

a training	**d** move	**g** exam
b spend	**e** cost	**h** role
c study	**f** take	

2

Groupwork. If you have a multinational class, put students from the same country in the same group. Ask the students to discuss whether the statements in Exercise 1 are true for their country or not, and then report back to the class on their decisions.

Pronunciation (SB page 73)

1 2.08

- Focus the students' attention on the table and remind the students that the large circles show stressed syllables and the small circles unstressed syllables.
- Play the recording and ask the students to listen and repeat the school subjects.
- When they've done this chorally, ask individual students to repeat the subjects. Check that everyone understands them. Find out which subjects the students study or studied at school.

2

- **Pairwork.** Go through the categories with the class and then put the students into pairs to discuss and categorize the school subjects in Exercise 1.
- Ask some pairs to report back to the class about what they decided.

Speaking: anecdote (SB page 73)

1 2.09

- Ask the students to look at the picture. Explain that Andy, the man in the picture, is going to talk about his favorite school subject.
- Go through the questions and the answer choices with the class. Explain any unknown vocabulary and ask the students to listen and underline the answers Andy gives.
- Check answers with the class and ask them whether their art classes are/were as enjoyable as Andy's.

ANSWERS:

a Art
b I was good at it
c Ms. Lewis
d had long, black hair and wore bright colors
e interesting and varied
f three
g still love taking pictures

2.09

I wasn't very academic at school, but I loved art. Yes, art was my favorite subject because I was good at it. We had a wonderful teacher—her name was Ms. Lewis, and I remember the first day she arrived at school. She didn't look like a teacher. She had long, black hair, and she wore bright colors. She was pretty young—thirty, thirty-one, something like that, and we all fell in love with her—boys and girls! She wasn't just beautiful—she was a really good teacher, too. Her classes were interesting and varied. We only had three hours of art each week, on Wednesday afternoons. Ms. Lewis loved photography and she taught us how to develop our own pictures. I really enjoyed that, and for a while I wanted to be a professional photographer. In the end, I realized that it was difficult to make a living as a photographer, so I went to college and studied engineering. But I still love taking pictures, and recently I won a competition—Ms. Lewis would be proud of me!

2

- Give the students a minute or two to decide what they're going to talk about. Then ask them to look at the questions in Exercise 1 again and decide how they'd answer them about the school subject they're going to talk about. Allow them to make notes on what they're going to say and how they're going to say it, but discourage them from writing a paragraph that they can simply read out. Go around, monitoring and giving help.
- **Pairwork.** Put the students into pairs and ask them to take turns telling their partner about their favorite school subject. Encourage them to ask each other follow-up questions to get further information.
- Ask some pairs to report back to the class about what they found out about their partners.

Reading (SB page 74)

1

- Focus the students' attention on the picture and ask them what they can see (*a TV set*). Ask the students if it is new or old (*old*) and how they know (*the dials, the screen, the size*).
- Ask them to look at the list of items and say how these have changed from when they were at school. Lead this as a whole class discussion, eliciting technology-related vocabulary (e.g. laptops, high-definition televisions, smart phones).
- Refer the students to the introduction and ask them if they are surprised by the results. Then ask the students to read the comments quickly and decide if any of these are similar to their own views. Point out that there is no right or wrong answer and that they are only skimming for gist at this point.
- After the students have read, ask them to share their findings.

2

- Explain that the students are now going to read the comments more closely and slowly. Focus their attention on the comprehension questions and deal with any difficult vocabulary.
- Ask the students to complete the task individually and then check the answers with the whole class. Ask the students to say where they found the information.

ANSWERS:

a They didn't have computers or the internet.
b They could only take out 6 books at a time / to make notes.
c He had to leave school and get a job.
d Tuition fees
e To be able to buy ink and paper.
f She had to help around the house (and get married young).

3

- Ask the students if any of the comments surprised them.
- **Pairwork.** Put the students into pairs and ask them to discuss the question. Encourage them to use the vocabulary from the comments (e.g. *generation gap, freedom, college, tuition, etc* ...)
- Wrap up the task by asking by asking several pairs to share their opinions in a whole class discussion on whether life is easier / better now than in the past.

Grammar (SB page 75)

could and *had to*

1

- Go through the information in the box with the class and explain the difference between *permission* (you're allowed to do something) and *obligation* (you're required to do something). Point out that the negative forms of *have to* mean *lack of obligation* rather than *prohibition*. Ask several students to read out the example sentences.
- Focus attention on the table and ask the students to complete it with the correct forms of *can* and *have to*.

ANSWERS:

1 can	**5** have to
2 could	**6** had to
3 can't	**7** don't have to
4 couldn't	**8** didn't have to

Language notes

Grammar: could

- *Could* is a modal verb. In this unit, *could* is used to talk generally about permission in the past (i.e. that you were allowed to do something over a period of time in the past).
- As with all other modal verbs, *could* is followed by the infinitive (without *to*), and doesn't use *do/did* to form questions and negative statements. *Could you smoke at school?* (i.e. *Were you allowed to smoke?*) *No, we couldn't. It was against the rules.* (i.e. *We weren't allowed to smoke.*)

Grammar: have to

- *Have to* is used to talk about obligation/ necessity (i.e. you're required to do something).
- *Have/had to* is followed by the infinitive. You use *do/did* to form questions and negative statements. *Did you have to do homework every day?* (i.e. *Was it necessary to do homework every day?*) *No, we didn't have to do it every day. Three times a week, usually.* (i.e. *It wasn't necessary to do it every day.*)

2 2.10

- Go through the example with the class and then ask the students to work individually to complete the other sentences. Go around, monitoring and giving help.
- Play the recording for students to check their answers and repeat the sentences, before asking them to check with the text on page 74 and choose the correct answers to the questions.

2.10

ANSWERS:

a Did Allie have to go to the library?
<u>Yes, she did</u>. / No, she didn't.
b Could Allie take out eight books?
Yes, she could. / <u>No, she couldn't</u>.
c Did Allie have to write with pen and paper?
<u>Yes, she did</u>. / No, she didn't.
d Did Aldo have to leave school to get a job?
<u>Yes, he did</u>. / No, he didn't.
e Could Aldo get a job?
<u>Yes, he could</u>. / No, he couldn't.
f Could Laura's mom go to college?
Yes, she could. / <u>No, she couldn't</u>.

3

- Go through the example with the class and demonstrate how the questions need to be altered to make them suitable for asking other members of the class.
- **Pairwork.** Put the students into pairs to take turns asking and answering the questions.

4 Pairwork

- The pairwork exercise for this unit is on pages 123 and 128 of the Student's Book. Put the students into pairs and tell them who will be Student A, and who will be Student B.
- While they're doing the exercise, go around, monitoring and giving help. Take note of any errors which may need particular attention later, and also any examples of good language use which you can praise.

5 Grammar Extra, Part 1

Ask the students to turn to Grammar Extra 8, Part 1 on page 144 of the Student's Book. Here they'll find an explanation of the grammar they've been studying and further exercises to practice it.

ANSWERS:

1

a I didn't have to make my bed every morning.
b I couldn't wear whatever I wanted.
c I didn't have to keep my room neat and clean.
d I didn't have to help my parents at home.
e I didn't have to travel everywhere by bicycle.
f I couldn't invite friends home on weekends.
g I couldn't stay out after 10:00 p.m.
h I couldn't play my music as loud as I wanted.

2

a Did you have to make your bed every morning?
b Could you wear whatever you wanted?
c Did you have to keep your room neat and clean?
d Did you have to help your parents at home?
e Did you have to travel everywhere by bicycle?
f Could you invite friends home on weekends?
g Could you stay out after 10:00 p.m?
h Could you play your music as loud as you wanted?

Listening (SB page 75)

1 2.11

Focus the students' attention on the pictures. Play the recording and ask the students to note which of the topics Aldo and Paulie talk about.

ANSWERS:

They talk about: road travel, money, military service, appearance, air travel.

2.11

(A = Aldo; P = Paulie)

P: Buckle up, Grandpa.

A: All these rules and regulations. In my day, we didn't have to wear seatbelts at all.

P: And it was much more dangerous.

A: But we didn't drive so fast. And there weren't so many cars on the road. In my day, we couldn't drive fast because there weren't any highways.

P: I thought you drove a horse and cart in your day.

A: Hmm, very funny. Actually, I had a beautiful motorcycle—a Harley Davidson—and I didn't have to wear a helmet. Not like nowadays.

P: Do you really think life was better in your day, Grandpa?

A: Well, life was less complicated. For example, we didn't have all these credit cards in my day. We had to use cash to buy things.

P: But not everything was better, Grandpa. You had to do military service—I wouldn't like that.

A: I was proud to do military service. In my day, a man had to be a man. Not like these days—men and women look exactly the same to me. In my day, you couldn't have long hair, or wear earrings like some men do nowadays.

P: Ha-ha. But some things were more difficult in your day, Grandpa—like traveling.

A: That's right, we couldn't travel by plane like you do today—it was too expensive. But we traveled by train and bus. I remember the first time I went to Louisiana ...

2

- Go through the example with the class and emphasize the different forms of the verbs for "then" and "now."
- Ask the students to work individually to write sentences for the other prompts. Go around, monitoring and giving help.
- Play the recording again for the students to check and amend their answers if necessary. Then check answers with the class.

ANSWERS:

a Now: You have to wear a seatbelt.
Then: You didn't have to wear a seatbelt.
b Now: You have to wear a helmet.
Then: You didn't have to wear a helmet.
c Now: You don't have to use cash.
Then: You had to use cash.
d Now: You don't have to do military service.
Then: You had to do military service.
e Now: You can have long hair.
Then: You couldn't have long hair.
f Now: You can wear earrings.
Then: You couldn't wear earrings.

3

Elicit a few changes from the class and write them on the board before you put the students into pairs to discuss the differences. In multinational classes it may be helpful to have pairs of students from the same country. Encourage them to think of any other differences between then and now and to report back to the class.

Reading & Listening (SB page 76)

1

- Ask the students if they would like to tell the class about a situation in which they met a girlfriend's/boyfriend's parents for the first time.
- Explain the situation and tell them that they have to decide which of the pieces of advice is most important. Ask them to discuss this in pairs and report back to the class.

Language note

Vocabulary: *make a good first impression*

If you make a good first impression on someone, you make that person notice and admire you as soon as they meet you.

2

- Ask the students to read the comments and label each one with a hashtag from Exercise 1.
- Check answers with the class and ask them for ideas about any other advice to give.

ANSWERS:

1 b) #tellthetruth
2 c) #rightclothes
3 d) #NoControversialTopics
4 e) #research
5 a) #goodfirstimpression
6 f) #beprepared

Language note

Vocabulary: hashtag

A **hashtag** (#) is a type of symbol or "tag" used on social networks, e.g. Twitter, so users can find messages with a specific theme easily.

3 2.12

- Tell the students that they're going to hear the young man in the picture meeting his girlfriend's parents for the first time. Ask them to check the advice he follows and put an *X* next to the advice he doesn't follow.
- Allow the students to compare notes in pairs before checking answers. You may need to play the recording more than once. Then ask them as a class to suggest ideas about how the evening continued.

ANSWERS:

a ✓ b ✗ c ✓ d ✗ e ✓ f ✓

2.12

(L = Liza; M = Mike; J = John; A = Anne)

L: This is my mom, and this is my dad.
M: Hello, Mrs. Wilson ... Mr. Wilson.
J: Nice to meet you, Mike. Please call us John and Anne.
A: Come in. Have a seat.
J: That's a very nice suit. Have you come straight from work?
M: Oh, no, I usually wear jeans at work!
J: Oh ... what do you do?
M: Ah, er, I'm a, um, sort of interior design consultant.
L: He works in a furniture store.
A: Oh, that's nice. Um, Liza tells us you were in France recently.
M: Yes, that's right, I went to Paris last month.
A: Nice. Did you like it?
M: Well, it's a beautiful city, but the people were very rude.
A: Oh. Did you know John's mother's from Paris?
M: Oh, no, I didn't. I'm sorry. I didn't mean ... um ...
J: Don't worry, my mother's very rude, too. ... Now, Mike, would you like a beer?
M: Yes, please. Oh, is that a picture of Liza when she was younger?
J: Yes, she was ten here. Would you like to see some more pictures?
L: Oh, Dad!
M: Oh, yes, please, er ... John.
A: OK, John, you get the photo albums out, and I'll talk to Mike. So, Mike, what are you going to do in the future?
M: Well, in my free time, I'm studying at college ...

Vocabulary (SB page 76)

1

- Remind the students that the words and phrases in the box come from the comments on this page.
- Ask the students to work individually to complete the sentences with the items in the box. Then allow them to compare with a partner.

ANSWERS:

a common **c** career
b effort **d** share

2

Pairwork. Ask the students to discuss whether the sentences are true for them. Invite them to report back to the class.

Grammar (SB page 77)

should and *must*

1

- Read out the sentences in the margin with *should* and *must*. Then focus the students' attention on the matching exercise.
- Allow the students to work in pairs to match the sentences and their meanings. Go around, monitoring and giving help. Then check answers with the class and ask them to choose the correct alternative in the sentence.

ANSWERS:

a 4 **b** 1 **c** 2 **d** 3

When you are giving advice, *must* is stronger than *should*.

Language notes

Grammar: *should*

- *should* is a modal verb. In this unit, should is used to give advice.
  A: I don't feel good.
  B: You should see a doctor.
- As with all other modal verbs, *should* is followed by the infinitive (without *to*), and doesn't use *do/ did* to form negative statements. Note that the negative form is usually contracted (*shouldn't* NOT ~~*should not*~~), except in formal writing. *You shouldn't smoke. It's bad for you.*

Grammar: *must*

- In this unit, *must* is used to give advice which is stronger and more authoritative than using *should*.
- As with all other modal verbs, *must* is followed by the infinitive (without *to*), and doesn't use *do/did* to form negative statements. Note that the negative form is usually used only in writing and is usually contracted (*mustn't* NOT ~~*must not*~~), except in formal writing. *You mustn't smoke in a gas station.*

2

- Go through the sentences with the class. Point out that the choice of *should* or *must* depends largely on the importance of the situation in which the advice is given or the status of the person giving it. Ask them to decide which situations require *must* and which *should*.
- Ask the students to complete the sentences. Check answers with the class, then put the students into pairs to discuss situations where they've heard similar sentences.

ANSWERS:

a should do
b must do
c must hold
d mustn't forget
e must speak (or should speak)
f shouldn't watch (or mustn't watch)

3 Grammar Extra 8, Part 2

Ask the students to turn to Grammar Extra 8, Part 2 on page 144 of the Student's Book. Here they'll find an explanation of the grammar they've been studying and further exercises to practice it.

ANSWERS:

1
a should **b** should **c** shouldn't **d** must **e** should **f** shouldn't **g** must

2

a a co-worker	**e** an old man
b a doctor	**f** a best friend
c a teenage boy	**g** an airport announcer
d a parent	

Reading & Speaking (SB page 77)

1

Ask the students for a couple of ideas about what they think the perfect girlfriend or boyfriend would be like. Ask them to read the webpage. Then ask the students to work in pairs and complete the text with the words in the box. Go around, monitoring and giving help.

2 2.13

Play the recording for the students to check their answers to Exercise 1. Then have a class discussion about whether or not they agree with the advice. Elicit ideas about what makes a successful date and put them on the board. (If the subject of dating is too sensitive an issue in your class, choose one of the subjects from the extra activity below instead.)

ANSWERS:

1 clothes	**4** funny
2 stomach	**5** work
3 directions	

Extra activity

Work with a partner. Choose one of the following topics and write three pieces of advice.

- How to be the perfect neighbor
- How to give a great party
- How to stay in shape

Language for Life (SB page 78)

1 2.14

- Focus the students' attention on the illustration. Explain that the students are going to hear a conversation between the women in the picture. Go through the list of topics and ask the students to try to predict which ones they'll talk about.
- Play the recording for them to listen to and check the topics mentioned. Check answers before going to the next exercise.

ANSWERS:

a Taking care of children ✓
c Marriage ✓
d Leaving home ✓

2.14

(W1 = Woman 1; W2 = Woman 2)
W1: How are your children?
W2: Oh, Jenny's great. She's a dentist now.
W1: Oh, very good.
W2: Yes, it's a good job, but I don't think she should work.
W1: Oh, why?
W2: Well, her son's only three. I think mothers should stay at home and take care of the children.
W1: Oh, yes, I agree. I think children need their mothers at home.
W2: Absolutely. My daughter thinks fathers should stay at home and take care of the children.
W1: Oh, no, I don't agree with that. It's a woman's job.
W2: Exactly. Now, what about your son? Is he married yet?
W1: No, but he's living with his girlfriend.
W2: Oh. I don't think couples should live together before they get married.
W1: Oh, I'm not so sure. I don't think my son's ready to get married.
W2: No, he's like my Sam. He's thirty-six and he's still living at home.
W1: Really? I think young people should leave home when they're eighteen.
W2: Well, it depends. Sam can't afford to leave home.
W1: Well, when we were young ...

2

- Ask the students to work in pairs and discuss how they think each of the sentences should be completed.
- Play the recording again for them to listen and check their answers. Focus the students' attention on the language for expressing opinions and for agreeing and disagreeing with someone else's opinion.

ANSWERS:

a I think
b I think
c My daughter thinks
d I don't think
e I think

3 2.15

Ask the students to listen and repeat the useful phrases.

4

Put the diagram on the board and ask the students to call out their answers or come to the board and put the phrases in the correct place.

ANSWERS:

Agree - Absolutely. - Oh, yes, I agree. - Well, it depends. - Oh, I'm not so sure. - Oh, no, I don't agree with that. - Disagree

5

Ask the students to work individually to rewrite the statements according to their own opinions. Then put them into pairs to compare notes and discuss the statements.

Life Skills (SB page 78)
Giving advice: Education options

Explain that going to college is a big decision for students and that they have to think carefully before making a decision. It is common to ask for advice from family, counselors, and friends. This lesson focuses on problems and advice regarding education options. Before starting the task, ask the students what kind of problems young people might have when making decisions about their college education.

1 2.16

- Focus the students' attention on the rubric and point out that they are only making short notes on the decisions that the three friends have to make.
- Play the recording once and ask the students to check their answers in pairs. Play the recording again if necessary.
- Ask several students to share their answers with the rest of the class. Write these on the board. Ask the students to explain what helped them understand.

ANSWERS:

1 Susie
Decision 1: what to study (Art History or Business)
Decision 2: what to take (take belongings or buy there)
2 Robbie
Decision 1: where to study (in state or out of state)
Decision 2: where to live (on campus or in the city)
3 Katie
Decision 1: go to college or get a job
Decision 2: how to pay for college (parents or a loan)

2.16

(S = Susie; R = Robbie; K = Katy)

S: It's so hard to know what to do.
R: I know. I still don't know if I should attend college in the state, or go out of state where it's more expensive but possibly a better experience.
S: I can't decide what to study. I really enjoy art history but I think business is going to be more useful. Do you choose something you enjoy or something that will help you get a job?
R: Right. Then I have to decide where to live. Should I try to get a place on campus, or should I stay in the city?
S: You also need to decide what to take? My brother took so much stuff. Or should I take a couple of bags and buy stuff when I get there? How about you, Katy?
K: All of this is very confusing. I'm not sure if I want to go to college. Maybe should I try to get a job? And I'm not sure how we're going to pay for college. Should I ask my parents to pay, or should I take out student loans? I'm not sure what is best...
S: Yeah, it's hard. We really need to get some good advice.

2

- Refer the students to the rubric and then to the problems listed on the board. Before starting the task, elicit from the students different ways of giving advice and write these on the board, e.g. *you should ..., why don't you ..., how about ...,* Give the students a few minutes to choose one problem and write down one piece of advice. Stronger students can choose more than one problem.
- Go through the problems on the board one at a time and ask the students to offer their advice. Compare solutions where students have chosen the same problem. Encourage the students to use different expressions when giving advice.

3

- **Pairwork.** Give the students some time to prepare what they are going to say before starting the task.
- Put the students into pairs and tell them they should swap roles. Time permitting, have the pairs change partners so they are working with a new student and can practice a new dialogue. Go around, monitoring and giving help and monitoring.
- Wrap up by asking a few pairs to perform their dialogue for the class.

Vocabulary Extra (SB page 79)

Stages of education

1

- Focus the students' attention on the pictures and look at the list of stages. Read these aloud and ask the students to match them to the pictures.
- Check answers with the class, and explain any new vocabulary.

ANSWERS:

1 Age 14–18 ...
4 Age 3–4 ...
5 Age 18+ ...
3 Age 5 ...
2 Age 21+ ...
6 Age 11 ...
7 Age 21+ ...

2

In single-nationality classes, put the students into pairs and ask them to discuss the question and report back to the class. In multinational classrooms, have a class discussion with people from different countries volunteering information.

3

Give the students a few minutes to think about their own education and to decide how they would describe it. Allow them to make notes but discourage them from writing a script. Then ask several students to describe their education to the class.

Focus on words used with education

1

- Allow the students to work in pairs to complete the sentences.
- Check answers and explain any difficult vocabulary.

ANSWERS:

a go	**d** many	**g** taken
b elementary	**e** apply	**h** fail
c leave	**f** study	

2

Ask the students to answer the questions individually and then compare their answers with a partner. Encourage them to report back to the class any particularly interesting information.

Further Practice Material

Need more classroom practice activities?
Photocopiable resource materials in the Teacher's Presentation Kit / Extra Resources

Need more tests?
Test Generator
Teacher's Presentation Kit / Extra Resources / Tests

Need more on important teaching concepts?
Key concepts in *American Inside Out Evolution* pages xxi-xxxvii

Need student self-study practice?
Workbook pages 32–35

Need more information and ideas?
American Inside Out Evolution website www.macmillan.com.br/americaninsideoutevolution

Need to check what your students can do by the end of this unit?
Self-evaluation checklists on pages xxxix-xliii

9 Smile *Overview*

Section	Aims	What the students are doing
Reading SB page 80	Reading for detail	Discussing smiling for photographs. Reading and completing a post about smiling.
Vocabulary SB page 80	The face	Matching adjectives with parts of the face. Discussing facial features that they like.
Reading SB page 81	Reading for gist	Making guesses about what people are like. Matching photos to conversations. Matching descriptions to people they know.
Vocabulary SB page 81	Character adjectives	Repeating adjectives and matching them with their meanings. Listening and choosing adjectives to describe six people. Doing a personality test.
Reading SB page 82	Reading for detail	Reading survey results and drawing a conclusion. Writing true sentences about themselves and comparing them with a partner.
Grammar & Vocabulary SB page 82	Verb patterns	Underlining the correct structures in sentences. Writing more true sentences about themselves.
Reading & Speaking SB page 83	Fluency practice	Describing their country. Completing a text about Thailand and discussing vacation destinations.
Listening SB page 83	Listening for specific information	Completing statements about vacations with the correct names. Writing true sentences about classmates.
Listening SB page 84	Listening for specific information	Identifying people's jobs from a podcast. Identifying true and false statements. Talking about countries they'd like to live in.
Grammar SB page 84	Present perfect: simple & progressive; *for*, *since*, and *been*	Completing sentences with *for* or *since* and completing a table. Studying the use of *been*. Writing true sentences about their own experiences and comparing them in pairs.
Grammar SB page 85	Present perfect: simple & progressive	Studying the form and use of the present perfect. Completing sentences with the present perfect: simple and progressive. Asking and answering questions with *How long ...?*
Pronunciation SB page 85	Sentence stress	Underlining stressed words in sentences. Listening to and repeating a chant.
Speaking SB page 85	Fluency practice	Talking about how long they have known people, been going to places, etc.
Language for Life SB page 86	Useful body idioms	Reading conversations and underlining the correct alternatives. Matching phrases with their meanings and writing a conversation.
Life Skills SB page 86	Collecting information: *Have you ever ...?*	Completing a form with things they want to experience. Writing questions and interviewing classmates.
Vocabulary Extra SB page 87	Parts of the body, verbs + *ing*-form or *to*-infinitive	Matching pictures with words. Choosing the correct alternatives and completing a table. Writing their own examples.
Writing WB page 39		Listing points. Using adverbs of attitude. Writing a travel blog.

9 Smile *Teacher's notes*

Warm-up

Write on the board: What's the longest word in the English language? Give the students a minute or two to make suggestions. Then write the word *smiles* on the board and ask why this might be the longest word. (Because there's a mile between the first and last letters.)

Reading (SB page 80)

1

- Focus the students' attention on the speech bubble. Ask the students to discuss the questions in groups. You'll need to check that they know the answer to the first one (they say it when they want people to smile for a photograph) before they go on to answer the others.
- In a multinational class, you may get several answers to the second question. Ask the students to write the words used in their language up on the board. Then let them all take a turn saying them. Find out which one produces the best smile.

2

- Give the students time to look at the picture and the facial features that are labeled.
- Ask the students to read the rubric and point out that the first gap is done for them. Encourage the students to guess the missing word from the context before looking at the word box.
- Ask the students to read the article and complete it with words for facial features from the picture. Allow them to compare their answers in pairs or small groups before checking with the class.

ANSWERS:

1 tooth	**4** wrinkles	**7** eyebrows
2 cheeks	**5** dimples	
3 eyes	**6** mouth	

3

Put the students into pairs to practice doing all the smiles. Choose any particularly talented students to demonstrate their smiles to the class. Ask the others to guess what kind of smile they are doing.

Vocabulary (SB page 80)

1

Ask the students to work individually to match the adjectives to the features. Then let them compare their results in pairs before checking with the class.

ANSWERS:

a 2 **b** 6 **c** 5 **d** 3 **e** 1 **f** 4

2

Groupwork. Ask the students to discuss the question in groups and then report back to the class. Find out how much agreement there is within the class about features liked on a man and on a woman.

3 Pairwork

- The pairwork exercise for this unit is on pages 123 and 128 of the Student's Book. Put the students into pairs and tell them who will be Student A, and who will be Student B.
- While they're doing the exercise, go around, monitoring and giving help. Take note of any errors which may need particular attention later, and also any examples of good language use which you can praise.

ANSWERS:

Picture 1
Student A: the man has straight, blond hair and thin eyebrows.
Student B: the man has curly, dark hair and thick eyebrows.
Picture 2
Student A: the woman has long, blonde hair, blue eyes, and dimples.
Student B: the woman has short, blonde hair, green eyes, and no dimples.
Picture 3
Student A: the woman has big, brown eyes and full lips.
Student B: the woman has big, blue eyes and thin lips.
Picture 4
Student A: the man has some black/crooked teeth and wrinkles on his forehead and cheeks.
Student B: the man has straight, white teeth and no wrinkles.

Extra activity

Get the students to describe the people shown in the pictures in other units of the book.

Reading (SB page 81)

1 2.18

- Focus the students' attention on the conversation boxes and explain that the students are going to listen to two people describing the pictures and they should match the photos with the conversation.

- Play the recording and encourage stronger students to cover the scripts while they listen.
- Play the recording a second time if necessary. Then nominate for answers and ask the students to explain what helped them understand.

ANSWERS:			
4a	1b	2c	3d

2

- Focus the students' attention on the task and demonstrate the activity by describing a member of your family and matching their smile to one of the smiles in Exercise 2. Show a picture of your family member if possible.
- **Groupwork.** Put the students in small groups and ask them to describe a member of their family or a friend to each other using the vocabulary seen in this unit. Go around, monitoring and taking notes of any new vocabulary to write on the board.
- You can also extend the task by asking the students to describe someone in the class without saying their name and the others must guess who is being described.

Vocabulary (SB page 81)

1 2.19

- This exercise focuses on adjectives describing character, which were used in the reading text in the previous section.
- Play the recording and ask the students to listen to the adjectives and repeat them.
- Encourage the students to find the adjectives in the reading text and use the context to work out what they mean.

ANSWERS:				
a 3	**c** 1	**e** 6	**g** 10	**i** 8
b 9	**d** 7	**f** 2	**h** 4	**j** 5

Language note

Vocabulary: *sensible* vs. *sensitive*

Although the word *sensible* isn't featured in this unit, it could cause problems when dealing with the word *sensitive*. In many Latin languages, the word *sensible* has the same meaning as the word *sensitive* in English. In English, the word *sensible* describes someone who is reasonable or practical. The word has nothing to do with emotion.

2 2.20

- Tell the students that they'll hear six people talking. They should listen and choose the most appropriate adjective to describe each one. You may need to play the recording more than once and pause it between speakers to allow the students time to decide which adjective they'll use.
- Allow the students to compare their results in pairs before checking answers with the class.

ANSWERS:	
1 sociable	**4** ambitious
2 bossy	**5** easygoing
3 confident	**6** sensitive

2.20

1. I'd love to meet your friends—let's make a date now. We could try that new restaurant downtown.
2. No, no, don't do it like that. Do it like this. Go ahead, do it again, and, oh, then get me some coffee.
3. No problem—I'm sure I can win. I know I'm faster than the others.
4. I'm working here to get some experience, but I'm going to start up my own company soon.
5. Yeah, whatever—I really don't mind. I'll be happy if we go out. I'll be happy if we stay in. Let's do whatever you want to do.
6. Look, are you sure you're OK? Because I can stay longer if you want. Anyway, you know where I am if you need me. Take care.

3 2.21

- Ask the students to work individually to choose and write down the adjectives they'd use to describe each thing. Remind them that they can use their own ideas if none of the adjectives in the box is right for them.
- Play the recording so the students can find out the meaning of their choices. Put them into pairs to discuss whether or not they agree with the analysis.

2.21

Your description of a dog is your own personality.
Your description of a cat is your partner's personality.
Your description of a rat is your enemy's personality.
Your description of coffee is how you see love.
Your description of an ocean is your own life.

Reading (SB page 82)

1

- Ask the students the meaning of "survey" (*when you ask different people the same questions to compare results*). Explain that they are going to read survey results on happiness.
- Focus the students' attention on the pictures of Aranya and Stevie and ask them to predict who is happier. Ask them to explain why.

- Ask the students to read the survey quickly and scan for the answer. Was their prediction right? Do they agree with the "Happiness Index"?

2

- Tell the students they are now going to answer the survey questions for themselves. Give them some time to read the questions and make notes on their answers.
- **Pairwork.** Put the students into pairs and ask them to tell each other how they completed the sentences. Each pair must then decide who is happier.
- Encourage a few students to share their answers with the rest of the class. How did they decide who is happier?
- Time permitting, extend the discussion by asking if we are happier today than in the past? Has our definition of "happiness" changed over time?

Grammar & Vocabulary (SB page 82)

Verb patterns

1

- Focus attention on the information in the box. Read out the example sentence for the verbs which take the *ing*-form, or ask a student to read it aloud. See if the students can come up with example sentences for one or two of the other verbs in the list.
- Do the same for the verbs which take *to*-infinitive.
- Ask the students to look at the sentences in the exercise and underline the correct structures. Remind them that they can look at the examples in the survey in the previous section to help them.
- Refer the students to the follow-up question and demonstrate the task with one of the stronger students by asking *"Do you hope to get a new job soon?"*. If the students says yes, ask a follow-up question, such as, *"Really, what job do you hope to get?"*
- Put the students into pairs and ask them to take turns in asking and answering the questions. Remind them to ask follow-up questions in order to extend the conversation and keep it natural. Go around, monitoring and making sure they are using the right structures. Then ask a few students to report back to the rest of the class what they found out about their partner.

ANSWERS:

a to get	**c** speaking	**e** worrying
b to travel	**d** to spend	**f** going out

Language notes

Grammar: verbs with *ing*-form and *to*-infinitive

- Although the Grammar section on page 82 doesn't deal with those verbs which can take either the *ing*-form or the *to*-infinitive, there's work in the *Focus on ...* section of the Vocabulary Extra on page 87 which does.
- Verbs like *begin, hate, like, love, prefer,* and *start* can take both the *ing*-form and the *to*-infinitive with virtually no change in meaning: *It started to rain at lunchtime. It started raining at lunchtime.*
- With *stop, try,* and *remember/forget* there's a marked difference in meaning depending on whether you use the *ing*-form or the *to*-infinitive:
He stopped reading the letter. (= *He finished reading it.*) Refers to the action someone has finished.
He stopped to read the letter. (= *He stopped what he was doing in order to read the letter.*) The sentence refers to the reason why someone has stopped an action.
Sue remembered feeding the cat. (= *Sue fed the cat and, at a later date, she recalled doing it.*)
Sue remembered to feed the cat. (= *Sue had to feed the cat and she did.*)

2

- Read the example sentence with the class and give the students examples of sentences that are true for you. Then ask them to write their sentences. Allow them to compare them in pairs or small groups and ask some students to read their sentences out to the class.

Reading & Speaking (SB page 83)

1

- **Pairwork.** If you have a multinational class, try to form pairs with students from the same country.
- Ask the students to take each topic in turn and note down some of the adjectives they'd use to describe them to people from another country. Then ask the students to form sentences using those adjectives.
- Get several pairs to read thewwir sentences to the class.

2

- Focus the students' attention on the picture and the title of the article. Find out if anyone has been to Thailand. If so, ask them if they agree that it's "the land of smiles."
- Give the students time to read the article and complete it with the words in the box in Exercise 1.
- Check answers with the class and answer any questions the students may have.

ANSWERS:

1 The capital city	**4** The food
2 The mountains	**5** The beaches
3 The people	**6** The historic sites

3

- **Pairwork.** Give the students a few minutes to decide which places they're going to talk about and the language they'll need to do this. Go around, giving help with vocabulary where necessary.

- Put the students into pairs and ask them to take turns describing the various places they've chosen. Go around, monitoring and giving help. Take note of any particularly good descriptions and ask the students to repeat them to the class.

Listening (SB page 83)

1 2.22

- Focus the students' attention on the pictures and explain that all the people shown are on vacation in Thailand. Ask the students to think about what kind of people they are and what their interests might be. Go through the statements and ask the students to guess which people match each statement.
- Play the recording and ask the students to complete the statements with the names. You may need to play the recording more than once or pause it after each speaker to give the students time to make their choices.

ANSWERS:

a Cindy
b Hans
c Cindy
d Kay
e Kay and Ramiro
f Hans

2.22

(I = Interviewer; K = Kay; R = Ramiro; C = Cindy; H = Hans)

P: Welcome to The Vacation Station. We start off with a report from Thailand. For this report, we spoke to tourists on the beach in Ao Nang in the south of Thailand. We asked them what they were doing in Thailand. First, we spoke to Kay and Ramiro.

K: We're on our honeymoon and we're staying in the Rayavadee Hotel. It's wonderful. They put rose petals in our bathtub.

R: Next week we want to go to the north. I want to go trekking in the jungle, and Kay wants to take a cooking class. We both love Thai food, so I think it's a great idea.

P: Then we spoke to Cindy.

C: I'm on vacation and I'm taking a scuba diving class. I like swimming in the ocean, so I spend most of my day on the beach, and then in the evening I go shopping. I have a store back home in Sydney so I'm always looking for things to take back there.

P: Finally, we spoke to Hans.

H: I'm living here right now. I come from Germany but I've rented a house here for six months because I'm writing a novel. I think Thailand is a perfect place to live—it's cheap, hot, and inspiring. My girlfriend isn't very happy about it, though—I have a dog in Germany, and she has to stay at home and take care of it!

2

- Elicit the kinds of questions the students will need to find out the necessary information from their classmates. With weaker classes, put these on the board. Then let the students mingle to ask questions and note down names.
- When they've got all the information they need, ask them to rewrite the sentences in Exercise 1, using the names of students in the class. Find out who has the most sentences and ask this student to read them aloud and get the students named to confirm that the information is correct.

Listening (SB page 84)

1 2.23

- Focus the students' attention on the pictures of Becky and Jeff. Explain that Becky and Jeff went to Thailand on vacation and liked it so much that they decided to stay.
- Tell the students that they're going to hear a radio show about tourists who have stayed in Thailand and that they should listen and note down what jobs Becky and Jeff now do in Thailand.

ANSWERS:

Becky runs a bar.
Jeff works in a dive center.

2.23

(P = Presenter; B = Becky; J = Jeff)

P: For our second report from Thailand, we met two people who came here on vacation and never went home. Becky, how long have you been here in Thailand?

B: I arrived here in 2004. I only came here on vacation, but I liked it so much I stayed.

P: What have you been doing here since 2004?

B: I've been running a bar on the beach. It was difficult at first because I opened my bar two months before the tsunami in December 2004. Our bar was OK, but tourists stayed away for a long time after that, and I almost had to close the bar. But I've had a lot of support from my husband, and now the bar is going very well.

P: Did you get married here?

B: Yes, my husband's Thai, and we've been married for two years now.

P: Do you go back to the USA very often?

B: I haven't been to the USA for a few years.

P: What do you miss about home?

B: I guess I miss my family and friends, but they love coming here.

P: Jeff, how long have you been here?

J: For about six months.

P: What have you been doing here since you arrived?

J: I've been working in a dive center.

P: Have you learned the language?

J: Thai? Ha-ha. No, it's really difficult. I've been taking lessons for a few months, but I'm not a very good student.

> **P:** What do you like most about living in Thailand?
> **J:** Apart from the obvious things like the weather, the food, and the laid-back lifestyle, I like the fact that it's close to other interesting places. I've been to Laos, Cambodia, Bali, and Malaysia. But I always like coming back to Thailand. I'm not going home for a long time.

Cultural notes

Thailand

- There is currently a large number of US citizens living as permanent residents in Thailand.
- In 2004, the Indian Ocean tsunami devastated the west coast of Thailand and claimed the lives of 230,000 people in Thailand, India, Sri Lanka, Myanmar, and Indonesia.

2

- Go through the statements with the class. As you read each one aloud, ask the students to raise their hands if they think it's true and to do nothing if they think it's false. Encourage students who disagree to try to convince the others of their point of view. Note the majority decision on the board.
- Play the recording again for the students to check their answers. Encourage individual students to correct the false statements.

ANSWERS:

a False (She came on vacation.)
b True
c False (She says her bar was OK.)
d True
e True
f False (He says he's not going home for a long time.)

3

- Give the students a minute or two to think of their answer. Remind them that they'll need to give reasons as well as simply naming the country.
- Put the students into pairs and ask them to take turns talking about which country they'd like to live in and why. Go around, monitoring and encouraging students to answer the question as fully as they can.

Grammar (SB page 84)

for, *since*, and *been*

1

- Focus attention on the information about *for* and *since* in the margin. Explain the difference between *a period of time* (*24 hours, three days, ten minutes, six years*, etc.) and *a point in time* (*yesterday, this morning, last week, Saturday, last year*, etc.).
- Ask the students to complete the two sentences in the exercise and check their answers.

ANSWERS:

a since
b for

2

- Look at the diagram with the class and ask the students to work individually to complete the table.
- Go around, monitoring and checking that everyone has understood the difference between *for* and *since*.
- Ask the students to add more examples of expressions used with *for* and *since* to the table. Get several students to read theirs aloud to the class.

3

- Focus attention on the information about been in the margin and read out the two example sentences.
- **Pairwork.** Put the students into pairs to discuss the questions.

ANSWERS:

a Present perfect.
b Sentence b.
c Sentence a.

Language notes

Grammar: *been* and *gone*

- You may need to explain that *gone* and *been* are both used as past participles of *go*. Write on the board: *John has gone to New York. John has been to New York.*
- The first sentence means that John went to New York and he's still there. The second means that at some time in his life, John went to New York, but he isn't necessarily there right now.

4

- Go through the examples with the class, then ask them to work individually to write three true sentences for each item. Go around, monitoring and giving help. Make sure that everyone is using *for* and *since* and the present perfect correctly.
- Put the students into pairs to compare their sentences. Ask some students to read theirs aloud to the class.

Extra activity

Ask the students to note down the names of some good shops, restaurants, bars, or night clubs in their city. Write the following conversations on the board and ask them to have similar conversations about the places they've chosen, finding out as much information about them as they can:

Student A	Student B
Have you ever been to Chico's?	No, never. What/Where is it?
Have you been to Chico's recently?	Yes, I went there last Saturday.

Grammar (SB page 85)

Present perfect: simple & progressive

1

- Go through the information in the margin with the class. Remind the students that they studied verbs with dynamic and stative meanings on page 66.
- Ask them to look at the table in the exercise and decide which facts describe how long each activity has continued. Allow them to compare their answers in pairs before checking with the class.

ANSWER:
3 Present perfect facts

Language notes

Grammar: present perfect: simple and progressive

- The present perfect can be used to talk about past experience (completed actions in the past). *I've been to California, but I haven't been to New York*. Note that no precise time is given for the action in the past and only the simple present perfect is used when speaking about past experience.
- The present perfect can also be used to speak about actions which started in the past and are still happening now. In these cases it's possible to mention time, using *for* and *since*. Use *for* when you give the length of time–duration–(*for a few days, for years*). Use *since* when you give the beginning of the time–starting point–(*since Tuesday, since 1967*). You usually use the progressive form for verbs with dynamic meanings (*I've been going to the same dentist for years*). However, you can't use the progressive form for verbs with stative meanings (*I've known him since he was born*, NOT *I've been knowing him since he was born*). See page 142 in the Student's Book for a list of verbs with stative meanings.
- Occasionally you can use the simple form with verbs with dynamic meanings to indicate unchanging, "permanent" situations. Compare: *I've been working here since the beginning of summer* with *I've worked here all my life*.

2

Pairwork. Ask the students to discuss the questions in pairs.

ANSWERS:
a be
b the simple form
c work
d the progressive form

3

- Ask the students to work individually to complete the sentences. Go around, checking that everyone is using the correct verb forms.
- Allow the students to compare their answers in pairs before checking with the class. Then ask them to make changes to the sentences to make them true. Ask several students to read out their new sentences to the class.

ANSWERS:
a 've been studying
b 've been
c 've known
d 've had
e 've been using
f 've wanted

4

Pairwork. Put the students into pairs to discuss how long they've been doing the things in Exercise 3. Go through the example question with the class first, and with weaker classes, elicit more of the questions they'll need. If necessary, write the questions up on the board.

5 Grammar Extra 9

Ask the students to turn to Grammar Extra 9 on page 146 of the Student's Book. Here they'll find an explanation of the grammar they've been studying and further exercises to practice it.

ANSWERS:

1
a for **b** for **c** since **d** for **e** since **f** since
g since **h** for

2
a stealing, stolen
b growing, grown
c selling, sold
d driving, driven
e sending, sent
f paying, paid
g feeling, felt
h getting, got
i telling, told
j costing, cost
k hearing, heard
l losing, lost
m building, built
n lending, lent

3
a We've been married since 2007.
b I've been reading the newspaper for half an hour.
c He's liked jazz since he was at college.
d She's been learning to swim since September.

e She's worked/been working in a store since last May.
f They've lived/been living together since last summer.
g I've been playing the guitar since I was eight.
h We've had a motorcycle for three years
4
a How long have you known your best friend?
b How long have you been wearing the same sunglasses?
c How long have you been going to the same dentist?
d How long have you been listening to the same kind of music?
e How long have you been in the same job?
f How long have you been driving the same car?
g How long have you been living in the same house?
h How long have you been doing your shopping in the same grocery store?

Pronunciation (SB page 85)

1

- Explain that two words in each line of the chants should be stressed. Ask the students to decide which two words these are and to underline them.
- Allow the students to compare their answers in pairs but don't check them with the class at this stage.

2 2.24

Play the recording for the students to check their answers to Exercise 1. Then play it again for them to repeat the chants.

ANSWERS:

A
How long has she been cooking?
How long has she been cleaning?
How long has she been shopping?
How long have you been sleeping?
B
How long has he been reading?
How long has he been playing?
How long has he been eating?
How long have you been waiting?

Speaking (SB page 85)

1

Ask the students to work individually to write the names of all the places, people, and things.

2

- Focus the students' attention on the verbs in Exercise 1 and go through the example, showing them how these words can be used to write sentences describing how long each activity has gone on.
- Ask the students to work individually to write sentences for each of the places, people, and things they chose in Exercise 1. Go around, monitoring and giving help. Remind them to use the underlined words to help them.
- Put the students into pairs and ask them to take turns telling their partner about what they've written.

Extra activity

- Set up a class survey to find out who in the class has done each activity in Exercise 1 the longest.
- Ask each student to choose one "fact" from Exercise 2 and practice the questions they'll ask. For example, *What is your neighbor's name? How long have you known him/her?*
- Tell the students to ask everybody in the class their questions and make a note of the answers. They should then report the results back to the class.

Language for Life (SB page 86)

1

- Focus the students' attention on the pictures and ask them to speculate about the situation. Then tell them to read the conversations in pairs and decide who is getting married.

ANSWER:
Adam and Darina

2 2.25

- Focus the students' attention on the alternatives given in the conversations. Ask them what all these have in common (they're all body parts). Explain that there are several expressions (called idioms) in English which use parts of the body. An idiom is a fixed expression whose meaning cannot always be guessed from an understanding of the meaning of its constituent parts.
- Ask the students to underline the correct alternative to complete each phrase.
- Play the recording for the students to check and ask if anyone was surprised by the answers. Find out if they have any similar expressions in their own language(s).

ANSWERS:

a fingers
b an arm and a leg
c leg
d a hand
e eye to eye

3

- Ask the students to work individually to match the phrases and their meanings.
- Check answers with the class and then play the recording for the students to listen and repeat.

- When they've done this chorally, ask for individual repetition of the useful phrases.

ANSWERS:				
a 3	**b** 1	**c** 4	**d** 5	**e** 2

4

- **Pairwork.** Ask the students to work in pairs to write their conversations. Go around, monitoring and giving help with vocabulary. Make sure the useful phrases are being used correctly.
- Ask the pairs to perform their conversations for the class.

Life Skills (SB page 86)

Collecting information: Have you ever ...?

Explain to the students that finding out about people's experiences in life is a good way to make conversation. We usually ask questions starting with *"Have you ever...?"* Point out that this lesson focuses on asking about and sharing personal experiences.

1

- Explain that the students are going to write down some experiences. Give the students a few minutes to complete the form. Remind them that they are only writing short answers.

2

- Write the first heading on the board (country you've visited) and complete this for yourself. Then, in a different color marker, write *"Have you ever (visited)...?"* and elicit the full question (*Have you ever visited (country)?*)
- Explain that the students will now write questions for each of the headings using the information they wrote for themselves in Exercise 1. You might like to give further examples with stronger students, forming questions based on the information they filled in on their forms and then write examples on the board to draw attention to the use of the past participle.
- Ask students to work individually and then check answers as a whole class.

3

- Demonstrate the task by asking one of the stronger students the question you wrote on the board (*Have you ever visited (country)?* If the student answers *Yes*, then cross out your question and write "1". If the student answers *No*, then leave the question as it is.
- Point out that the higher the score, the less unique your experience list is.
- Students work in pairs and complete the form. Go around, giving support where necessary and noting down interesting experiences for the feedback session.
- Ask several students to report back to the whole class on what they found out about their classmates from the activity. Then lead on to a discussion about who has the most interesting experiences in life.

Vocabulary Extra (SB page 87)

Parts of the body

1

Ask the students to match the pictures with the words. Let them use dictionaries if they wish. Check answers with the class. Then check that the students can pronounce the words correctly.

ANSWERS:	
14 ankle	**12** knee
11 bottom	**3** lip
2 cheek	**18** nail
7 chest	**5** neck
4 chin	**6** shoulder
20 elbow	**8** stomach
16 finger	**17** thumb
1 forehead	**13** toe
15 heel	**9** waist
10 hip	**19** wrist

2

Ask the students to discuss the questions in pairs and then present their lists to the class.

ANSWERS:

bottom
chest
chin (unless someone has a "double chin," a fold of skin which gives the appearance of two chins!)
forehead
neck
stomach
waist

Focus on verbs + *ing*-form or *to*-infinitive (with a change in meaning)

1

- Remind the students that they studied verbs which take *ing*-form or the *to*-infinitive on page 82. Explain that so far they've practiced using verbs with either *ing*-form or the *to*-infinitive. However, there are some verbs which can use either structure, depending on the context, though the meaning changes.
- Ask the students to choose and underline the correct alternatives.

ANSWERS:

a to mail	**d** raining
b getting	**e** to lock
c kissing	**f** to get

2

- Go through the table with the class. Ask them to complete it with the sentences from Exercise 1.
- Check answers with the class, then ask the students to write their own sentences using the same verbs. Go around, monitoring and giving help. Write some of their sentences on the board.

ANSWERS:

1 Sentences b and c
2 Sentences a and e
3 Sentence d
4 Sentence f

Writing

Workbook page 39

Listing points.

Using adverbs of attitude.

Writing a travel blog.

Further Practice Material

Need more classroom practice activities?
Photocopiable resource materials in the Teacher's Presentation Kit / Extra Resources

Need more tests?
Test Generator
Teacher's Presentation Kit / Extra Resources / Tests

Need more on important teaching concepts?
Key concepts in *American Inside Out Evolution* pages xxi-xxxvii

Need student self-study practice?
Workbook pages 36-39

Need more information and ideas?
American Inside Out Evolution website www.macmillan.com.br/americaninsideoutevolution

Need to check what your students can do by the end of this unit?
Self-evaluation checklists on pages xxxix-xliii

Review C *Teacher's notes*

These exercises act as a check of the grammar and vocabulary that the students have learned in Units 7–9. Use them to find any problems that students are having, or anything that they haven't understood and which will need further work.

Grammar (SB page 88)

Remind the students of the grammar explanations they read and the exercises they did in the Grammar Extra on pages 42 to 47.

1

This exercise reviews subject and object questions from Unit 7.

ANSWERS:

- **a** What did Al Gore make a movie about?
- **b** Which country is the world's biggest polluter?
- **c** How much garbage does the USA produce every year?
- **d** Who wants Virgin Airlines to go green?
- **e** How many people travel on passenger jets every year?
- **f** Which organization protests against global warming?

Cultural notes

Al Gore (born 1948)

A US businessman, politician, and environmentalist, Al Gore was the 45th Vice President of the United States from 1993 to 2001, under Bill Clinton. In 2000, he ran for President against George W. Bush in the US Presidential elections, but lost. Since then he's emerged as champion of environmental causes and won the Nobel Peace Prize, as well as an Oscar for his movie about climate change, *An Inconvenient Truth*, in 2007.

Richard Branson (born 1950)

A British businessman, who started up Virgin Records when he was 20 years old. In 1984, the Virgin brand grew when he formed Virgin Atlantic Airways. His worth is estimated today at around $8 billion.

Alliance for Climate Protection

A US organization which aims to persuade people that it's important to make changes to the way we live in order to reduce the negative effect we're having on the world's climate. The founder of the alliance is former US Vice President Al Gore.

2

This exercise reviews verbs with dynamic and stative meanings from Unit 7.

ANSWERS:

- **a** 's having
- **b** have
- **c** don't believe
- **d** look
- **e** 're thinking
- **f** thinks

3

This exercise reviews future forms for arrangements and intentions from Unit 7. Check answers with the class before asking the students to check the sentences that are true for them and to compare with a partner.

ANSWERS:

- **a** 'm seeing
- **b** 'm going to visit
- **c** 'm going
- **d** are coming
- **e** 'm going to buy
- **f** 'm having

4

This exercise reviews verbs which take *ing*-form or the *to*-infinitive from Unit 9. Check answers with the class before asking the students to check the sentences that are true for them and to compare with a partner.

ANSWERS:

- **a** walking
- **b** to take
- **c** taking
- **d** to go
- **e** watching
- **f** to spend

5

This exercise reviews *could* for permission, and *had to* and *should* for obligation from Unit 8. Check answers with the class. Then ask the students for their views on the clothes they have to or had to wear at school.

ANSWERS:

1. Did you have to
2. couldn't
3. had to
4. didn't have to
5. should
6. shouldn't

6

This exercise reviews the present perfect, simple or progressive, with *for* and *since* from Unit 9.

ANSWERS:

a They've been living in Venezuela since 2005.
b We've been learning the violin for two months.
c She's wanted to be a vet since she was six.
d He's been studying French for a year.
e I've known him since we were at school.
f She's had a motorcycle for three weeks.

Vocabulary (SB page 89)

1

This exercise reviews words connected to protesting and demonstrations from Unit 7.

ANSWERS:

1 buzzing	4 away	7 action
2 part	5 swarming	
3 way	6 slogans	

Cultural notes

Pennsylvania Avenue

This street in Washington, DC runs from the White House (see below) to the US Capitol. It is the location of many official parades and processions, as well as protest marches.

The White House

The White House is the official home of the President of the United States. It is situated in central Washington, DC. It was built between 1792 and 1800 from white-painted sandstone.

The Washington Monument

The Washington Monument is one of the most famous of the city's monuments. It is a large, tall, white-colored obelisk situated in the National Mall, a large park in downtown Washington, DC. Construction of the monument began in 1848, but was not completed until 1884 because of a lack of funds, and the intervention of the civil war.

2

Go through the example with the class first and then ask them to complete the exercise by putting the other sentences in order. Check answers with the class before asking the students to check the statements which they agree with and then compare with a partner.

ANSWERS:

a I'm anti nuclear power.
b I'm against using big cars in the city.
c I feel strongly about global warming.
d I'm in favor of more money for farmers.
e I really care about protecting our environment.
f I support the protection of wild animals.

3

This exercise reviews vocabulary to do with education and training from Unit 8. Check answers with the class before asking the students to think about their own country and check the statements which are true. They should then compare with a partner.

ANSWERS:

a 3 b 1 c 4 d 2 e 6 f 5

4

This exercise reviews adjectives for describing facial features from Unit 9.

ANSWERS:

1 curly	3 full	5 square
2 thick	4 rosy	6 white

5

This exercise reviews character adjectives from Unit 9.

ANSWERS:

a ambitious	e independent
b bossy	f loyal
c confident	g mysterious
d easygoing	h selfish

Pronunciation (SB page 89)

1

Remind the students that the boxes show the syllables in a word and the large boxes indicate the stressed syllables. Here the students are being asked to classify words from Units 7–9 according to how many syllables they have and where the main stress falls. Encourage them to say each word aloud to get a feeling for what sounds right. Don't confirm answers at this stage.

2 2.26

Point out the main stresses in the example words which are underlined. Ask the students to do the same for the other words in the table. Play the recording for the students to check their answers. Then play it a second time for them to listen and repeat the words.

ANSWERS:

1 and 2

A: curly, eyebrows, forehead, pointed
B: against, believe, degree, support
C: confident, earlier, sociable, tourism
D: affectionate, biology, democracy, responsible

Reading & Listening (SB page 90)

1

- Ask the students which modern day gadgets / objects they could not live without. You might want to suggest a few yourself, e.g. a cell phone, a car, fast food. Brainstorm and write a few ideas on the board.
- Explain that the students are going to read about a family that decided to leave the city and live "off the grid", i.e. without all modern conveniences. You might like to elicit what type of changes living "off the grid" would involve.
- Refer the students to the three questions in Exercise 1 and point out that the students will need to infer, that is to say read between the lines, in order to identify who said what.
- Ask the students to complete the task individually then check with a partner before whole class feedback. Ask the students to share their answers with the rest of the class and ask them what helped them understand who said what.

ANSWERS:

a Elli (...was still dreaming of a way to grow chocolate.)
b the kids / Tom
c Patricia (...feels better about things now– she knows we made the right choice)

2

- Tell the students they are going to read the article again, but this time they are scanning for specific information.
- Encourage the students to read quickly and set this as a timed exercise.
- Allow the students to compare their answers in pairs before checking answers with the whole class. Ask the students to say where the answer can be found in the text.

ANSWERS:

a A place where there was no outside water or electricity (far from the city). Possibly a rainforest.
b Mobile phones and TV
c Chickens and a (pet) goat
d Because they are growing their own food and have a chicken and a goat so they don't have to do much shopping.
e To celebrate their first year "off the grid".

3

- Ask the whole class to consider the changes Tom and his family have made and consider if they could make the same changes.
- **Pairwork**. Ask them to discuss this in pairs. Go around, monitoring and offering help. Then lead a whole class discussion on the students' views.

Extra activity

Desert Island

Play *Desert Island* with the students. Tell the students to imagine they are shipwrecked on a desert island and they can only take 3 objects with them. They must debate and agree on what those 3 items are. Depending on the level of the class, you can either have them think of the objects to save or provide a list to choose from, e.g. a box of matches, a bottle of water, a knife, a first aid kit, a radio, a blanket, a pen and paper, etc. ...

Language note

Vocabulary: *off the grid*

Off the grid is a way of life where people live without the support of infrastructure, such as an electrical grid. Off-grid electricity can be supplied by a stand-alone power system, such as solar panels.

4 2.27

Go through the choices with the students before playing the recording. Ask them to underline the correct information.

ANSWERS:

a is **b** is

5

Go through the statements before you play the recording again and ask the students to think about whether they are true or false. Then play the recording for them to check. Encourage them to correct the false statements.

ANSWERS:

a False. (He worked for an oil company.)
b True.
c False (She was very happy about the changes.)
d False. (He says he would like to get a motorcycle.)
e True.
f False. (He says his friends agree that climate change is a real problem.)

2.27

(I = Interviewer; F = Frank; E = Elli)
I: Tell me, Frank, how did your family decide to go green?
F: It was Dad's idea, really. When we were young, Dad had an important job with an oil company. He was very ambitious, and we didn't see him a lot, because he was always flying around the world. But when he was forty-three, he lost his job. After he lost his job, he changed completely. He started working as a gardener, met new friends, and that's how he became interested in green issues.

E: Very different from his old life?
F: Yeah. He actually became a bit of a rebel. So when he asked us about going off the grid, I wasn't surprised.
I: How did you feel about the changes you had to make, Elli?
E: I was very happy. Last year, Dad and I took part in a demonstration about climate change in Washington, DC. It was fun, and I had a great day, but when I went back home I felt I needed to do more. These are serious problems. We all have to make changes to our lives now!
I: What about you, Frank?
F: Mostly it's OK. I don't mind walking and cycling. But I get tired of eating potatoes, salad, and apples. Sometimes I just want to eat a hamburger, turn all the lights on in every room in the house, and take a jacuzzi bath. And I'd really like to get a motorcycle when I'm older.
I: What about your friends, what do they think?
E: They're all very worried about climate change. At my school, I've started an environmental group. We're trying to persuade people to change their lives. My friends think I'm very bossy, but all this is too important! We have to do something before it's too late. We can't close our eyes to this problem.
F: My friends think my dad is crazy – I think he's crazy too sometimes – but all my friends agree that climate change is a real problem and we should do everything we can to stop it. I hope the changes my family is making can help, but I'm not sure.

Writing & Speaking (SB page 91)

1

Ask the students to read the email and complete it with the words in the box.

ANSWERS:

Paragraph 1
I bought a lottery ticket **last** week ...
I'**m** so excited.

Paragraph 2
... starting with **my** job.
I've always wanted to be a doctor, **but** my parents ...
Now I **can** finally do it!

Paragraph 3
We **have** nothing in common, ...
I'm going to **be** too busy with my studies!

Paragraph 4
I'm looking **forward** to that.
Do you think I **should** give some money to my sister?

Paragraph 5
I'm **going** to give some money to Greenpeace.
But first I'm planning a **vacation** in a warm place.
I'll pay **for** your ticket!

Paragraph 6
Don't **tell** Kenny I won this money.

2

Ask the students to read the text again and match the headings to the paragraphs.

ANSWERS:

a Paragraph 4
b Paragraph 5
c Paragraph 2
d Paragraph 1
e Paragraph 3

3

Explain the situation and ask the students to work individually to decide on the changes they're going to make to their lives. Go around, offering help with vocabulary, and encouraging them to put something for each of the items in Exercise 2.

4

Pairwork. Go through the example sentence with the class and then ask the students to work in pairs and take turns to tell each other about the changes they plan for their lives following their big win.

5

Remind the students that they can use the text in Exercise 1 as a model. Go around, monitoring and giving help. Encourage the use of the headings in Exercise 2 for structuring the email

Further Practice Material

Need more classroom practice activities?
Photocopiable resource materials in the Teacher's Presentation Kit / Extra Resources

Need more tests?
Test Generator
Teacher's Presentation Kit / Extra Resources / Tests

Need more on important teaching concepts?
Key concepts in *American Inside Out Evolution* pages xxi-xxxvii

Need more information and ideas?
American Inside Out Evolution website www.macmillan.com.br/americaninsideoutevolution

10 Lifestyle Overview

Section	Aims	What the students are doing
Reading & Vocabulary SB page 92	Reading for detail Collocations	Predicting a text by guessing answers to questions. Completing collocations. Discussing lifestyles.
Listening & Grammar SB page 93	Listening for gist *will*	Answering questions about a telephone inquiry. Completing questions and answers. Talking about health spas.
Grammar SB page 93	Future time clauses	Studying future time clauses. Completing questions and short answers and repeating them. Discussing the questions in pairs. Underlining the correct structures and rewriting the sentences so they are true for them.
Vocabulary SB page 94	Food and cooking	Checking items bought in a shopping list. Discussing their own shopping lists and habits.
Pronunciation SB page 94	Vowel sounds in food words	Listening and repeating food words. Matching words according to pronunciation of vowel sounds.
Reading & Vocabulary SB page 95	Reading for detailed information	Reading a text and categorizing vocabulary. Talking about their favorite dish.
Speaking: anecdote SB page 95	Fluency work	Underlining the correct information from a description. Talking about the healthiest person they know.
Reading SB page 96	Reading for detail	Matching descriptions with pictures. Answering questions about the text from memory. Talking about first experiences with cars.
Vocabulary SB page 97	Cars and driving	Finding names of car parts in a reading text. Putting features of cars in order of importance.
Grammar SB page 97	*used to* + infinitive	Identifying the meaning and usage of *used to* + infinitive. Replacing the simple past with *used to* + infinitive and changing the sentences so they are true for them.
Speaking: anecdote SB page 97	Fluency practice	Underlining the correct information about a woman's dream car. Talking about their own dream car.
Language for Life SB page 98	Idioms with food	Matching conversations with pictures. Underlining the correct alternatives. Replacing phrases in sentences with food idioms. Listening to and repeating sentences.
Life Skills SB page 98	Self-knowledge: Do you have a healthy lifestyle?	Identifying their own healthy and unhealthy activities. Discussing how to lead a healthier lifestyle. Comparing lifestyles with a partner's.
Vocabulary Extra SB page 99	Review of words from the unit: cars; words used with driving	Matching pictures with words. Asking and answering questions about the pictures. Matching sentence halves to complete definitions. Completing questions, then discussing them with a partner.

10 Lifestyle *Teacher's notes*

Warm-up

- Ask the students what they think about growing old. Do they fear it? Are they looking forward to it? What problems do they think they'll experience when they are old? What age would they like to live to?
- Find out who in the class has the oldest relative and how old that person is.

Reading & Vocabulary (SB page 92)

1

- Ask the students to cover the text and look at the picture. Go through the questions with the class and ask them to guess the answers. Allow them to discuss in pairs or small groups if they wish. Find out how much consensus there is in the class, particularly with regard to the man's age. Note the highest and lowest estimates of his age on the board.
- Give the students time to read the text and find out if their guesses were correct. Ask them if they're surprised by how old Roberto is. Answer any questions they may have about vocabulary.

ANSWERS:

a 6:00 a.m.
b 104 years old.
c Cuba (but has lived in the USA since he was a teenager).
d Martial arts: tai chi.
e No.

Language notes

Vocabulary: martial arts

A sport that is a traditional form of fighting, such as: karate, kung fu, judo, tae kwon do, and tai chi.

2

- Ask the students if they can complete any of the collocations without looking back at the article. For number 2 they may suggest *live a healthy life*; point out that this is possible, but the word used in the article is more common. When they've done all they can, allow them to look through the article and complete the remainder.
- Check answers with the class before putting the students into pairs to discuss their answers to the questions and the similarities and differences between their lives and Roberto Salazar. Get several pairs to report back to the class on their discussions.

ANSWERS:

a brisk	**d** hurry	**g** network
b lead	**e** sunset	**h** stay
c arts	**f** family	

Listening & Grammar (SB page 93)

1 2.28

- Ask the students to look at the picture and describe what they see. Prompt them to say which of the people shown they think is the healthiest. What might the man do to get in shape?
- Tell the students that they're going to hear the woman's phone conversation with the receptionist at the New Life Center, a health spa. Explain health spa and ask the students to suggest a few of the things that you might find in a health spa (a gym, a pool, therapy rooms, etc.). Before you play the recording, go through the questions with the class so they know what they are listening for.
- Play the recording and ask the students to answer the questions.

ANSWERS:

a She wants to give her husband a surprise for his birthday.
b Possible answer: No, he won't, because he isn't in shape.

2.28

(M = Man; W = Woman)
M: New Life Center. Can I help you?
W: Yes. Could you give me some information about your center?
M: Sure. When would you like to come?
W: Actually, it's not for me. It's for my husband. It's a surprise for his birthday.
M: Ah, lucky man!
W: Yes ... Could you tell
M: Sure. As soon as he arrives here, he'll take a fitness test.
W: OK. Umm, he isn't in great shape.
M: Well, we start every day at 7:30 a.m. He'll do a yoga class before breakfast.
W: Ha-ha. He usually has sweets before breakfast!
M: Oh, no. If he has sweets here, he'll be in big trouble. We have a strict "No Sugar" diet.

W: Well, it's a good idea for him to give up sugar. He says he'll give up as soon as he feels more relaxed.
M: Oh, well, this is the ideal place to relax. After the morning walk, he'll have a sauna and jacuzzi.
W: Oh, he'll enjoy that. But what's this walk?
M: They go for a brisk walk in the morning from 8:30 to 12:30. That's four hours.
W: Four hours! He hates walking. He only walks from the front door to his car.
M: Oh, don't worry. When they get to the top of the mountain, they have a twenty-minute break before they come down again.
W: And what about the afternoon? Will he relax?
M: No, not really. He'll go to the gym in the afternoon. But he'll have time to relax in the evening.
W: Oh, my goodness. I don't think he'll thank me for this.
M: Believe me, when he finishes the week, he'll feel like a new man.

will

2 2.29

- Go through the information about *will* in the margin and explain that it's used to talk and ask questions about the future. So far the students have used *going to* to talk about decisions that have been made for the future and the present progressive for future arrangements. Here, the future isn't definitely decided or arranged yet—*will* is a more general way of referring to the future. Spend some time making sure the students can pronounce *won't* /woʊnt/ correctly and make sure that they can distinguish it from *want* /wɑnt/.
- Ask the students to complete the questions and answers and then play the recording for them to check.

Language notes

Grammar: *will*

- *Will* is a modal verb and is used to express a number of functions such as offers (*I'll help her*), promises (*She'll be there at 10:00 a.m.*), requests (*Will you get me a newspaper?*), restaurant orders (*I'll have the steak*) and predictions (*It'll rain tomorrow—it always rains on the weekend*). *Will* is also used to make general statements (of fact) about the future (*The stadium will be used for all national events*). In this unit *will* is used to express predictions and to make statements of fact about the future.
- The negative of *will* is *will not*. The contraction of *will* is *'ll* and the contraction of *will not* is *won't*. The contractions *'ll* and *won't* are more commonly used than the full form in statements, while in questions and short answers the full form is always used.
- Statement: *He'll do a yoga class.*
  Question: *Will he relax?*
  Short answer: *Yes, he will.* (NOT ~~*Yes, he'll.*~~)
- *Will* is always followed by the infinitive without *to*.

ANSWERS:

a Will he take a fitness test?
Yes, he will. / No, he won't.
b Will he do yoga?
Yes, he will. / No, he won't.
c Will he have sweets?
Yes, he will. / No, he won't.
d Will he have a sauna and a jacuzzi?
Yes, he will. / No, he won't.
e Will he go for a four-hour walk?
Yes, he will. / No, he won't.
f Will he have time to relax in the afternoon?
Yes, he will. / No, he won't.

3

- **Pairwork.** Ask the students to take turns to ask and answer the questions in Exercise 2 according to what they heard on the recording.
- Still in pairs, students discuss health spas or the equivalent in their country and whether or not they would like to go to one. Go around, monitoring and giving help with vocabulary.

ANSWERS:

a Yes, he will.
b Yes, he will.
c No, he won't.
d Yes, he will.
e Yes, he will.
f No, he won't.

Grammar (SB page 93)

Future time clauses

1

- Focus the students' attention on the information in the margin. Read out the first two example sentences and make sure everyone notices the present form verb in the subordinate clause and the future form in the main clause. Point out that the order of the clauses can be reversed.
- Go through the examples in the table with the class and ask them to discuss the questions in pairs.

ANSWERS:

a Future time.
b will
c Simple present
d if
e when
f as soon as

Language notes

Grammar: future time clauses with *if, as soon as, when*

- It is important to establish that in future time clauses, after the conjunctions *if, as soon as,* and *when*, you use a simple present form. (*If it rains, we'll play inside* NOT ~~*If it will rain, we'll play inside*~~).
- It is the main clause that takes the future form and can be placed at the beginning or at the end of a sentence. For example: *He'll take a fitness test as soon as he arrives. As soon as he arrives, he'll take a fitness test.* Note the difference in punctuation in the two sentences.

2

- Ask the students to work individually to underline the correct verb forms.
- Go around as they do this, and help anyone who's having difficulty. Check answers with the class before asking them to rewrite the sentences so that they are true for them. Ask several students to read out their new sentences.

ANSWERS:

a 'll go	**d** 'm
b finishes	**e** have
c go	**f** 'll go

3 Grammar Extra 10, Part 1

Ask the students to turn to Grammar Extra 10, Part 1 on page 148 of the Student's Book. Here they'll find an explanation of the grammar they've been studying and further exercises to practice it.

ANSWERS:

1	2
a I'll lend	**a** finishes
b you won't be	**b** arrives
c will love	**c** gets home
d **will get**	**d** rains
e We won't arrive	**e** goes
f They won't play	**f** finishes

Vocabulary (SB page 94)

1

- Ask the students to look at Nick's shopping list and the pictures. Tell them to check the items on the shopping list which are shown in the pictures (the items that Nick bought). They should then have five items unchecked (the ones he forgot). If you wish, you could have the students work in pairs and make this a race, with the first pair to identify the five forgotten items as the winners.
- Check answers with the class and help them with any items that presented difficulties.

ANSWERS:

He forgot: tomatoes, carrots, sardines, tea, soup

2

Ask the students to work individually to look at the list again and follow the instructions in the task. When they've finished, allow them to compare their results in pairs. Then have a class feedback session. Find out which are the most popular and the least popular food items on the shopping list.

Pronunciation (SB page 94)

1 2.30

- Point out that the vowel sounds which are featured here are printed in red. Focus attention on the example. Students may be surprised that *lettuce* and *lemon* both contain the same vowel sound /ɪ/.
- Play the recording and ask the students to listen and repeat, paying particular attention to the vowel sounds in red.
- When they've done this chorally, ask for individual repetition. Make sure everyone can pronounce the more difficult items, such as *lettuce* /ˈlet̬.ɪs/ *spinach* /ˈspɪn.ɪtʃ/, and *cauliflower* /ˈkɑː.ləˌflaʊ.ɚ/ correctly.

2 2.31

- Ask the students to work individually to match the words in the two columns. Encourage them to say the words aloud as they do this in order to get a feel for what sounds right.
- Play the recording for them to check their own answers and then check with the class.
- See if everyone agrees on which word is the most difficult to say. Give extra practice in saying this word.

ANSWERS:

a 3 **b** 1 **c** 5 **d** 2 **e** 4

Reading & Vocabulary (SB page 95)

1

- Find out by a show of hands who in the class likes or doesn't like eggplants. Ask them to give details about how they eat them. For example, do they peel them, boil them, grill them? If students show interest in this, extend the questions to how they prepare and eat other vegetables, such as zucchini or peppers (e.g. Do they eat them raw? Can they peel them?).
- Ask the students to read the recipes and mark the dishes they would and wouldn't like to try.
- In a feedback session, find out if there is consensus on which dishes are preferred and if the students know of any other dishes that are made with eggplants.

2

- Ask the students to work individually to find the words in the text.
- Allow them to compare their results in pairs before checking with the class.

ANSWERS:

a slice, mix, peel, cut, chop
b grill, boil, bake, broil, fry
c raw

Extra activity

- Ask the students to think about food items from the previous page which they can boil, peel, fry, etc. For example, you can peel an orange, an apple, a potato, a carrot, etc.
- Select one item of food and ask the students to decide how many things you can do with it, e.g. an onion–peel it, slice it, chop it, fry it, etc.

3

- Give the students a minute or two to think about their favorite dish. Emphasize that it doesn't have to contain eggplant. Ask them to think about the questions and make brief notes (but not write down whole sentences). Go around, monitoring and giving help with vocabulary.
- **Pairwork.** Put the students into pairs and ask them to use their notes as prompts to help them talk about their favorite dishes.

Speaking: anecdote (SB page 95)

For more information about how to set up, monitor, and repeat Anecdotes, see page xviii-xx in the Introduction.

1 2.32

- Ask the students to look at the picture of Darren. Explain that someone called Josh is going to talk about Darren, who's the healthiest person he knows.
- Go through the questions and the answer choices with the class. Explain any unknown vocabulary and then ask the students to listen and underline the answers Josh gives.
- Check answers with the class and ask them whether they know anyone like Darren.

ANSWERS:

a cousin
b 26
c an army officer
d tall and well built
e runs up mountains
f high-calorie
g really lazy

2

- Give the students a minute or two to decide who they're going to talk about. Then ask them to look at the questions in Exercise 1 again and decide how they'd answer them about the person they're going to talk about. Allow them to make notes of what they're going to say and how they're going to say it, but discourage them from writing a paragraph that they can simply read out. Go around, monitoring and giving help.
- **Pairwork.** Put the students into pairs and ask them to take turns to tell their partner about the healthiest person they know. Encourage them to ask each other follow-up questions to get further information.
- Ask some pairs to report back to the class about what they found out.

Reading (SB page 96)

1

- Go through the instructions with the class and then ask them to read the descriptions and match them to the pictures.
- Check answers with the class and answer any questions about vocabulary.

ANSWERS:

a 1 **b** 3 **c** 2

2

Ask the students to cover the descriptions and see if they can answer the questions from memory. Read each question aloud in turn and ask the students to say which car they think it is. Allow people with different opinions to try to persuade each other to change their minds. At the end, ask them to uncover the descriptions and check their answers.

ANSWERS:

a BMW
b Porsche
c Fiat 500
d Porsche
e Fiat 500
f BMW

3

Pairwork. Put the students into pairs to talk about their first car or their first experience of traveling in a car. Encourage them to report any interesting experiences to the class.

Vocabulary (SB page 97)

1

- You could set this up as a race with the first student or pair of students to find all six car parts as the winners.

ANSWERS:

windshield wiper, sunroof, engine, seats, trunk, roof

Extra activity

Draw the outline of a car on the board and ask the students to label it with the words from Exercise 1. Then invite them to add any other car parts they know.

2

Go through the features in the box with the class and make sure that they understand all of them. Then ask the students to work individually to categorize the features according to how important they think they are. Put them into pairs to compare answers and find out how much consensus there is around the class.

Grammar (SB page 97)

used to + infinitive

1

- Go through the information in the margin with the students and explain that you use *used to* to talk about repeated actions that happened (or states that were true) in the past, but which no longer happen (or are true) now. Draw their attention to the fact that the question form is *Did he use to ...?* and not ~~*Did he used to ...?*~~
- Ask the students to look at the extracts from the texts on page 96 in pairs and to match the underlined verbs with the descriptions.
- Check answers with the class and then ask them if it's possible to use *used to* + infinitive to talk about a single action in the past.

> **ANSWERS:**
>
> **a** 2 **b** 1 **c** 3
>
> No, it isn't possible to use the structure to talk about a single action in the past.

Language note

Grammar: *used to*

- You can use *used to* when you want to talk about past habits or states. It's always followed by the infinitive. It can't be used to talk about 1) something in the past which happened once, or 2) something which is still true. Compare:
  We used to live in Puebla (*but we don't now*). (past state)
  He used to smoke (*but he doesn't now*). (past habit)
  We went to Texas last year. (single action, so ~~*We used to go to Texas last year*~~ is not possible)
- The question form is *Did you use to...?* (NOT ~~*Did you used to..?*~~)

2

- **Pairwork.** Go through the example with the class. You may like to point out that the simple past has been underlined in each sentence. Ask the students to work in pairs to replace it with *used to* or *didn't use to* + infinitive where this is possible.
- Check answers with the class and then ask the students to work individually to change the sentences so that they are true for them. They can then compare with a partner before you ask several students to read out their altered sentences.

> **ANSWERS:**
>
> **a** My parents used to have a big old car.
> **b** My mother used to drive me to school every day.
> **c** I didn't use to like going on long trips. I used to get car sick.
> **d** -
> **e** My father never used to wash the car. It always used to look dirty.
> **f** -

3 Pairwork

- The pairwork exercise for this unit is on pages 124 and 129 of the Student's Book. Put the students into pairs and tell them who will be Student A, and who will be Student B.
- While they're doing the exercise, go around monitoring and giving help. Take note of any errors which may need particular attention later, and also any examples of good language use which you can praise in a feedback session.

4 Grammar Extra 10, Part 2

Ask students to turn to Grammar Extra 10, Part 2 on page 148 of the Student's Book. Here they'll find an explanation of the grammar they've been studying and further exercises to practice it.

> **ANSWERS:**
>
> **1**
> **1** did your dad use to do
> **2** used to be
> **3** Did he use to enjoy
> **4** used to say
> **5** didn't use to like
> **6** used to leave
> **7** didn't use to arrive
> **8** used to get
> **9** Did your dad use to earn
> **10** used to have
> **11** used to eat out
> **12** used to tell
>
> **2**
> **a** -
> **b** used to live
> **c** used to share
> **d** used to have
> **e** used to watch
> **f** used to give
> **g** -
> **h** didn't use to

Speaking: anecdote (SB page 97)

For more information about how to set up, monitor, and repeat Anecdotes, see page xviii–xx in the Introduction.

1 2.33

- Ask the students to look at the picture. Tell them that a woman called Patti is going to talk about her dream car. Explain that the expression a dream car is used to refer to the car that you'd most like to own, not to a car you've seen in a dream. Similar common expressions include *dream kitchen*, *dream vacation*, *dream job*, etc.
- Go through the questions and the answer choices with the class. Explain any unknown vocabulary and ask the students to listen and underline the answers Patti gives.
- Check answers with the class and ask them whether their dream car would be like Patti's.

ANSWERS:

a Chevrolet
b old
c black
d spacious
e Brown leather
f Elvis
g My friends
h Down Fifth Avenue in New York

2.33

My dream car is an old car. I love cars from the fifties or sixties, and my favorite is a Chevrolet. A really big, old Chevrolet. It has to be black—definitely black—with a silver bumper and big, flashy headlights. Inside, it's really spacious with plenty of room to stretch your legs. The seats are soft and made of leather.
Red leather. No, brown leather. Brown is more sophisticated. Oh, and there's a beautiful old radio with Elvis playing really loud. I love Elvis. I'd like to take all my friends out in my car. I can imagine wearing glamorous evening clothes and going to a fancy restaurant in New York. As we drive down Fifth Avenue, everybody turns to look at our fabulous car ...

Cultural notes

Elvis Presley (1935–1977)

A US singer, musician, and actor, Elvis Presley is known as "The King" (of Rock 'n' Roll). The teenage Presley got his break in 1953. Over the next two decades Presley became an international star with recordings like *Jailhouse Rock* (1957), *It's Now or Never* (1960), and *Suspicious Minds* (1969). From 1973, Presley's health declined. He put on weight and became increasingly dependent on prescription drugs. In 1977 he died of a heart attack at the age of forty-two.

2

- Give the students a minute or two to decide what their dream car would be like. Then ask them to look at the questions in Exercise 1 again and decide how they'd answer them about their dream car. Allow them to make notes of what they're going to say and how they're going to say it, but discourage them from writing a paragraph that they can simply read out. Go around, monitoring and giving help.
- **Pairwork.** Put the students into pairs and ask them to take turns to tell their partner about their dream car. Encourage them to ask each other follow-up questions to get further information.
- Ask some pairs to report back to the class about what they found out.

Language for Life (SB page 98)

1

- Focus the students' attention on the pictures and ask the students what they can see.
- Ask the students to read the conversations and match them to the pictures. Tell them not to worry about the alternatives at this point.

ANSWERS:

a 3 **b** 1 **c** 2

2 2.34

- Focus the students' attention on the choices in the conversations. Point out that these are parts of idioms involving food. Ask them what they think the first one means: they should be able to guess from the context that it is a collocation with *a cup of* that means something you like.
- Ask the students to work in pairs or small groups and to use the same technique (deciding on meaning from context and then choosing the most likely-sounding option) to complete the remaining expressions.
- Play the recording for the students to check their answers. You may need to point out that *packed*

in like sardines comes from the way sardines are traditionally sold in the USA, lying in tight rows in a tin. Ask them if they think any of the idioms are particularly appropriate, and whether they have any idioms like these in their own language(s).

ANSWERS:
a tea
b cake
c sardines

3
Put the students into pairs to complete the exercise, then check answers.

ANSWERS:
a 3
b 1
c 2

4 2.35
- Ask the students to work individually to replace the underlined phrases with the food idioms from the conversations in Exercise 1.
- Play the recording for them to check their answers and then play it a second time for them to listen and repeat the sentences.
- Ask the students to discuss in pairs whether the sentences are true for them or not.

ANSWERS:
a a piece of cake
b packed in like sardines
c not my cup of tea

2.35

a I think that learning English is a piece of cake.
b I hate places where you are packed in like sardines.
c Going clubbing is not my cup of tea.

Extra activity
Ask the students to write another conversation using at least two of the useful phrases.

Life Skills (SB page 98)
Self-knowledge: Do you have a healthy lifestyle?

Ask the students what characterizes a healthy lifestyle. Elicit a few ideas. Explain that in this lesson they will find out about healthy living and test their own lifestyle.

1
- Refer the students to the instructions and give them a few minutes to complete the task about themselves.
- Then, put the students into pairs and ask them to compare their answers with their partners and focus on the items they crossed to say what they will do in the future to lead a healthier lifestyle. Refer to the example in the box and remind the students to use the 1st conditional form (*if* + simple present / *will* + verb). Go around, monitoring and giving help with vocabulary.
- Get several pairs to report back to the class on their answers. Ask if the students can add any other healthy activities to the list.

2
- Now explain that the students will consider aspects of an unhealthy lifestyle. Elicit a few examples of unhealthy activities.
- Focus the students' attention on the pictures and the instructions. Ask them to complete the task individually.
- Then ask the students to compare their answers with a partner and focus on the items they crossed to say what they will stop doing in the future to lead a healthier lifestyle. Refer to the example in the box and remind the students to use the 'ing' form after *stop* as well as the 1st conditional form (*if* + simple present / *will* + verb). Go around, checking the structures are being used correctly.
- In the class feedback session, ask several pairs to share their answers with the rest of the class. Lead a discussion on what other unhealthy activities they would add to the list.

3
- Pair the students with a different partner to compare their lifestyles and discuss how healthy (or unhealthy) they are. Go around, helping with vocabulary.
- Ask a few pairs to share their findings with the rest of the class and hold a class vote on who has the healthiest lifestyle, and why.

Vocabulary Extra (SB page 99)
Cars

1
- Focus the students' attention on the list of words and point out that they're all to do with parts of a car. Remind students that the underlining indicates the syllable of the word that has the strongest stress. Check that the students can pronounce the words correctly.
- Ask students to look at the pictures and ask them to match the numbers in the pictures with the car parts.

ANSWERS:

5 bumper
14 emergency brake
7 headlights
4 hood
6 license plate
15 seat
13 seatbelt
11 steering wheel
12 stick shift
1 sunroof
8 tire
3 trunk
9 wheel
2 windshield
10 windshield wipers

2

Pairwork. Ask the students to cover the words and take turns to test each other by pointing at parts of the pictures and asking what the things are. Go through the example questions with the class first.

Focus on words used with driving

1

Go through this exercise with the class, reading out each sentence half in turn and asking the students to match it with the correct ending.

ANSWERS:

a	2	**c**	1	**e**	3
b	5	**d**	6	**f**	4

2

Ask the students to work individually to complete the questions. Check answers before putting them into pairs to take turns asking and answering the questions.

ANSWERS:

a passing
b down
c gas
d hour
e jams
f ride

Further Practice Material

Need more classroom practice activities?
Photocopiable resource materials in the Teacher's Presentation Kit / Extra Resources

Need more tests?
Test Generator
Teacher's Presentation Kit / Extra Resources / Tests

Need more on important teaching concepts?
Key concepts in *American Inside Out Evolution* pages xxi-xxxvii

Need student self-study practice?
Workbook pages 40–43

Need more information and ideas?
American Inside Out Evolution website www.macmillan.com.br/americaninsideoutevolution

Need to check what your students can do by the end of this unit?
Self-evaluation checklists on pages xxxix-xliii

11 Animals *Overview*

Section	Aims	What the students are doing
Reading & Speaking SB page 100	Reading for detail	Reading opinions about animals. Discussing opinions about animals. Giving feedback about their discussions.
Listening SB page 101	Listening for specific information	Talking about animals they like and dislike. Listening and checking the animals the people mention. Underlining correct information and rewriting the sentences so they are true for people in the class.
Vocabulary SB page 101	Adjective + preposition	Adding prepositions to sentences and completing them to make some true and some false. Guessing which of a partner's statements are true.
Vocabulary SB page 102	Animals	Matching animals with their defining characteristics. Listing animals or insects for every letter of the alphabet.
Reading & Vocabulary SB page 102	Reading for gist and detail	Matching animals to descriptions and checking answers in a text. Identifying true and false sentences. Replacing words in sentences with expressions from stories.
Grammar SB page 103	Defining relative clauses	Studying the structure and use of defining relative clauses. Using *that* to combine sentences and replacing *that* with *which* or *who*. Correcting sentences.
Pronunciation SB page 104	Words with the same sound but different meaning	Listening to and repeating pairs of words. Matching words with the correct meanings.
Listening SB page 104	Listening for detail	Identifying the questions which an interviewer asks about pets. Checking the characteristics of pets mentioned. Talking about characteristics they look for in pets and people.
Grammar SB page 105	Unreal conditionals	Studying the structure and meaning of unreal conditional sentences. Completing a table with conditional sentences. Completing "moral dilemmas" and discussing their answers.
Speaking: anecdote SB page 105	Fluency practice	Listening and underlining the correct information. Talking about pets.
Language for Life SB page 106	Useful conversational phrases for making polite requests	Finding out who's going to look after someone's pet snake. Completing a table with useful phrases. Listening to and repeating useful phrases. Writing and practicing conversations.
Life Skills SB page 106	Giving opinions: Animals: Use or abuse?	Discussing how humans use animals. Agreeing or objecting to statements. Discussing their opinions about the "use" or "abuse" of animals.
Vocabulary Extra SB page 107	Review of words from the unit: animals; insects; that	Matching pictures with words. Asking and answering questions. Completing a table with examples using *that* and writing their own examples.
Writing WB page 47		Linking: giving examples. Giving opinions.

11 Animals *Teacher's notes*

Warm-up

Find out: Do any of the students have pets? If so, ask them how long they have had it and what the challenges are. If you have a pet yourself, you could take in a picture and tell the students something about it and whether it is easy or difficult to take care of it.

Reading & Speaking (SB page 100)

1

- Focus the students' attention on the pictures and find out what the students' attitudes to animals are.
- Tell the students to read the comments and decide which one(s) they agree with. Ask them to work individually.

2

Groupwork. Look at the example with the class and then ask the students to work in small groups and discuss their opinions. Go around, monitoring and giving help with vocabulary. Ask one student in each group to make notes of their discussion as these will be needed for the next exercise.

3

Ask a representative from each group to present the results of their discussion to the class.

Listening (SB page 101)

1

- Ask the students to look at the animals and insects in the pictures. Ask them which ones are pets, which ones you can find in a zoo, and which in the wild.
- **Pairwork.** Ask the students to discuss which animals they like or dislike.

Language note

Vocabulary: *mice*

The plural of mouse is *mice*, not *mouses*. This is the only irregular noun in this list, but one of a number of irregular animal plurals. Other irregular animal nouns are: *goose/geese*, *sheep/sheep*, *fish/fish*.

2 2.36

- Ask the students to listen to three people talking about animals and to check the animals in Exercise 1 that they mention. You may need to play the recording more than once.

ANSWERS:

bull, lion, crocodile, mouse, frog, eagle, cat, horse, dog

2.36

(P = Presenter; R = Ricardo; A = Alicia; H = Hank)

Ricardo

P: So, Ricardo, which animals do you like or dislike?
R: I like dogs and I hate cats.
P: Oh, why?
R: Because I'm allergic to cats.
P: Oh, I see.
R: But I'm interested in wild birds. In fact, I'm writing a book on South American eagles. I find the Black-chested Buzzard Eagle particularly fascinating.
P: Gosh. Are there any animals you're afraid of?
R: Yes, bulls. I once went camping in the south of Argentina. When I put the tent up, there weren't any animals in the field, but when I woke up, I could see this shadow outside the tent—a big shadow. And I could hear heavy breathing.
P: Oh, my goodness. A bull?
R: No, actually it was a cow. A very big cow. But I thought it was a bull.

Alicia

P: Which animals do you like or dislike, Alicia?
A: Well, I like most animals, but I'm really crazy about horses. I think they're wonderful, beautiful animals. I don't like mice, obviously. And I really can't stand frogs. Urgh, they're gross.
P: Are you afraid of frogs?
A: Afraid? I'm terrified of them.
P: Are there any other animals you're afraid of?
A: Well, most wild animals. I don't think I'd like to meet a lion or a crocodile in the street. I enjoy watching documentaries about them, but I wouldn't have one as a pet.

Hank

P: And Hank, which animals do you like or dislike?
H: I'm fascinated by all animals.
P: Have you ever had any experience with wild animals?
H: Yes. I used to work in a zoo.
P: Oh, great.
H: You wouldn't think it was great if you were an animal. How would you like to live in a cage?
P: Oh, no, that would be, um ... Are there any animals you're afraid of?
H: No, I'm afraid of humans.
P: Well, thank you for your help. Bye.

3

- Go through the sentences with the class and make sure everyone understands them. You may need to explain *allergic* (a condition in which certain things, such as cats, pollen, certain foods, etc. make the sufferer come out in a rash, start sneezing, or make their eyes water, etc.).
- Play the recording again and ask the students to underline the correct alternatives. Check answers with the class before asking the students to rewrite the sentences using the names of people in the class. Then go through the example question and answer with the class, and with weaker classes elicit the questions they'll need to find out the other information. Allow the students to mingle and check how many they got correct.

ANSWERS:

a cats **c** horses **e** all animals
b wild birds **d** frogs **f** humans

Vocabulary (SB page 101)

1

- Focus the students' attention on the example and point out that the sentence has been completed with a preposition (*about*) and a noun (*soccer*). Ask various students around the class if they're crazy about soccer, crazy about animals, etc.
- Ask the students to work individually to complete the remaining sentences. Remind them that they need a preposition and a noun each time and that some of their sentences should be true and some false. Go around, monitoring and giving help.

ANSWERS:

a about **c** by **e** to
b in **d** of **f** of

2

- **Pairwork.** Ask the students to work in pairs and to exchange the statements they wrote in Exercise 1.
- Ask them to read their partner's statements and to decide which ones they think are true and which false. They can then check with their partner.

Vocabulary (SB page 102)

1

- Look at the example with the class and then give the students time to read the defining characteristics and match them to the animal they refer to.
- Allow the students to compare results in pairs before checking answers with the class. Answer any questions about vocabulary and ask if the students know any more surprising facts about animals. If they know a lot, perhaps they could prepare a matching activity like the one in this exercise to test other students.

ANSWERS:

a 4 **b** 6 **c** 2 **d** 1 **e** 3 **f** 5

2

- **Groupwork.** Look at the example with the class and then give the groups three minutes to prepare their lists.
- When the three minutes is up, stop the class and find out which group has the longest list. Ask them to read out their list to the class. Invite other teams to call out alternative animals that they put on their lists.
- If you want to make this more of a competition, award one point for every correct animal or insect that each team has listed, and an extra point if it's an animal or insect that no other team got. Explain the points system in advance so that the teams can choose whether to spend time thinking of unusual animals for each letter, or to simply list as many as they can in the time limit.

Extra activity

As an alternative to Exercise 2, students could be encouraged to brainstorm as many animals as they know in the following categories:

- in homes (domestic)
- in the countryside
- on a farm
- in the ocean / rivers
- in the wild / a zoo

Reading & Vocabulary (SB page 102)

1

- Focus the students' attention on the three pictures.
- Read out the three descriptions, or get individual students to read them out, and ask the students to decide which animal goes best with each description.
- Play the recording and ask the students to read the stories as they listen.

ANSWERS:

1 c **2** a **3** b

2

- Give the students time to read the stories again. Then ask them to decide if the statements are true or false. (Tell them to ignore the underlined words at this stage.) You might like to read each one aloud in turn and get the students to vote on whether it's true or false.
- Check answers with the class and explain any difficult vocabulary.

ANSWERS:

- **a** True
- **b** True
- **c** False (Samantha lived near an animal sanctuary.)
- **d** True
- **e** False (Tommy often travels away from home on business, not Ricky.)
- **f** False (He took care of his brother's pet canary.)

3

Ask the students to look at the underlined words in each statement in Exercise 2. Ask them to look back at the stories and find words and expressions which they can use instead of the underlined parts. Check answers before asking the students to comment on the stories and tell a partner any other animal stories they know.

ANSWERS:

- **a** an area with lots of trees – wooded area
- **b** left – walked away
- **c** a safe place – a sanctuary
- **d** thief – burglar
- **e** travels away from home – goes away
- **f** take care of – keep an eye on

Grammar (SB page 103)

Defining relative clauses

1

- Go through the information in the box with the class and read out the example sentences. Point out that the relative clauses are used to combine ideas to make one sentence. Do the first part of the exercise with the class, reminding them to refer to the information in the box to see which relative pronouns can and can't be used.
- Then ask the students to work individually to complete the rules.

ANSWERS:

a that/~~which~~/who **b** that/which/~~who~~

1 who **2** which **3** that

Language notes

Grammar: defining relative clauses

- A defining relative clause gives essential information about the noun or noun phrase it describes. The defining relative clause joins two ideas together with a relative pronoun (*who, which, that*). For example, these two sentences: *I've got a friend. He lives in the United States,* become one sentence when the relative pronoun *who* replaces the pronoun *he*: *I've got a friend who lives in the United States.*
- The relative pronoun *who* is used when talking about people (and replaces the pronoun *he* or *she*); *which* is used when talking about things (and replaces the pronoun *it*). The relative pronoun that can be used to talk about people or things in a defining relative clause, although it's mainly used in spoken English rather than written.

2

- Go through the example with the class and then ask the students to work individually to combine the other sentences. Go around, monitoring and giving help.
- Check answers with the class before asking the students to do the second part of the exercise. When checking answers, find out which sentences are true for the students.

ANSWERS:

- **a** I've got a dog that likes going for long walks.
- **b** I've got a car that isn't very easy to park.
- **c** I've got a sister that works in a store.
- **d** I've got an espresso machine that makes great coffee.
- **e** I've got a friend that lives in Panama.
- **f** I've got some shoes that are too small for me.

a	which	**c**	who	**e**	who
b	which	**d**	which	**f**	which

3

- Look at the example with the class and explain that each definition has one word that isn't needed.
- Check answers to the first part of the exercise before asking the students to match the words to the definitions.

ANSWERS:

- **a** a person who ~~she~~ treats sick animals
- **b** the only animal–apart from humans–which ~~it~~ gets sunburn
- **c** a word to describe people who ~~they~~ are afraid of spiders
- **d** a person who ~~he~~ studies birds
- **e** the scientist who ~~he~~ developed the theory of evolution
- **f** the largest animal that ~~it~~ has ever lived

1 c **2** d **3** a **4** e **5** b **6** f

Cultural notes

Charles Darwin (1809–1882)

A British naturalist whose travels by sea around the world resulted in his theory of evolution as set out in the book *On the Origin of Species* (1859). Darwin's work had a tremendous impact on religious thought. Many people strongly opposed the idea of evolution because it conflicted with their religious convictions.

4 Pairwork

- The pairwork exercise for this unit is on pages 124 and 129 of the Student's Book. Put the students into pairs and tell them who will be Student A, and who will be Student B.
- While they're doing the exercise, go around monitoring and giving help.

5 Grammar Extra 11, Part 1

Ask students to turn to Grammar Extra 11, Part 1 on page 150 of the Student's Book. Here they'll find an explanation of the grammar they've been studying and further exercises to practice it.

ANSWERS:

1
a A camel is a horse **that** has been designed by a committee.
b Everybody knows how to raise children—except the people **who** have them.
c How can you govern a country **that** has 246 varieties of cheese?
d Go on, get out! Last words are for fools **who** haven't said enough.
e Life is something **that** happens when you can't get to sleep.
f A bank is a place **that** will lend you money if you can prove you don't need it.
g Women **who** want to be equal with men don't have ambition.
h People **who** get nostalgic about childhood were obviously never children.

2
a Most of the people who work with me speak perfect English.
b People who complain all the time make me angry.
c I've met lots of people who have the same name as me.
d We should ban cars that use too much gas.
e I think dictionaries that don't give good examples are useless.
f The family that lives next door has a dog and a cat.

Pronunciation (SB page 104)

1 2.37

- Focus the students' attention on the pairs of words in the left-hand column. Play the recording once and ask the students to say what they notice about the pairs of words.
- Play the recording again and ask the students to listen and repeat the pairs of words. When they've done this chorally, ask for individual repetition of the words.

ANSWER:
The two words are pronounced the same but are spelled differently.

Language notes

Pronunciation: homophones

Words which are pronounced the same but have different spellings are called *homophones*. This activity focuses on some common homophones.

2

- Ask the students to match the words in Exercise 1 with their meanings.
- Check answers with the class and then ask about words in their own language(s) which sound the same but have different spellings and meanings.

ANSWERS:
a 3 **b** 1 **c** 2 **d** 4

Listening (SB page 104)

1 2.38

- Ask the students to look at the pictures and explain that they show three people and their pets. Ask them to say what kind of animal each pet is (pig, spider, hamster) and whether they think these are unusual pets or not. You might like to ask if they'd like any of these animals as a pet.
- Explain that they're going to listen to the three people being interviewed about their pets. Ask them to read the questions and then listen and decide which questions the interviewer asked.
- Check answers with the class and see what the students can remember about what each person said about their pet.

ANSWERS:
a, c, e, and f

2.38

(P = Presenter; T = Tim; G = Gus; M = Maxine)
Tim
P: Can you describe your pet?
T: She's very fat and not very pretty. But she's got a cute, curly tail.
P: Is she a good companion?
T: Yes, absolutely. I always tell her my problems, and she listens.
P: Do you and your pet look alike?
T: I hope not.
P: If you were an animal, what would you like to be?
T: A dolphin. I love the ocean, and dolphins are intelligent and funny—like me!

Gus
P: Can you describe your pet?
G: He's black and has eight hairy legs.
P: Is he a good companion?
G: Yeah. He's like a friend. But other people are afraid of him. He scares people away.
P: Do you and your pet look alike?
G: I'm not that hairy—but I think he looks cool, like me.
P: If you were an animal, what would you like to be?
G: A lion, because they're big and tough, and they rule.

Maxine
P: Can you describe your pet?
M: She's very fluffy and very lovable. My boyfriend doesn't like her because she bit him—she doesn't like men.
P: Is she a good companion?
M: Yes, she's good company for me when my boyfriend goes away on business. And she enjoys doing the same things as me—she loves to sleep all day and party all night long.
P: Do you and your pet look alike?
M: I think that she's better looking than me—who could resist those brown eyes?
P: If you were an animal, what would you like to be?
M: I am an animal.

Extra activity

In pairs, students interview each other about their pets using the questions in Exercise 1.

2

- Go through the characteristics with the class and ask them to check the things that they think Tim, Gus, and Maxine mentioned in their interviews. Allow them to work in pairs if they wish.
- Play the interviews again for the students to check their answers.

ANSWERS:

✓: a), b), d), f), g)

3

- **Pairwork.** Ask the students to discuss the questions in pairs. Go around, monitoring and giving help. Ask several pairs to report back to the class.
- In a follow-up feedback session, allow students to share information about their own pets if they wish.

Grammar (SB page 105)

Unreal conditionals

1

- Remind the students that one of the questions in the interviews in the previous section was *If you were an animal, what would you like to be?* Ask the students if it's possible to be an animal. Point out that it's possible to talk about imaginary situations: it's true that no one can actually be an animal, but they can talk about what kind of animal they'd like to be if they could be one.
- Go through the example sentences in the box and ask the students what they'd like to be *if* they were animals.
- Focus the students' attention on the table and go through the structure of unreal conditional sentences with the class. Elicit answers to the questions under the table.
- Check answers and then ask the students to make further questions using the words in the box or their own ideas. Put them into pairs to take turns asking and answering their questions.

ANSWERS:

a Imaginary situation
b Now
c Simple past

Language note

Grammar: unreal conditionals

- The type of conditional in this unit is also known as the "second conditional." There are two clauses in this type of sentence: the *if* clause (*if* followed by the verb in the simple past form), and the main clause (*would* followed by the infinitive without *to*).
  For example: *If I was an animal*, (*if* + simple past form) *I'd be a cat*. (*would* + infinitive).
- The clauses can be reversed without changing the meaning, but the punctuation changes: When the *if* clause comes after the main clause they aren't separated by a comma. When the *if* clause comes before the main clause they are separated by a comma.
- The examples in this unit relate to a hypothetical or imaginary present, and not the past. If is followed by the simple past form to "remove it one step from reality," not because the situation relates to the past.

2

- Ask students to look again at the table and replace the word animal with words in the box and their own ideas.
- **Pairwork.** Put the students into pairs. Students then ask their partner the questions.

3

- Introduce the idea of a "moral dilemma": a situation in which several courses of action are possible and a person is required to choose what to do. That choice may be "moral," in that it's the right thing to do (by society's standards of right and wrong), or the thing that will cause the least harm to anyone. Alternatively, some people may choose the course of action that will benefit themselves the most.

- Go through the situations with the class and make sure that everyone understands them. Ask the students to complete them with the correct verb forms. Check answers with the class before moving on to the next stage of the exercise.
- Put the students into small groups to discuss what they'd do in these situations. When they've finished, ask them to think of some more moral dilemmas. Get them to write these out properly and check that they've formed their questions correctly. You can then ask them to exchange them with other groups and discuss each other's new moral dilemmas. Have a feedback session in which groups report back to the class on what they decided.

ANSWERS:

a	found	c	gave
b	would you call	d	would you look

4 Grammar Extra 11, Part 2

Ask students to turn to Grammar Extra 11, Part 2 on page 150 of the Student's Book. Here they'll find an explanation of the grammar they've been studying and further exercises to practice it.

ANSWERS:

a could sing; 'd join
b won; 'd give
c was/were; wouldn't be
d had; 'd read
e didn't work; wouldn't be
f lost; 'd have to

Speaking: anecdote (SB page 105)

For more information about how to set up, monitor, and repeat Anecdotes, see pages xviii–xx in the Introduction.

1 2.39

- Ask the students to look at the picture. Explain that someone called Mandy is going to talk about her friend in the picture and his pet.
- Go through the questions and the answer choices with the class. Explain any unknown vocabulary and then ask the students to listen and underline the answers Mandy gives.
- Check answers with the class and ask them whether they know anyone like Angus who has an unusual pet.

ANSWERS:

a	iguana	f	the drapes
b	Angus	g	Vegetables
c	Iggy	h	goes for walks in the park
d	five		
e	green and almost a meter long		

2.39

I know somebody who has an iguana as a pet. It's a man I work with named Angus. The iguana's name is Iggy and it's probably about five years old–that's how long I've known Angus and he got it soon after we met. It was a birthday gift from his wife. It's almost a meter long from the tip of its nose to the end of its tail and it's a beautiful green color. Like all reptiles, iguanas never stop growing, so Iggy will get bigger and bigger. It's kind of shy and nervous, which is exactly the opposite of Angus, who's very outgoing and confident. It's definitely better looking than Angus, though. Iggy doesn't sleep in a cage. Right now, it lives at the top of the drapes in Angus' living room.
When it was young, it ate crickets, but now that it's adult, it doesn't need so much protein–in fact, it's completely vegetarian. Angus takes it for walks in the park on a leash. It's funny–when it's scared, it runs up Angus' body and sits on his head.

2

- Give the students a minute or two to decide what they're going to talk about. Then ask them to look at the questions in Exercise 1 again and decide how they'd answer them about the pet they're going to talk about. Allow them to make notes of what they're going to say and how they're going to say it, but discourage them from writing a paragraph that they can simply read out. Go around, monitoring and giving help.
- **Pairwork.** Put the students into pairs and ask them to take turns to tell their partner about their pet or a pet they know. Encourage them to ask each other follow-up questions to get further information.
- Ask some pairs to report back to the class about what they found out.

Language for Life (SB page 106)

1 2.40

- Focus the students' attention on the illustration. Explain that the students are going to hear telephone conversations between Sarah, the woman in the picture, and four people she's going to ask to take care of her pet this weekend.
- Play the recording for them to listen, read, and decide who will look after Mona. Check answers with the class and ask if any of the students would be willing to look after a friend's pet snake.

ANSWER:

Mrs. Harvey is going to take care of Mona.

2 2.41

- Ask the students to work in pairs to complete the table.
- Check answers with the class, then play the recording for them to listen and repeat the useful phrases.

ANSWERS:
1 Could you take care of Mona?
2 Oh, I'm afraid I can't.
3 Do you think you could take care of Mona?
4 I'd really like to help, but I'm afraid I can't.
5 Oh, yes, that's no problem at all.
6 That's wonderful!

Ask the students to look closely at the phrases in the completed table in Exercise 2 and to choose the correct alternative to complete the sentence (write the sentence on the board): If you want to be formal or more polite, you usually use more/less words?

ANSWER:
more

3

- **Pairwork.** Go through the situations with the class. Then ask them to work in pairs and to choose one of the situations to write a conversation about.
- As they write their conversations, go around, giving help with vocabulary and making sure that they incorporate some of the useful phrases.
- When they've finished, ask them to practice their conversations. It may help to have them sitting back-to-back to simulate a real phone conversation. Choose some pairs to perform their conversations to the class.

Life Skills (SB page 106)

Giving opinions: Animals: Use or abuse?

Explain that there many different ways to express opinions. Write on the board AGREE and DISAGREE. Elicit from the students phrases they know to express either concept. Tell the students that they will see more ways to express opinions during the lesson as this section focuses on giving opinions about the way we use animals.

1

- **Pairwork.** Ask the students to work in pairs to complete more uses for each animal. Encourage pairs to join other pairs if they are short of ideas. Go around, helping with vocabulary.
- Then encourage several pairs to share their ideas with the rest of the class.

2

- Refer the students to the expressions for giving opinions and compare these to those suggested by the students in the introduction. Go through any expressions they don't know.
- Focus the students' attention on the exercise and ask them to complete the task individually. Go around, offering help, especially with the two additional sentences that the students have to write.

Vocabulary Extra (SB page 107)

Animals

1

Focus the students' attention on the pictures and the names of the baby animals. Read these aloud and ask the students to match them to the names of the adult animals.

ANSWERS:
a kitten: a cat 5
a calf: a cow 2
a puppy: a dog 1
a chick: a hen 6
a foal: a horse 4
a lamb: a sheep 3

2

Pairwork. Put the students into pairs. Go through the example question and answer with the class and then ask them to cover the words and pictures and take turns to test each other with similar questions.

Extra activity

Ask the students:

- Which of these animals would you like as a pet?
- Which of these animals would you like to eat?

Insects

1

- Focus the students' attention on the pictures and the insect names. Remind students that the underlining indicates the syllable of the word that has the strongest stress. Read the insect names aloud and ask the students to match the pictures to them.
- Check answers with the class and check that everyone can pronounce the names correctly.

ANSWERS:

an ant 4
a bee 5
a butterfly 1
a cockroach 6
a fly 8
a mosquito 7
a spider 3
a wasp 2

2

Pairwork. Put the students into pairs. Go through the example question and answer with the class and then ask them to cover the words and take turns to test each other with similar questions.

Extra activity

Ask the students: Which of these insects have bitten or stung you?

Focus on *that*

1

- Allow the students to work in pairs to complete the table.
- Check answers and explain any difficult vocabulary.

ANSWERS:

1 What's that strange noise?
2 Look at that car. It's going too fast.
3 The woman that called me spoke French.
4 Where are the pictures that were on my desk?
5 Yes, that's right.
6 That's all right.

2

Ask the students to write their own example sentences. Go around, monitoring and giving extra help to anyone.

Writing

Workbook 47

Linking: giving examples.

Giving opinions

Before the next lesson ...

You'll need dice for each pair of students for the activity for the Reading & Speaking activity on page 109 of the Student's Book. Depending on the size of your class, you may need to ask the students to bring their own to the next lesson.

Further Practice Material

Need more classroom practice activities?
Photocopiable resource materials in the Teacher's Presentation Kit / Extra Resources

Need more tests?
Test Generator
Teacher's Presentation Kit / Extra Resources / Tests

Need more on important teaching concepts?
Key concepts in *American Inside Out Evolution* pages xxi-xxxvii

Need student self-study practice?
Workbook pages 44-47

Need more information and ideas?
American Inside Out Evolution website www.macmillan.com.br/americaninsideoutevolution

Need to check what your students can do by the end of this unit?
Self-evaluation checklists on pages xxxix-xliii

12 Incredible *Overview*

Section	Aims	What the students are doing
Reading SB page 108	Reading for detail	Reading two stories and inserting missing sentences. Identifying true and false statements. Discussing incredible but true stories.
Grammar SB page 109	Past perfect	Studying the form and use of the past perfect. Underlining actions that happened first in sentences. Talking about emotions and what had happened previously to cause them.
Vocabulary SB page 109	Collocations with *have*, *make*, and *take*	Finding collocations in stories and completing statements with them. Discussing the statements.
Reading SB page 110	Reading for specific information	Matching pictures with reviews. Answering questions on the text. Discussing good and bad hotels they have stayed in.
Grammar SB page 111	Passives	Studying the form and use of the passive. Completing questions and answers. Asking and answering questions.
Speaking: anecdote SB page 111	Fluency practice	Listening and underlining the correct information. Talking about the most incredible building they have ever seen.
Vocabulary & Listening SB page 112	The weather	Completing a table with weather words. Underlining the correct information in a weather forecast. Inventing a weather forecast for their own country.
Grammar SB page 112	*will* and *might* for future and possibility	Completing predictions about the weather with *will* and *might*. Changing the predictions so they are true about where they live.
Reading & Speaking SB page 113	Reading for detail	Discussing predictions for the future. Writing sentences about their future.
Language for Life SB page 114	Useful conversational expressions for making comments	Listening to a conversation and underlining the topics. Completing a conversation with *very* and *absolutely*. Listening to and repeating useful expressions. Completing a table with adjectives and using them to continue the conversation.
Life Skills SB page 114	Achieving goals: In five years	Completing a table with goals for the next five years and how they could be achieved. Discussing goals with a partner and looking for similarities.
Vocabulary Extra SB page 115	Review of words from the unit: weather; *do*, *get*, *go*, *have*, *make*, and *take*	Matching pictures with words. Completing a table of nouns and adjectives to do with the weather. Studying expressions for talking about temperature. Completing collocation tables with *do*, *get*, *go*, *have*, *make*, and *take*.

12 Incredible *Teacher's notes*

Warm-up

Explain that the title of this unit is *Incredible* and this word can be used to refer to anything that is so amazing that it's difficult to believe. Elicit from the students any amazing stories from their own country or culture. If they don't have any specific examples, they may be able to talk about TV shows that they've watched which tell incredible stories.

Reading (SB page 108)

1 2.43

- Focus the students' attention on the pictures, tell them that they're going to read two incredible stories and ask them to predict what might be in these stories.
- Give the students a time limit to read the stories and then ask them to decide where the missing sentences might go. Allow them to discuss this in pairs before playing the recording for them to check their answers.
- Teach the word *coincidence* (when two things unexpectedly happen at the same time) and ask what the coincidences were in Story B (Lucy and Stevie were born on the same day, in the same hospital).

ANSWERS:

a - Story A. Position 2
b - Story B. Position 2

2

Ask the students to work individually to mark the statements true or false. Allow them to compare in pairs before checking with the class. Encourage them to correct the false statements.

ANSWERS:

a False (They didn't know each other, but turned out to be brothers.)
b True
c True
d True
e False (They were born in the same hospital.)
f True

3 Pairwork

- The pairwork exercise for this unit is on pages 124 and 129 of the Student's Book. Put the students into pairs and tell them who will be Student A, and who will be Student B.
- While they're doing the exercise, go around, monitoring and giving help. Take note of any errors which may need particular attention later, and also any examples of good language use which you can praise in a feedback session.

ANSWERS:

Text before marriage
A clairvoyant had once told Emilia Sanchez that she would meet her husband when she was 21. She was now almost 22 and hadn't met the love of her life yet. One day, she tapped the text message, "Do you want to talk?" into her cell phone. She then invented a number and sent the message. She didn't know that the number belonged to her future husband. Pedro Gonzales was at work 140 kilometers away when he got the message. He called Emilia, and they talked for about an hour. They found that they had a lot in common and made plans to meet. They got married six months later.

4

Groupwork. Put the students into groups to discuss the questions. Go around, monitoring and giving help with vocabulary. Ask a representative from each group to present any interesting stories to the class.

Extra activity

Ask students to write and illustrate some unusual stories, and then display them in the classroom.

Grammar (SB page 109)

Past perfect

1

- Go through the form of the past perfect in the box with the class. Then put the students into pairs to look at the sentences and answer the questions. As they do this, go around, giving extra help to students who need it.
- Check answers with the class and make sure that everyone understands that the past perfect is used to help express the order in which actions happened in the past.

ANSWERS:

a canceled = simple past; had planned = past perfect
b The past perfect
c 1 It wasn't canceled
2 Was it canceled?
3 Paul hadn't planned.
4 Had Paul planned?

Language note

Grammar: past perfect

You use the past perfect when you're talking about the past and want to talk about something that happened before the time you're speaking about. It's an "earlier" past. It's formed with *had* + past participle.

2

- Go through the example with the class. Explain that in the first sentence, the person had breakfast in the office after they arrived at work. In the second, they had breakfast, probably at home, before they arrived at work. Ask the students to read the other pairs of sentences and decide which actions happened first. As they do this, go around, offering extra help to students who are having difficulty.
- Check answers with the class and then read out the example sentence using *already* with the class. Ask the students to rewrite the other sentences using *already*. Go around, monitoring and giving help. Check answers with the class and ask the students which sentences are true for them.

ANSWERS:

a 1 I had breakfast when I got to work this morning.
2 I'd had breakfast when I got to work this morning.
b 1 When I got home yesterday, my mom made dinner.
2 When I got home yesterday, my mom had made dinner.
c 1 When I started learning English, I'd been to the USA several times.
2 When I started learning English, I went to the USA several times.
d 1 This lesson started when I arrived.
2 This lesson had started when I arrived.

a 2 I'd already had breakfast when I got to work this morning.
b 2 When I got home yesterday, my mom had already made dinner.
c 1 When I started learning English, I had already been to the USA several times.
d 2 This lesson had already started when I arrived.

3

- Go through the emotions with the class and make sure everyone understands them. As you read each one aloud, you could ask the students to mime the feeling or show by their facial expression that they understand it.
- Give the students a few minutes to think about times when they've felt these emotions and what had happened to make them feel that way. Allow them to make brief notes if they wish.
- Put the students into pairs. Read the example aloud and point out the use of the past perfect to say what the person had done to make them feel really tired. Then ask the students to take turns to tell each other about the emotions and what had caused them. Go around, monitoring and taking note of any particularly good sentences which can be put on the board or reported to the class.

4 Grammar Extra 12, Part 1

Ask students to turn to Grammar Extra 12, Part 1 on page 152 of the Student's Book. Here they'll find an explanation of the grammar they've been studying and further exercises to practice it.

ANSWERS:

1	had lived	7	had died
2	had died	8	had seen
3	were	9	met
4	had been	10	hadn't seen
5	had lived	11	reminded
6	realized	12	had been

Vocabulary (SB page 109)

1

- Remind the students that collocations are words that frequently occur together. Point out that have, make, and take are very common verbs in English and that they occur in several fixed expressions.
- Ask the students to work individually to find the collocations in the stories on page 108 and to complete the sentences. Go around, monitoring and giving help. Check answers with the class and then ask the students if they know of any other collocations with these verbs. They may know take a shower, have dinner, make plans, etc.

ANSWERS:

take another flight, have a first date, had the same interests

a have dinner
b take pictures
c make money
d make a promise
e have a good time

Language note

Vocabulary: collocations

Many words in English exist as part of a group of words which commonly occur together in a certain order. Verbs like *have*, *make*, *take*, and *do* are all commonly used in collocations. *Have breakfast* is much more natural than eat *breakfast*; you *make a mistake*, you don't ~~*do a mistake*~~; you *take a picture*, you don't ~~*make a picture*~~ and you *do your homework*, you don't ~~*make your homework*~~.

Reading (SB page 110)

1

- Focus the students' attention on the pictures and tell them that these are pictures of special or unusual hotels around the world. Give them a minute or two to look at the pictures and then ask them what they think is unusual about each hotel, e.g. *It's shaped like a dog.*
- Tell the students that they are going to read a review of each hotel and they must match a description to each picture. Point out that the students are only reading for gist so they should read quickly for general meaning and not worry about any new words at this point. Encourage the students to look at the names of the hotels for clues.
- Have the students complete the task individually then ask students to share their answers with the rest of the class. Ask them to say what helped them understand the answer.

ANSWERS:

1 d
2 b
3 a
4 c

Cultural notes

The Dog Bark Park Inn, USA

The Dog Bark Park Inn is located in Idaho. It is built in the shape of a beagle and has only 2 rooms. The local residents call the hotel Sweet Willy.

Capsulevalue, Japan

A capsule hotel, or a pod hotel, is a type of hotel developed in Japan that features a large number of extremely small "rooms" (capsules). The hotel offers cheap, basic overnight accommodation.

Arctic Tree House Hotel, Finland

The Arctic Tree House Hotel is a luxury located in Lapland, near Santa Claus Village. The guests can enjoy views of the surrounding forest over the tree tops and see the Northern Lights.

The Hobbit Motel, New Zealand

The Hobbit Motel rooms are all self-contained with kitchens, shower and toilet facilities. The rooms can accommodate between 2-6 people and each has specially designed furniture and décor modelled after the set of the films *The Hobbit and Lord of the Rings.*

2

- Explain that the students will now read the reviews more carefully and look for specific information.
- Focus the students' attention on the scan questions and deal with any new vocabulary.
- Ask the students to complete the task individually then compare answers with a partner. Ask several pairs to go through the answers and ask them to say where in the text the answers can be found.
- Time permitting, ask the class to vote for the hotel they would most like to visit and why.

ANSWERS:

1 Arctic Tree House Hotel, Finland
2 The Hobbit Motel, New Zealand
3 Osaka
4 The Dog Bark Park Inn, USA

Grammar (SB page 111)

Passives

1

- Focus attention on the information in the box and explain that the sentences are all examples of the passive. You may like to point out that all the sentences they've studied in earlier units have been in the active, but that the questions in Exercise 2 of the previous section were in the passive. The reviews on page 110 have many examples of the passive in use. You could ask the students to look through the reviews and underline the passive sentences
- Go through the sentences in the table with the class and point out the differences between the active sentences and the passive ones.
- Ask the students to decide if statements a–c are true or false.

ANSWERS:

a True
b True
c True

Language note

Grammar: passives

You use the passive when the person, people, or thing that does an action isn't important. Compare: *This bridge was built in 1750* with *Someone built this bridge in 1750*. It's natural to want to make the bridge the subject of the sentence (as in the first example) and by using the passive this is achieved. It's formed with the verb *be* in the correct form (*will be*, *is/are going to be* to talk about the future; *is* or *are* to talk about the present; *was* or *were* to talk about the past) + the past participle.

2 2.44

- Go through the first example with the class and ask several students this question about their own houses. Then ask them to complete the remaining questions and answers.
- Play the recording for the students to check their answers. Then play it again for them to listen and repeat the questions and answers. When they've done this chorally, ask individual students to repeat the questions and answers.

ANSWERS:

a Was your house built before 1980?
Yes, it was. No, it wasn't.
b Were your shoes designed in Italy?
Yes, they were. No, they weren't.
c Is your salary paid by check?
Yes, it is. No, it isn't.
d Were you invited to any parties last week?
Yes, I was. No, I wasn't.
e Is your name spelled the same in English?
Yes, it is. No, it isn't.
f Was your cell phone made in Japan?
Yes, it was. No, it wasn't.

3

Pairwork. Put the students into pairs and ask them to take turns asking and answering the questions in Exercise 2.

Extra activity

Ask students who answered *No* to any of the questions in Exercise 2 to correct the information using the passive. So, for example, for question a) they might say, *No, it wasn't. It was built in 1995.*

4 Grammar Extra 12, Part 2

Ask students to turn to Grammar Extra 12, Part 2 on page 153 of the Student's Book. Here they'll find an explanation of the grammar they've been studying and further exercises to practice it.

ANSWERS:

1

a was opened
b is parked
c is cleaned
d was painted
e is pronounced
f was made

2

a Was this school opened in the 1990s?
b Is your car parked outside your house every day?
c Is your house cleaned once a week?
d Was our classroom painted recently?
e Is your name pronounced differently in English?
f Was your watch made in Switzerland?

3

1 is called
2 was built
3 is connected
4 was started
5 was completed
6 was designed
7 is considered

Speaking: anecdote (SB page 111)

For more information about how to set up, monitor and repeat Anecdotes, see page xviii-xx in the Introduction.

1 2.45

- Ask the students to look at the picture. Explain that this is Curro and he's going to talk about the most incredible building he's ever seen.
- Go through the questions and the answer choices with the class. Explain any unknown vocabulary and then ask the students to listen and underline the answers Curro gives.
- Check answers with the class and ask them whether they've ever been to the Alhambra and if so, what they thought of it.

ANSWERS:

a Alhambra
b the south of Spain
c When I was eighteen
d In the 13th or 14th century
e The style is Moorish
f location
g Four times

2.45

The most incredible building I've ever seen is the Alhambra. It's a beautiful palace in Granada in the south of Spain. The first time I saw the Alhambra Palace was when I was eighteen—I went to visit my brother who was studying in Granada. I think it was built in the thirteenth or fourteenth century for the Moorish kings. Alhambra is an Arabic name—it means "red," probably because of the color of the walls. It's an enormous building. I don't know who the architect was, but the style is Moorish, or Islamic. I love the gardens - water is very important. You can hear water running wherever you go. But it isn't only the building that's so great. I think the location is the most incredible thing about it. It's built on a hill overlooking Granada with the Sierra Nevada mountains in the background. I've been there four times, and each time I think it is more beautiful. In my opinion, it is definitely one of the seven wonders of the modern world.

Cultural notes

Colosseum, Rome

A Roman amphitheater built between 70 AD and 80 AD, the Colosseum could seat 50,000 spectators and was used for public spectacles such as dramas and gladiator fights. Although the last known entertainment took place in 465 AD, it remained in use, even inhabited, until the early 19th century. In 2000, a new floor was installed in part of the arena for smaller events. Larger events are played outside, using the Colosseum as a backdrop.

The Alhambra Palace

Situated in Granada, in Andalusia, southern Spain, the Alhambra Palace is the fortress of the Moorish monarchs of Granada. It's a wonderful example of Islamic architecture and dates back to 900 AD, although much of the present structure is probably from the 14th century.

2

- Give the students a minute or two to decide which building they're going to talk about. Then ask them to look at the questions in Exercise 1 again and decide how they'd answer them about the building they're going to talk about. Allow them to make notes of what they're going to say and how they're going to say it, but discourage them from writing a paragraph that they can simply read out. Go around, monitoring and giving help with vocabulary.
- **Pairwork**. Put the students into pairs and ask them to take turns to tell their partner about the most incredible building they've ever seen. Encourage them to ask each other follow-up questions to get further information.
- Ask some pairs to report back to the class about what they found out.

Vocabulary & Listening (SB page 112)

1

- Ask the students how they'd describe the weather today. Elicit words for temperature as well as weather conditions. Then focus their attention on the table. Ask them to work individually to try to complete it with suitable words to describe the weather.
- Ask the students to compare notes with a partner before checking answers with the class.

ANSWERS:

1 sun
2 cloudy
3 rain
4 foggy
5 wind
6 storm

2 2.46

- Ask the students to look at the picture of the North Pole in winter. Tell them to read the text and decide which of the alternatives is most likely.
- Allow them to compare their answers in pairs before playing the recording for them to listen and check. Ask the students whether they would prefer to live in a very hot climate or a very cold climate.

ANSWERS:

1 cold
2 minus 30
3 windy
4 snow
5 dark
6 warmer

Cultural notes

North Pole

The North Pole is the most northerly point on Earth and is in the middle of the Arctic Ocean in waters that are usually covered with ice. As the ice is constantly moving, it isn't possible to build any permanent structure on it (unlike the South Pole, which is located on the continent of Antarctica, and on which there's a permanent structure, the Amundsen-Scott South Pole Station).

3

- Remind the students that they can use the text in Exercise 2 as a model and just change the highlighted words to match a particular season in their own country. Encourage them to work individually to do this.
- Put the students into pairs to read the weather forecasts and guess the season. Alternatively, collect in the forecasts and read them aloud to the class, asking the students to guess collectively which season is being described.

Grammar (SB page 112)

will and *might* for future possibility

1

- Go through the sentences in the margin and explain that *will* and *might* are both used to talk about future possibility. (See Language notes below.) Ask the students to look at the weather forecast in Exercise 2 of the previous section and underline *will* and *might*.
- Go through the example with the class, then ask the students to complete the remaining predictions. As they do this, go around, checking that everyone has understood. Point out that *probably* (in sentences b and f) expresses less certainty than *definitely*, but still gives an idea of what the speaker is pretty sure will happen.
- Check answers with the class before asking the students to rewrite the sentences so they are true for them and to compare them in pairs.

ANSWERS:

a The south will definitely have better weather than the north.
b Tomorrow will probably be warmer than today.
c I think we'll have a lot of snow next winter.
d It might rain later today.
e I don't think there will be any storms tomorrow.
f It probably won't be so sunny tomorrow.
g It definitely won't freeze tomorrow.

Language notes

Grammar: *will* and *might*

- *Will* and *might* are both modal verbs and so they follow the same grammatical rules as other modal verbs. They're followed by the infinitive without *to* and they don't take the third person *s*. For example: *It might rain tomorrow*. NOT: ~~*It might to rain tomorrow. It mights rain tomorrow. It might rains tomorrow.*~~
- The meaning of *will* and *might* can differ depending on the context in which they're used. In this unit, *will* and *might* are used to make predictions about the future. *Might* is used to express a 50% possibility, whereas the meaning of *will* is broader and depends on other words (*definitely*, *probably*, *think*, *don't think*) that are used with it and which modify it:
  - *It will definitely happen* is a strong prediction and indicates a degree of certainty from the speaker.
  - *It will probably happen* indicates confidence, but isn't as strong.
  - *I think it will happen* is less confident than the previous two examples but still more confident than *It might happen*.
- The modifying words *definitely* and *probably* come after *will* but before *won't*: *It will definitely happen. It definitely won't happen.*

2

- **Pairwork.** Go through the prompts with the class and then ask the students to discuss which people in the class they can make these predictions about.
- Go around, monitoring and giving help. Encourage them to use all the expressions in the box at least once.
- Check answers by having pairs read their sentences aloud and ask the people named whether or not they agree with the prediction.

Reading & Speaking (SB page 113)

1

- Ask the students to read the article quickly and say whether they agree with the predictions. Remind them that they are only reading for gist so they should not worry about any new words at this point.
- Wrap up the task by asking a few students to share their opinions with the rest of the class and go over any new vocabulary.

2

- Ask the students to work individually to write their sentences. As they work, go around offering extra help to anyone who is having difficulties with the concept or structure of making predictions.
- When they've finished, ask them to compare their sentences with a partner and discuss their predictions. Put any particularly good sentences on the board.

Language for Life (SB page 114)

1 ▶ **2.47**

- Focus the students' attention on the illustration and ask the students where Alma and Betty, the two women, are (at the hairdresser's). Ask the students if women at the hairdresser's in their country talk to each other. Teach the word *gossip* and ask for other situations in which people gossip and the sorts of things they gossip about.
- Go through the list of topics, then play the recording and ask the students to check the topics that the two women talk about.

> **ANSWERS:**
>
> They talk about: celebrities, clothes, and houses.

2

- Explain that *very* and *absolutely* are both used to make adjectives stronger. Ask the students to read the conversation and try to complete it with *very* and *absolutely*.
- Play the recording again for the students to check their answers. Ask them if they notice anything about when you use *very* and when you use *absolutely*. They may notice that you use *absolutely* with adjectives which are already strong.

> **ANSWERS:**
>
> **1** very
> **2** absolutely
> **3** very
> **4** absolutely
> **5** very
> **6** absolutely
> **7** very
> **8** absolutely
> **9** very
> **10** absolutely
> **11** very
> **12** absolutely
> **13** very
> **14** absolutely

3 ▶ **2.48**

- Ask the students to look closely at the useful phrases. Point out that some adjectives are stronger than others. For example, *pretty* and *gorgeous* have similar meaning, but *gorgeous* is much stronger than *pretty*. Here the adjectives are paired by meaning. In each pair, *very* is used with the weaker adjective and *absolutely* with the stronger one.
- Play the recording and ask the students to repeat the phrases, trying to imitate the intonation of the speakers. When they've done this chorally, ask individual students to repeat the words and encourage them to exaggerate their intonation to match the speakers.

4

- Remind the students that Alma and Betty were looking at a magazine at the hairdresser's. Ask them to imagine that they're now looking at a different page of the magazine and to continue their conversation. Practicing their new conversations will be easier if you allow them to work in pairs to do this. Go around, offering help with ideas and vocabulary. Encourage them to use the adjectives in Exercises 3 and the ones in the box or their own ideas.
- Ask the students to practice their conversation aloud using appropriate intonation and then perform them for the class. Allow them to sit side by side at the front of the class with magazines open as if in a hairdresser's as they do this.

Life Skills (SB page 114)

Achieving Goals: In Five Years

1

Ask the students to work individually to complete the table with their goals for the next five years.

2

Students consider how they might achieve their goals and fill in the table.

3

Ask the students to work in pairs to discuss their goals and find out how many are similar.

Vocabulary Extra (SB page 115)

Weather

1

- Focus the students' attention on the list of words and point out that they're all to do with the weather. Check that the students can pronounce all the words correctly.
- Ask the students to look at the pictures and match each one to the weather words. Point out that the first one has been done for them.

2

Go through the example with the class and explain that you can say such things as *There is a breeze today* or *It is breezy today*. Ask students to complete the table with the other corresponding nouns and adjectives.

ANSWERS:

1 and 2

Noun	Adjective	
breeze	breezy	9
cloud	cloudy	11
drizzle	drizzly	1
fog	foggy	6
heat	hot	7
humidity	humid	8
ice	icy	4
mist	misty	5
rain	rainy	2
storm	stormy	3
sun	sunny	12
wind	windy	10

3

- Read the words on the scale aloud to the class or get one or two of the students to read them out. Ask them to work individually to decide what temperature is, for them, the equivalent of each of these terms.
- You might like to point out that the terms are in order on the scale, with *freezing* referring to extreme cold and *boiling* to extreme heat, and that when you say *It's freezing* or *It's boiling*, this isn't a literal statement of fact.
- Allow the students to compare results with a partner and see if they agree on the temperatures.
- You could review *very* and *absolutely* with the class. Ask the students which adjectives they can use with *very* (*cold/chilly*, *warm* and *hot*) and which with *absolutely* (*freezing* and *boiling*).

Focus on *do, get, go, have, make, take*

1

- Allow the students to work in pairs to complete the tables, if they wish. Encourage them to say each of the collocations aloud to see what sounds right.
- Check answers and answer any questions the students may have.
- Note: there's some overlap in the use of these verbs. For example, you could also say *get lunch* or *get a bus* or *get the shopping* or *get home*. However, the collocations given here are the most frequent ones.

ANSWERS:

a get
b have
c take
d make
e do
f go

2

Ask the students to use their dictionaries to find other collocations for these verbs.

Extra activity

Ask the students to produce sentences using some of the collocations.

Further Practice Material

Need more classroom practice activities?
Photocopiable resource materials in the Teacher's Presentation Kit / Extra Resources

Need more tests?
Test Generator
Teacher's Presentation Kit / Extra Resources / Tests

Need more on important teaching concepts?
Key concepts in *American Inside Out Evolution* pages xxi-xxxvii

Need student self-study practice?
Workbook pages 48–51

Need more information and ideas?
American Inside Out Evolution website www.macmillan.com.br/americaninsideoutevolution

Need to check what your students can do by the end of this unit?
Self-evaluation checklists on pages xxxix-xliii

Review D *Teacher's notes*

These exercises act as a check of the grammar and vocabulary that the students have learned in Units 10–12. Use them to find any problems that students are having, or anything that they haven't understood and which will need further work.

Grammar (SB page 116)

Remind the students of the grammar explanations they read and the exercises they did in the Grammar Extra on pages 148 to 153.

1

This exercise reviews *will* (future) from Unit 10.

ANSWERS:

a	will help	d	Will Sara be
b	won't have	e	won't eat
c	'll send	f	Will you see

2

This exercise reviews future time clauses from Unit 10.

ANSWERS:

a	If	d	When
b	When	e	If
c	as soon as	f	as soon as

3

This exercise reviews *used to* and *didn't use to* from Unit 10. Check answers with the class before asking the students to write new sentences, including one false one. They then see if they can identify their partner's false sentence.

ANSWERS:

- **a** I used to live in an apartment.
- **b** -
- **c** -
- **d** my family didn't use to watch TV.
- **e** I didn't use to like classical music.

4

This exercise reviews defining relative clauses from Unit 11.

ANSWERS:

- **a** She has a cat which never stops eating.
- **b** I have a friend who lives in Peru.
- **c** Where are the eggs which were in the refrigerator?
- **d** Those are the people who bought my old house.
- **e** She has a son who is a doctor.

5

This exercise reviews unreal conditionals from Unit 11. When you've checked the answers, ask the students to practice the conversation in pairs.

ANSWERS:

1	would you do	5	'd get
2	won	6	wouldn't buy
3	'd buy	7	Would you give
4	won	8	had
		9	'd give

6

This exercise reviews the past perfect from Unit 12.

ANSWERS:

a	4	d	3
b	1	e	2
c	5	f	6

7

This exercise reviews the past passive from Unit 12. Check answers with the class before asking the students to answer the questions. Then put them into pairs to compare their results.

ANSWERS:

- **a** Was your car made in Brazil?
- **b** Was your house built in the 20th century?
- **c** Were your shoes made in Argentina?
- **d** Was your jacket designed by Armani?
- **e** Was your watch made in Japan?
- **f** Was your computer manufactured in China?

Cultural notes

Giorgio Armani (born 1934)

The Italian fashion designer Giorgio Armani has given his name to a range of perfumes and (mainly men's) clothing, creating one of the most famous designer labels in the world. He has a number of trademarks including: Giorgio Armani, Emporio Armani, Armani Cosmetics, and Armani Jeans.

Vocabulary (SB page 117)

1

This exercise reviews words connected to lifestyles from Unit 10. Check answers with the class before asking the students to check the statements that are true for them and then compare with a partner.

ANSWERS:

a	a healthy life	d	in a hurry
b	extended family	e	a good network
c	a brisk walk	f	in shape

2

This exercise reviews food vocabulary from Unit 10.

ANSWERS:

Fruit and vegetables: beans, garlic, lettuce, onion, orange, peach, tomato
Meat and fish: chicken, sausage, shrimp, trout
Other: coffee, nuts, soup

3

This exercise reviews vocabulary to do with food preparation from Unit 10.

ANSWERS:

1 Peel, Boil
2 Chop
3 Put
4 Slice
5 Bake

4

This exercise reviews prepositions. Check answers with the class before asking the students to check the statements that are true for them and then compare with a partner.

ANSWERS:

a of
b about
c in
d to
e of

5

This exercise reviews collocations with take and make from Unit 12. Check answers with the class before asking the students to answer the questions and then compare with a partner.

ANSWERS:

a make **b** take **c** make **d** take

Pronunciation (SB page 117)

1

Remind the students that the boxes show the syllables of a word and the large boxes indicate the stressed syllables. Here the students are being asked to classify words from Units 10–12 according to how many syllables they have and where the main stress falls. Encourage them to say each word aloud to get a feeling for what sounds right.

2 2.49

Point out the main stresses in the example words which are underlined. Ask the students to do the same for the other words in the table. Then play the recording for them to check their answers. Play it a second time for them to listen and repeat.

ANSWERS:

1 and 2
A: fitness, healthy, lettuce, promise, rainy
B: afraid, arrive, enjoy, relax, sardine
C: animal, dangerous, gardening, politics, terrified

Reading & Listening (SB page 118)

1 2.50

Give the students plenty of time to read and listen to the article. Then ask them to match the animals to the places. Make sure the students can pronounce the names of the animals and the numbers correctly. Ask them which journey they find most surprising.

ANSWERS:

a 2 **b** 4 **c** 1 **d** 3 **e** 5

2

Go through the items with the students before they read the texts again and see if they can identify which animals they refer to. Then ask them to read the text again and find any remaining answers.

ANSWERS:

a polar bear
b pigs
c duck
d manatee
e giraffe

3 2.51

Go through the statements with the students before playing the recording. Then ask them to listen and say which statements are true and which false. Encourage them to correct the false statements.

ANSWERS:

a False (Emma went on vacation with Dom.)
b True
c True
d False (They didn't sleep well because they were woken at 3 a.m. and had to get off the train and wait for a bus.)
e False (The coffee was terrible.)
f True
g False (It rained when they were setting off on the boat, but it stopped quickly and the sun came out.)

2.51

(L = Lou; D = Dom)

L: Have you ever been on an animal adventure, Dom?
D: Yes, we went scuba diving in Thailand. The journey there was so long!
L: Oh, yeah?
D: Emma and I were living in Bangkok and we decided to go to Koh Tao on vacation.
L: Koh Tao?
D: Yeah. It means "Turtle Island" in Thai. It's near Koh Samui.
L: Ah, I see.
D: Anyway, we had to take a night train from Bangkok to Chumphorn in the south of Thailand and then a boat from there to Koh Tao.
L: How exciting!
D: So, we were taken to the train station in Bangkok and then we waited there for two hours. We left the station at around 7:30 p.m.
L: Oh.
D: Yeah. At first we felt really excited, but after about an hour we started feeling pretty tired. It was noisy and hot. I think I got to sleep at around 11:30 p.m.
L: Oh, that's not so bad.
D: Mm. The next morning at three o'clock, the train stopped, and we were told to get off. It was the middle of the night, so it was still dark. We had to wait in a small station for a bus to take us to the boat.
L: How did you feel?
D: Really tired! And hungry and thirsty, but the only place we could get a drink was from an old lady who served terrible coffee.
L: Oh, poor you.
D: Then the mosquitoes started biting us—and they were hungry, too! Well, they bit me but they didn't really bite Emma.
L: Oh, no!
D: Four hours later the bus arrived, and we were taken to the boat. Then it started raining as the boat moved out into the ocean.
L: Oh, how annoying!
D: Suddenly, as quickly as it had started, the rain stopped, and the sun came out.
L: Aha! A happy ending!
D: Yes, it was. Eventually we arrived at Koh Tao, seventeen hours after our journey had begun.
L: Ahh. Were you tired?
D: Absolutely exhausted, but really happy.

4

Go through the choices with the students before playing the recording again. Ask them to match the linkers to the correct events.

ANSWERS:

a 2
b 6
c 5
d 4
e 3
f 1

Writing & Speaking (SB page 119)

1

Ask the students to read the story and complete it with the words in the box.

ANSWERS:

1 Two years ago
2 At first
3 The next day
4 four days
5 Then
6 suddenly
7 Eventually

2

Ask the students to put the words in order to make questions. Check answers with the class before asking them to look back through the text and see which of these questions it answers.

ANSWERS:

a Where did you start your trip?
b Where did you go?
c How did you get there?
d Where did you stay at night?
e Did you have any problems?
f Did you enjoy your trip?
g How long did the trip take?
h Would you do it again?

Questions **a** - **e** were answered in the text.

3

Go through the instructions with the class and make sure everyone understands what they have to do. Ask them to work individually at first to think of ideas. Allow them to make brief notes if they wish, but discourage them from writing out a script. Remind them to look at the expressions in Exercise 1. Go around, offering help with vocabulary. Then ask the students to get into pairs and take turns to describe their trips.

4

Remind the students that they can use the text in Exercise 1 as a model and should incorporate some of the organizing expressions in the box. Go around, monitoring and giving help, and encourage them to use the questions in Exercise 2 to help them structure their work. You could then display the finished accounts around the classroom.

Further Practice Material

Need more classroom practice activities?
Photocopiable resource materials in the Teacher's Presentation Kit / Extra Resources

Need more tests?
Test Generator
Teacher's Presentation Kit / Extra Resources / Tests

Need more on important teaching concepts?
Key concepts in *American Inside Out Evolution* pages xxi-xxxvii

Need more information and ideas?
American Inside Out Evolution website www.macmillan.com.br/americaninsideoutevolution